ORGANIZATIONAL PSYCHOLOGY

ORGANIZATIONAL PSYCHOLOGY

Dr. Punam Singh

CENTRUM PRESS
NEW DELHI-110002 (INDIA)

CENTRUM PRESS
H.O.: 4360/4, Ansari Road, Daryaganj,
New Delhi-110002 (India)
Tel: 23278000, 23261597, 23255577, 23286875
B.O.: No. 1015, Ist Main Road, BSK IIIrd Stage,
IIIrd Phase, IIIrd Block, Bangalore-560085 (INDIA)
Tel: 080-41723429
Email: centrumpress@gmail.com
Visit us at: www.centrumpress.com

Organizational Psychology

First Edition, 2011

ISBN 978-93-80921-62-4

PRINTED IN INDIA

Printed at Tarun Offset Printers, Delhi-110053

Contents

Preface

Organizational Psychology is a subject which applies the principles of psychology into one of the most important areas of people's life – work. Specifically, we work with the human aspects of the workplace and aim at improving people's efficiency, and hence organizational effectiveness, through our knowledge about human functioning. There exist a group of professionals who share a similar aim and are working closely with us, the human resource professionals. Despite the close relationship with HR professionals, Organizational Psychologists are distinctive professionals. Unfortunately, there is always some confusion among the general public that people just cannot tell who is who. More importantly, even some HR professionals do not know what we are doing and what can we offer them. When we tell them we are Psychologists, a frequent reply is "but we don't have any mental problems"!

As Organizational Psychologists, we work with a wide range of domains that are related to people's everyday work life. We design work activities, schedules and workplaces; we design reward principles that are based on human motivation theories; we develop training principles and train the trainers; we develop selection procedures and tools; we formulate performance appraisal systems; and we advise on organizational development issues as well as career development decisions. As you may recognise, our work reaches every working individual on the planet and our working field is very closely related with the work of HR professionals. Although there are quite a few overlapping areas between Organizational Psychology and Human Resource Management (HRM), there are fundamental differences between us. The first and perhaps the most obvious difference between us is the knowledge foundation. As psychologists, we base our work heavily on science. All work has to be backed up by scientific evidence and statistics is always in our toolbox. In contrast, HRM is essentially a business study which emphasises more on the practical side, with less focus on the scientific side. Moreover, in addition to working on overlapping areas, we work on different levels. Organizational Psychologists focus more on the design and development of procedures, tools and principles while HR professionals work more on the operational level, such as implementation of selection systems and applying training principles in real training scenarios. The discrepancy between the knowledgebase of Organizational Psychologists and HR professionals has been documented in academic journals. For example Sally Carless and colleagues pointed out that although there are important advancements in HR-related research, the everyday HR practice have benefited from it to a minimum level. They found that this is due to the lack of knowledge among HR professionals, especially when the training of the HR professionals emphasizes on general skill and knowledge in favour of science.

In contrast, the training of Organizational Psychologists is built upon the scientist-practitioner model which emphasizes on both research and practical skills and stipulates that practice must be supported by scientific evidence. Another reason may lie in the Continuous Professional Development (CPD) requirement. As Organizational Psychologists, CPD is a statutory condition for registration and this helps them to keep updated with the latest developments in the field. However there is no such requirement for HR professionals. Carless's study confirmed that Organizational Psychologists are experts in the field, especially in the area of selection and the authors articulated that "scientific integrity is a key differentiating feature of I/O (Organizational) psychologists."

Having closely related working areas, our work is actually complementary to each other. Without Organizational Psychologists in the design and development work of various HR processes and tools, the HR professional would not be enjoying these scientific and highly effective products. On the other hand, without the help of HR professionals we could never apply our work to such a broad range of people. Moreover, our relationship is much more complex and interactive than one might be aware of. Besides the above mentioned supplier-user relationship, HR professionals are also partners, advisors and sometimes suppliers for Organizational Psychologists.

This book has over all covered a new ideal in this subject so it is useful for students.

1

General Outline of the Psychology of Management

Definition of Psychology of Management

The Psychology of Management, as here used, means, — the effect of the mind that is directing work upon that work which is directed, and the effect of this undirected and directed work upon the mind of the worker.

Importance of the Subject

Before defining the terms that will be used more in detail, and outlining the method of treatment to be followed, it is well to consider the importance of the subject matter of this book, for upon the reader's interest in the subject, and his desire, from the outset, to follow what is said, and to respond to it, rests a large part of the value of this book.

Value of Psychology

First of all, then, what is there in the subject of psychology to demand the attention of the manager?

Psychology, in the popular phrase, is "the study of the mind." It has for years been included in the training of all teachers, and has been one of the first steps for the student of philosophy; but it has not, usually, been included among the studies of the young scientific or engineering student, or of any students in other lines than Philosophy and Education. This, not because its value as a "culture subject" was not understood, but because the course of the average student is so crowded with technical preparation necessary to his life work, and because the practical value of psychology has not been recognized.

It is well recognized that the teacher must understand the working of the mind in order best to impart his information in that way that will enable the student to grasp it most readily. It was not recognized that every man going out into the world needs all the knowledge that he can get as to the working of the human mind in order not only to give but to receive information with the least waste and expenditure of energy, nor was it recognized that in the industrial, as well as the academic world, almost every man is a teacher.

Value of Management

The second question demanding attention is; — Of what value is the study of management?

The study of management has been omitted from the student's training until comparatively recently, for a very different reason than was psychology. It was never doubted that a knowledge of management would be of great value to anyone and everyone, and many were the queer schemes for obtaining that knowledge after graduation. It was doubted that management could be studied otherwise than by observation and practice.

Few teachers, if any, believed in the existence, or possibility, of a teaching science of management. Management was assumed by many to be an art, by even more it was thought to be a divinely bestowed gift or talent, rather than an acquired accomplishment. It was common belief that one could learn to manage only by going out on the work and watching other managers, or by trying to manage, and not by studying about management in a class room or in a text book; that watching a good manager might help one, but no one could hope really to succeed who had not "the knack born in him."

With the advent of "Scientific Management," and its demonstration that the best management is founded on laws that have been determined, and can be taught, the study of management in the class room as well as on the work became possible and actual.

Value of Psychology of Management

Third, we must consider the value of the study of the psychology of management.

This question, like the one that precedes it, is answered by Scientific Management. It has demonstrated that the emphasis in successful management lies on the *man*, not on the *work*; that efficiency is best secured by placing the emphasis on the man, and modifying the equipment, materials and methods to make the most of the man. It has, further, recognized that the man's mind is a controlling factor in his efficiency, and has, by teaching, enabled the man to make the most of his powers. In order to understand this teaching element that is such a large part of management, a knowledge of psychology is imperative; and this study of psychology, as it applies to the work of the manager or the managed, is exactly what the "psychology of management" is.

Five Indications of This Value

In order to realize the importance of the psychology of management it is necessary to consider the following five points:—

1. Management is a life study of every man who works with other men. He must either manage, or be managed, or both; in any case, he can never work to best advantage until he understands both the psychological and managerial laws by which he governs or is governed.
2. A knowledge of the underlying laws of management is the most important asset that one can carry with him into his life work, even though he will never manage any but himself. It is useful, practical, commercially valuable.
3. This knowledge is to be had *now*. The men who have it are ready and glad to impart it to all who are interested and who will pass it on. The text books are at hand now. The opportunities for practical experience in Scientific Management will meet all demands as fast as they are made.
4. The psychology of, that is, the mind's place in management is only one part, element or variable of

management; one of numerous, almost numberless, variables.

5. It is a division well fitted to occupy the attention of the beginner, as well as the more experienced, because it is a most excellent place to start the study of management. A careful study of the relations of psychology to management should develop in the student a method of attack in learning his selected life work that should help him to grasp quickly the orderly array of facts that the other variables, as treated by the great managers, bring to him.

Purpose of This Book

It is scarcely necessary to mention that this book can hope to do little more than arouse an interest in the subject and point the way to the detailed books where such an interest can be more deeply aroused and more fully satisfied.

What this Book will not do

It is not the purpose of this book to give an exhaustive treatment of psychology. Neither is it possible in this book to attempt to give a detailed account of management in general, or of the Taylor plan of "Scientific Management" so-called, in particular.

All of the literature on the subject has been carefully studied and reviewed for the purpose of writing this book, — not only what is in print, but considerable that is as yet in manuscript. No statement has been made that is not along the line of the accepted thought and standardized practice of the authorities. The foot notes have been prepared with great care. By reading the references there given one can verify statements in the text, and can also, if he desires, inform himself at length on any branch of the subject that especially interests him.

What this Book will do

This book aims not so much to instruct as to arouse an interest in its subject, and to point the way whence instruction comes. If it can serve as an introduction to psychology and to management, can suggest the relation of these two fields of inquiries and can ultimately enrol its readers as investigators in a resultant great field of inquiry, it will have accomplished its aim.

Definition of Management

To discuss this subject more in detail —

First: What is "Management"?

"Management," as defined by the Century Dictionary, is "the art of managing by direction or regulation."

Successful management of the old type was an art based on no measurement. Scientific Management is an art based upon a science, — upon laws deducted from measurement. Management continues to be what it has always been, — the *art* of directing activity.

Change in the Accepted Meaning

"Management," until recent years, and the emphasis placed on Scientific Management was undoubtedly associated, in the average mind, with the *managing* part of the organization only, neglecting that vital part — the best interests of the managed, almost entirely. Since we have come to realize that management signifies the relationship between the managing and the managed in doing work, a new realization of its importance has come about. Inadequacy of the Terms Used

It is unfortunate that the English language is so poor in synonyms in this field that the same word must have two such different and conflicting meanings, for, though the new definition of management be accepted, the "Fringe" of associations that belong to the old are apt to remain. The thoughts of "knack, aptitude, tact, adroitness," — not to speak of the less desirable "Brute Force," "shrewdness, subtlety, cunning, artifice, deceit, duplicity," of the older idea of management remain in the background of the mind and make it difficult, even when one is convinced that management is a science, to think and act as if it were.

It must be noticed and constantly remembered that one of the greatest difficulties to overcome in studying management and its development is the meaning of the terms used. It is most unfortunate that the new ideas have been forced to content themselves with old forms as best they may.

Psychological Interest of the Terms

Psychology could ask no more interesting subject than a study of the mental processes that lie back of many of these terms. It is most unfortunate for the obtaining of clearness, that new terms were not invented for the new ideas. There is, however, an excellent reason for using the old terms. By their use it is emphasized that the new thought is a logical outgrowth of the old, and experience has proved that this close relationship to established ideas is a powerful argument for the new science; but such terms as "task," "foreman," "speed boss," "piece-rate" and "bonus," as used in the science of management, suffer from misunderstanding caused by old and now false associations. Furthermore, in order to compare old and new interpretations of the ideas of management, the older terms of management should have their traditional meanings only. The two sets of meanings are a source of endless confusion, unwarranted prejudice, and worse. This is well recognized by the authorities on Management.

The Three Types of Management

We note this inadequacy of terms again when we discuss the various *types* of Management.

We may divide all management into three types —

(1) Traditional

(2) Transitory

(3) Scientific, or measured functional.

Traditional Management, the first, has been variously called "Military," "Driver," the "Marquis of Queensberry type," "Initiative and Incentive Management," as well as "Traditional" management.

Definition of the First Type

In the first type, the power of managing lies, theoretically at least, in the hands of one man, a capable "all-around" manager. The line of authority and of responsibility is clear, fixed and single. Each man comes in direct contact with but one man above him. A man may or may not manage more than one man beneath him, but, however this may be, he is managed by but one man above him.

Preferable Name for the First Type

The names "Traditional," or "Initiative and Incentive," are the preferable titles for this form of management. It is true they lack in specificness, but the other names, while aiming to be descriptive, really emphasize one feature only, and in some cases with unfortunate results.

The Name "Military" Inadvisable

The direct line of authority suggested the name "Military," and at the time of the adoption of that name it was probably appropriate as well as complimentary. Appropriate in the respect referred to only, for the old type of management varied so widely in its manifestations that the comparison to the procedure of the Army was most inaccurate. "Military" has always been a synonym for "systematized", "orderly," "definite," while the old type of management was more often quite the opposite of the meaning of all these terms. The term "Military Management" though often used in an uncomplimentary sense would, today, if understood, be more complimentary than ever it was in the past. The introduction of various features of Scientific Management into the Army and Navy, — and such features are being incorporated steadily and constantly, — is raising the standard of management there to a high degree. This but renders the name "Military" Management for the old type more inaccurate and misleading.

It is plain that the stirring associations of the word "military" make its use for the old type, by advocates of the old type, a weapon against Scientific Management that only the careful thinker can turn aside.

The Names "Driver" and "Marquis of Queensberry" Unfortunate

The name "Driver" suggests an opposition between the managers and the men, an opposition which the term "Marquis of Queensberry" emphasizes. This term "Marquis of Queensberry" has been given to that management which is thought of as a mental and physical contest, waged "according to the rules of the game." These two names are most valuable pictorially, or in furnishing oratorical material. They are constant reminders of the constant desire of the managers to get all the work that is possible out of the men, but they are scarcely descriptive in any satisfactory sense, and the visions they summon, while they are perhaps definite, are certainly, for the inexperienced in management, inaccurate. In other words, they usually lead to imagination rather than to perception.

The Name "Initiative and Incentive" Authoritative

The term "Initiative and Incentive" is used by Dr. Taylor, and is fully described by him. The words themselves suggest, truly, that he gives the old form of management its due. He does more than this. He points out in his definition of the terms the likenesses between the old and new forms.

The Name "Traditional" Brief and Descriptive

The only excuses for the term "Traditional," since Dr. Taylor's term is available, are its brevity and its descriptiveness. The fact that it is indefinite is really no fault in it, as the subject it describes is equally indefinite. The "fringe" of this word is especially good. It calls up ideas of information handed down from generation to generation orally, the only way of teaching under the old type of management. It recalls the idea of the inaccurate perpetuation of unthinking custom, and the "myth" element always present in tradition, — again undeniable accusations against the old type of management. The fundamental idea of the tradition, that it is *oral*, is the essence of the difference of the old type of management from science, or even system, which must be written.

It is not necessary to make more definite here the content of this oldest type of management, rather being satisfied with the extent, and accepting for working use the name "Traditional" with the generally accepted definition of that name.

Definition of the Second Type of Management

The second type of management is called "Interim" or "Transitory" management. It includes all management that is consciously passing into Scientific Management and embraces all stages, from management that has incorporated one scientifically derived principle, to management that has adopted all but one such principle.

Preferable Name for Second Type of Management

Perhaps the name "Transitory" is slightly preferable in that, though the element of temporariness is present in both words, it is more strongly emphasized in the latter. The usual habit of associating with it the ideas of "fleeting, evanescent, ephemeral, momentary, short-lived," may have an influence on hastening the completion of the installing of Scientific Management.

Definition of the Third Type of Management

The third form of management is called "Ultimate," "measured Functional," or "Scientific," management, and might also be called, — but for the objection of Dr. Taylor, the "Taylor Plan of Management." This differs from the first two types mentioned in that it is a definite plan of management synthesized from scientific analysis of the data of management. In other words, Scientific Management is that management which is a science, i.e., which operates according to known, formulated, and applied laws.

Preferable Name of the Third Type of Management

The name "Ultimate" has, especially to the person operating under the transitory stage, all the charm and inspiration of a goal. It has all the incentives to accomplishment of a clearly circumscribed task. Its very definiteness makes it seem possible of attainment. It is a great satisfaction to one who, during a lifetime of managing effort, has tried one offered improvement after another to be convinced that he has found the right road at last. The name is, perhaps, of greatest value in attracting the attention of the uninformed and, as the possibilities of the subject can fulfil the most exacting demands, the attention once secured can be held.

The name "measured functional" is the most descriptive, but demands the most explanation. The principle of functionalization is one of the underlying, fundamental principles of Scientific Management. It is not as necessary to stop to define it here, as it is necessary to discuss the definition, the principle, and the underlying psychology, at length later.

The name "scientific" while in some respects not as appropriate as are any of the other names, has already received the stamp of popular approval. In derivation it is beyond criticism. It also describes exactly, as has been said, the difference between the older forms of management and the new. Even its "fringe" of association is, or at least was when first used, all that could be desired; but the name is, unfortunately, occasionally used indiscriminately for any sort of system and for schemes of operation that are not based on time study. It has gradually become identified more or less closely with

1. the Taylor Plan of Management
2. what we have defined as the "Transitory" plan of management
3. management which not only is not striving to be scientific, but which confounds "science" with "system." Both its advocates and opponents have been guilty of misuse of the word. Still, in spite of this, the very fact that the word has had a wide use, that it has become habitual to think of the new type of management as "Scientific," makes its choice advisable. We shall use it, but restrict its content. With us "Scientific Management" is used to mean the complete Taylor plan of management, with no modifications and no deviations.

We may summarize by saying that:

1. the popular name is Scientific Management,
2. the inspiring name is Ultimate management,
3. the descriptive name is measured Functional management,
4. the distinctive name is the Taylor Plan of Management.

For the purpose of this book, Scientific Management is, then, the most appropriate name. Through its use, the reader is enabled to utilize all his associations, and through his study he is able to restrict and order the content of the term.

Relationship Between the Three Types of Management

From the foregoing definitions and descriptions it will be clear that the three types of management are closely related. Three of the names given bring out this relationship most clearly. These are Traditional (i.e., Primitive), Interim, and

Ultimate. These show, also, that the relationship is genetic, i.e., that the second form grows out of the first, but passes through to the third. The growth is evolutional. Under the first type, or in the first stage of management, the laws or principles underlying right management are usually unknown, hence disregarded. In the second stage, the laws are known and installed as fast as functional foremen can be taught their new duties and the resistance of human nature can be overcome.

In the third stage the managing is operated in accordance with the recognized laws of management.

Psychological Significance of this Relationship

The importance of the knowledge and of the desire for it can scarcely be overestimated. This again makes plain the value of the psychological study of management.

Possible Psychological Studies of Management

In making this psychological study of management, it would be possible to take up the three types as defined above, separately and in order, and to discuss the place of the mind in each, at length; but such a method would not only result in needless repetition, but also in most difficult comparisons when final results were to be deduced and formulated. It would, again, be possible to take up the various elements or divisions of psychological study as determined by a consensus of psychologists, and to illustrate each in turn from the three types of management; but the results from any such method would be apt to seem unrelated and impractical, i.e., it would be a lengthy process to get results that would be of immediate, practical use in managing.

Plan of Psychological Study Used Here

It has, therefore, seemed best to base the discussion that is to follow upon arbitrary divisions of scientific management, that is —

1. To enumerate the underlying principles on which scientific management rests.
2. To show in how far the other two types of management vary from Scientific Management.
3. To discuss the psychological aspect of each principle.

Advantages of this Plan of Study

In this way the reader can gain an idea of:

1. The relation of Scientific Management to the other types of management.
2. The structure of Scientific Management.
3. The relation between the various elements of Scientific Management.
4. The psychology of management in general, and of the three types of management in particular.

Underlying Ideas and Divisions of Scientific Management

These underlying ideas are grouped under nine divisions, as follows: —

1. Individuality.
2. Functionalization.
3. Measurement.
4. Analysis and Synthesis.
5. Standardization.
6. Records and Programmes.
7. Teaching.
8. Incentives.
9. Welfare.

It is here only necessary to enumerate these divisions.

Derivation of these Divisions

These divisions lay no claim to being anything but underlying ideas of Scientific Management, that embrace varying numbers of established elements that can easily be subjected to the scrutiny of psychological investigation.

The discussion will be as little technical as is possible, will take nothing for granted and will cite references at every step.

This is a new field of investigation, and the utmost care is necessary to avoid generalizing from insufficient data.

Derivation of Scientific Management

There has been much speculation as to the age and origin of Scientific Management. The results of this are interesting, but are not of enough practical value to be repeated here. Many ideas of Scientific Management can be traced back, more or less clearly and directly, to thinkers of the past; but the Science of Management, as such, was discovered, and the deduction of its laws, or "principles," made possible when Dr. Frederick W. Taylor discovered and applied Time Study. Having discovered this, he constructed from it and the other fundamental principles a complete whole.

Mr. George Iles in that most interesting and instructive of books, "Inventors at Work," has pointed out the importance, to development in any line of progress or science, of measuring devices and methods. Contemporaneous with, or previous to, the discovery of the device or method, must come the discovery or determination of the most profitable unit of measurement which will, of itself, best show the variations in efficiency from class. When Dr. Taylor discovered units of measurement for determining, *prior to performance*, the amount of any kind of work that a worker could do and the amount of rest he must have during the performance of that work, then, and not until then, did management become a science. On this hangs the science of management.

Outline of Method of Investigation

In the discussion of each of the nine divisions of Scientific Management, the following topics must be treated:

1. Definition of the division and its underlying idea.
2. Appearance and importance of the idea in Traditional and Transitory Management.
3. Appearance and importance of the idea in Scientific Management.
4. Elements of Scientific Management which show the effects of the idea.
5. Results of the idea upon work and workers.

These topics will be discussed in such order as the particular division investigated demands. The psychological significance of the appearance or non-appearance of the idea, and of the effect of the idea, will be noted.

The results will be summarized at the close of each chapter, in order to furnish data for drawing conclusions at the close of the discussion.

Conclusions to be Reached

These conclusions will include the following: —

1. "Scientific Management" is a science.
2. It alone, of the Three Types of Management, is a science.
3. Contrary to a widespread belief that Scientific Management kills individuality, it is built on the basic principle of recognition of the individual, not only as an economic unit but also as a personality, with all the idiosyncrasies that distinguish a person.
4. Scientific Management fosters individuality by functionalizing work.
5. Measurement, in Scientific Management, is of ultimate units of subdivision.
6. These measured ultimate units are combined into methods of least waste.
7. Standardization under Scientific Management applies to all elements.
8. The accurate records of Scientific Management make accurate programmes possible of fulfilment.
9. Through the teaching of Scientific Management the management is unified and made self-perpetuating.
10. The method of teaching of Scientific Management is a distinct and valuable contribution to Education.
11. Incentives under Scientific Management not only stimulate but benefit the worker.
12. It is for the ultimate as well as immediate welfare of the worker to work under Scientific Management.
13. Scientific Management is applicable to all fields of activity, and to mental as well as physical work.
14. Scientific Management is applicable to self-management as well as to managing others.

15. It teaches men to cooperate with the management as well as to manage.
16. It is a device capable of use by all.
17. The psychological element of Scientific Management is the most important element.
18. Because Scientific Management is psychologically right it is the ultimate form of management.
19. This psychological study of Scientific Management emphasizes especially the teaching features.
20. Scientific Management simultaneously
    a. increases output and wages and lowers costs.
    b. eliminates waste.
    c. turns unskilled labour into skilled.
    d. provides a system of self-perpetuating welfare.
    e. reduces the cost of living.
    f. bridges the gap between the college trained and the apprenticeship trained worker.
    g. forces capital and labour to cooperate and to promote industrial peace.

Individuality

Definition of Individuality

"An individual is a single thing, a being that is, or is regarded as, a unit. An individual is opposed to a crowd. Individual action is opposed to associate action. Individual interests are opposed to common or community interests." These definitions give us some idea of the extent of individuality. Individuality is a particular or distinctive characteristic of an individual; "that quality or aggregate of qualities which distinguishes one person or thing from another, idiosyncrasy." This indicates the content.

For our purpose, we may define the study of individuality as a consideration of the individual as a unit with special characteristics. That it is a *unit* signifies that it is one of many and that it has likeness to the many. That it has *special characteristics* shows that it is one of many, but different from the many. This consideration of individuality emphasizes both the common element and the diverging characteristics.

Individuality as Treated in this Chapter

The recognition of individuality is the subject of this chapter. The utilization of this individuality in its deviation from class, is the subject of the chapter that follows, Functionalization.

Individuality as Considered by Psychology

Psychology has not always emphasized the importance of the individual as a unit for study. Prof. Ladd's definition of psychology, quoted and endorsed by Prof. James, is "the description and explanation of states of consciousness, as such." "By states of consciousness," says James, "are meant such things as sensation, desires, emotions, cognitions, reasonings, decisions, volitions, and the like." This puts the emphasis on such divisions of consciousness as, "attention," "interest," and "will." With the day of experimental psychology has come the importance of the individual self as a subject of study, and psychology has come to be defined, as Calkins defines it, as a "science of the self as conscious."

We hear much in the talk of today of the "psychology of the crowd," the "psychology of the mob," and the "psychology of the type," etc., but the mind that is being measured, and from whose measurements the laws are being deduced and formulated is, at the present the *individual* mind.

The psychology which interested itself particularly in studying such divisions of mental activity as attention, will, habit, etc., emphasizes more particularly the likenesses of minds. It is necessary to understand thoroughly all of these likenesses before one can be sure what the differences, or idiosyncrasies, are, and how important they are, because, while the likenesses furnish the background, it is the differences that are most often actually utilized by management. These must be determined in order to compute and set the proper individual task for the given man from standard data of the standard, or first-class man.

In any study of the individual, the following facts must be noted: —

1. The importance of the study of the individual, and the comparatively small amount of work that has as yet been done in that field.
2. The difficulty of the study, and the necessity for great care, not only in the study itself, but in deducing laws from it.
3. The necessity of considering any one individual trait as modified by all the other traits of the individual.
4. The importance of the individual as distinct from the type.

Many students are so interested in studying types and deducing laws which apply to types in general, that they lose sight of the fact that the individual is the basis of the study, — that individuality is that for which they must seek and for which they must constantly account. As Sully says, we must not emphasize "*typical developments* in a new individual," at the expense of "typical development *in a new individual.*" It is the fact that the development occurs in an individual, and not that the development is typical, that we should emphasize.

Individuality Seldom Recognized Under Traditional Management

Under Traditional Management there was little or no systematized method for the recognition of individuality or individual fitness. The worker usually was, in the mind of the manager, one of a crowd, his only distinguishing mark being the amount of work which he was capable of performing.

Selecting Workers Under Traditional Management

In selecting men to do work, there was little or no attempt to study the individuals who applied for work. The matter of selection was more of a process of "guess work" than of exact measurement, and the highest form of test was considered to be that of having the man actually tried out by being given a chance at the work itself. There was not only a great waste of time on the work, because men unfitted to it could not turn it out so successfully, but there also was a waste of the worker, and many times a positive injury to the worker, by his being put at work which he was unfitted either to perform, to work at continuously, or both. In the most progressive type of Traditional Management there was usually a feeling, however, that if the labour market offered even temporarily a greater supply than the work in hand demanded, it was wise to choose those men to do the work who were best fitted for it, or who were willing to work for less wages.

It is surprising to find in the traditional type, even up to the present day, how often men were selected for their strength and physique, rather than for any special capabilities fitting them for working in, or at, the particular line of work to be done.

Output Seldom Separated Under Traditional Management

Under Traditional Management especially on day work the output of the men was not usually separated, nor was the output recorded separately, as can be done even with the work of gangs.

Few Individual Tasks Under Traditional Management

Seldom, if ever, was an individual task set for a worker on day work, or piece work, and even if one were set, it was not scientifically determined. The men were simply set to work alone or in gangs, *as the work demanded*, and if the foreman was overworked or lazy, allowed to take practically their own time to do the work. If, on the other hand, the foreman was a "good driver," the men might be pushed to their utmost limit of their individual undirected speed, regardless of their welfare.

Little Individual Teaching Under Traditional Management

Not having a clear idea either of the present fitness and the future possibilities of the worker, or the requirements of the work, no intelligent attempt could be made at efficient individual teaching. What teaching was done was in the form of directions for all, concerning the work in general, the directions being given by an overworked foreman, the holding of whose position often depended more upon whether his employer made money than upon the way his men were taught, or worked.

Seldom an Individual Reward Under Traditional Management

As a typical example of disregard of individuality, the worker in the household may be cited, and especially the "general housework girl." Selected with no knowledge of her capabilities, and with little or no scientific or even systematized knowledge of the work that she is expected to do, there is little or no thought of a prescribed and definite task, no teaching specially adapted to the individual needs of the taught, and no reward in proportion to efficiency.

Cause of these Lacks Under Traditional Management

The fault lies not in any desire of the managers to do poor or wasteful work, or to treat their workers unfairly, — but in a lack of knowledge and of accurate methods for obtaining, conserving and transmitting knowledge. Under Traditional Management no one individual knows precisely what is to be done. Such management seldom knows how work could best be done; — never knows how much work each individual can do. Understanding neither work nor workers, it can not adjust the one to the other so as to obtain least waste. Having no conception of the importance of accurate measurement, it has no thought of the individual as a unit.

Individuality Recognized Under Transitory Management

Recognition of individuality is one of the principles first apparent under Transitory Management. This is apt to demonstrate itself first of all in causing the outputs of the workers to "show up" separately, rewarding these separated outputs, and rewarding each worker for his individual output.

Benefits of this Recognition

The benefits of introducing these features first are that the worker, (1) seeing his individual output, is stimulated to measure it, and (2) receiving compensation in accordance with his output, is satisfied; and (3) observing that records are necessary to determine the amount of output and pay, is glad to have accurate measurement and the other features of Scientific Management introduced.

Individuality a Fundamental Principle of Scientific Management

Under Scientific Management the individual is the unit to be measured. Functionalization is based upon utilizing the particular powers and special abilities of each man. Measurement is of the individual man and his work. Analysis and synthesis build up methods by which the individual can best do his work. Standards are of the work of an individual, a standard man, and the task is always for an individual, being that percentage of the standard man's task that the particular individual can do. Records are of individuals, and are made in order to show and reward individual effort. Specific individuals are taught those things that they, individually, require. Incentives are individual both in the cases of rewards and punishments, and, finally, it is the welfare of the individual worker that is considered, without the sacrifice of any for the good of the whole.

Individuality Considered in Selecting Workers

Under Scientific Management individuality is considered in selecting workers as it could not be under either of the other two forms of management. This for several reasons:

1. The work is more specialized, hence requires more carefully selected men.
2. With standardized methods comes a knowledge to the managers of the qualifications of the "standard men" who can best do the work and continuously thrive.
3. Motion study, in its investigation of the worker, supplies a list of variations in workers that can be utilized in selecting men.

Variables of the Worker

This list now includes at least 50 or 60 variables, and shows the possible elements which may demand consideration. When it is remembered that the individual selected may need a large or small proportion of most of the variables in order to do his particular work most successfully, and that every single one of these variables, as related to the others, may, in some way affect his output and his welfare in doing his assigned work, the importance of taking account of individuality in selection is apparent.

Scientific Management Needs Support in Studying Workers

The best of management is by no means at its ultimate stage in practice in this field. This, not because of a lack in the laws of management, but because, so far, Scientific Management has not received proper support from other lines of activity.

Present Lack of Knowledge of Applicants

At present, the men who apply to the Industries for positions have no scientifically determined idea of their own capabilities, neither has there been any effort in the training or experience of most of those who apply for work for the first time to show them how fit they really are to do the work which they wish to do.

Supplements Demanded by Scientific Management

Before the worker can be scientifically selected so that his individuality can be appreciated, Scientific Management must be supplemented in two ways: —

1. By psychological and physiological study of workers under it. By such study of the effect of various kinds of standardized work upon the mind and body, standard requirements for men who desire to do the work can be made.
2. By scientific study of the worker made before he comes into the Industries, the results of which shall show his capabilities and possibilities.

Whence this Help must Come

This study must be made

a. In the Vocational Guidance Work.

b. In the Academic Work, and in both fields psychological and physiological investigations are called for.

Work of Vocational Guidance Bureaus

Vocational Guidance Bureaus are, at present, doing a wonderful work in their line. This work divides itself into two parts:

1. Determining the capabilities of the boy, that is, seeing what he is, by nature and training, best fitted to do.
2. Determining the possibilities of his securing work in the line where he is best fitted to work, that is, studying the industrial opportunities that offer, and the "welfare" of the worker under each, using the word welfare in the broadest sense, of general wellbeing, mental, physical, moral and financial.

Work of Academic World

The Academic World is also, wherever it is progressive, attempting to study the student, and to develop him so that he can be the most efficient individual. Progressive educators realize that schools and colleges must stand or fall, as efficient, as the men they train become successful or unsuccessful in their vocations, as well as in their personal culture.

Need for Psychological Study in all Fields

In both these complementary lines of activity, as in Scientific Management itself, the need for psychological study is evident. Through it, only, can scientific progress come. Here is emphasized again the importance of measurement. Through accurate measurement of the mind and the body only can individuality be recognized, conserved and developed as it should be.

Preparedness of Experimental Psychology

Experimental psychology has instruments of precision with which to measure and test the minds and bodies brought to it, and its leading exponents are so broadening the scope of its activities that it is ready and glad to plan for investigations.

Method of Selection Under Ultimate Management

Under Ultimate Management, the minds of the workers,— and of the managers too, — will have been studied, and the results recorded from earliest childhood. This record, made by trained investigators, will enable vocational guidance directors to tell the child what he is fitted to be, and thus to help the schools and colleges to know how best to train him, that is to say, to provide what he will need to know to do his life work, and also those cultural studies that his vocational work may lack, and that may be required to build out his best development as an individual.

It is not always recognized that even the student who can afford to postpone his technical training until he has completed a general culture course, requires that his culture course be carefully planned. Not only must he choose those general courses that will serve as a foundation for his special study, and that will broaden and enrich his study, but also he must be provided with a counter-balance, — with interests that his special work might never arouse in him. Thus the field of Scientific Management can be narrowed to determining and preparing standard plans for standard specialized men, and selecting men to fill these places from competent applicants.

What part of the specialized training needed by the special work shall be given in schools and what in the industries themselves can be determined later. The "twin apprentice" plan offers one solution of the problem that has proved satisfactory in many places. The psychological study should determine through which agency knowledge can best come at any particular stage of mental growth.

Effect on Workers of Such Selection

As will be shown at greater length under "Incentives," Scientific Management aims in every way to encourage initiative. The outline here given as to how men must, ultimately, under Scientific Management, be selected serves to show that, far from being "made machines of," men are selected to reach that special place where their individuality can be recognized and rewarded to the greatest extent.

Selection Under Scientific Management today

At the present day, the most that Scientific Management can do, in the average case, is to determine the type of men needed for any particular kind of work, and then to select that man who seems, from such observations as can be made, best to conform to the type. The accurate knowledge of the requirements of the work, and the knowledge of variables of the worker make even a cursory observation more rich in results than it would otherwise be. Even such an apparently obvious observation, as that the very fact that a man claims that he can do the work implies desire and will on his part to do it that may overcome many natural lacks, — even this is an advance in recognizing individuality.

Effect of this Selection

The result of this scientific selection of the workman is not only better work, but also, and more important from the psychological side, the development of his individuality. It is not always recognized that the work itself is a great educator, and that acute cleverness in the line of work to which he is fitted comes to the worker.

Individuality Developed by Separating Outputs

Under Scientific Management the work of each man is arranged either so that his output shows up separately and on the individual records, or, if the Work is such that it seems best to do it in gangs, the output can often be so recorded that the individual's output can be computed from the records.

Purpose of Separating Outputs

The primary purpose of separating the output is to see what the man can do, to record this, and to reward the man according to his work, but this separating of output has also an individual result, which is even more important than the result aimed at, and that is the development of individuality.

Under Traditional Management and the usual "day work," much of the work is done by gangs and is observed or recorded as of gangs. Only now and then, when the work of some particular individual shows up decidedly better or worse than that of his fellows, and when the foreman or superintendent, or other onlooker, happens to observe this is the individual appreciated, and then only in the most inexact, unsystematic manner. Under Scientific Management, making individual output show up separately allows of individual recording, tasks, teaching and rewards.

Effect on Athletic Contests

Also, with this separation of the work of the individual under Scientific Management comes the possibility of a real, scientific, "athletic contest." This athletic contest, which proves itself so successful in Traditional Management, even when the men are grouped as gangs and their work is not recorded or thought of separately, proves itself quite as efficient or more efficient under Scientific Management, when the work of the man shows up separately. It might be objected that the old gang spirit, or it might be called "team" spirit, would disappear with the separation of the work. This is not so, as will be noted by a comparison to a baseball team, where each man has his separate place and his separate work and where his work shows up separately with separate records, such as "batting average" and "fielding average." Team spirit is the result of being grouped together against a common opponent, and it will be the same in any sort of work when the men are so grouped, or given to understand that they belong on the same side.

The following twelve rules for an Athletic Contest under Transitory System are quoted as exemplifying the benefits which accrue to Individuality.

1. Men must have square deal.
2. Conditions must be similar.
3. Men must be properly spaced and placed.
4. Output must show up separately.
5. Men must be properly started.
6. Causes for delay must be eliminated.
7. Pace maker must be provided.
8. Time for rest must be provided.
9. Individual scores must be kept and posted.
10. "Audience" must be provided.
11. Rewards must be prompt and provided for all good scores — not for winners only.
12. Appreciation must be shown.

This list shows the effects of many fundamental principles of Scientific Management, — but we note particularly here that over half the rules demand that outputs be separated as a prerequisite.

None of the benefits of the Athletic Contest are lost under Scientific Management. The only restrictions placed are that the men shall not be grouped according to any distinction that would cause hatred or ill feeling, that the results shall be ultimately beneficial to the workers themselves, and that all high scores shall win high prizes.

As will be brought out later under "Incentives," no competition is approved under Scientific Management which speeds up the men uselessly, or which brings any ill feeling between the men or any feeling that the weaker ones have not a fair chance. All of these things are contrary to Scientific Management, as well as contrary to common sense, for it goes without saying that no man is capable of doing his best work permanently if he is worried by the idea that he will not receive the square deal, that someone stronger than he will be allowed to cheat or to domineer over him, or that he will be speeded up to such an extent that while his work will increase for one day, the next day his work will fall down because of the effect of the fatigue of the day before.

The field of the contests is widened, as separating of the work of the individual not only allows for competition between individuals, but for the competition of the individual with his own records. This competition is not only a great, constant and helpful incentive to every worker, but it is also an excellent means of developing individuality.

Advantages to Managers of Separating Output

The advantages to the managers of separating the work are that there is a chance to know exactly who is making the high output, and that the spirit of competition which prevails when men compare their outputs to their own former records or others, leads to increased effort.

Advantages to Workers of Separating Output

As for advantages to the men:

By separation of the individual work, not only is the man's work itself shown, but at the same time the work of all other people is separated, cut away and put aside, and he can locate the man who is delaying him by, for example, not keeping him supplied with materials. The man has not only an opportunity to concentrate, but every possible incentive to exercise his will and his desire to do things. His attention is concentrated on the fact that he as an individual is expected to do his very best. He has the moral stimulus of responsibility. He has the emotional stimulus of competition. He has the mental stimulus of definiteness. He has, most valuable of all, a chance to be an entity rather than one of an un-discriminated gang. This chance to be an individual, or personality, is in great contradistinction to the popular opinion of Scientific Management, which thinks it turns men into machines. A very simple example of the effect of the worker's seeing his output show up separately in response to and in proportion to his effort and skill is that of boys in the lumber producing districts chopping edgings for fire wood. Here the chopping is so comparatively light that the output increased very rapidly, and the boy delights to "see his pile of fire wood grow."

With the separation of the work comes not only the opportunity for the men to see their own work, but also to see that of others, and there comes with this the spirit of imitation, or the spirit of friendly opposition, either of which, while valuable in itself is even more valuable as the by-product of being a life-giving thought, and of putting life into the work such as there never could be when the men were working together, more or less objectless, because they could not see plainly either what they were doing themselves, or what others were doing.

Separation of the output of the men gives them the greatest opportunity to develop. It gives them a chance to concentrate their attention at the work on which they are, because it is not necessary for them to waste any time to find out what that work is. Their work stands out by itself; they can put their whole minds to that work; they can become interested in that work and its outcome, and they can be positive that what they have done will be appreciated and recognized, and that it will have a good effect, with no possibility of evil effect, upon their chance for work and their chance for pay and promotion in the future. Definiteness of the boundaries, then, is not only good management in that it shows up the work and that it allows each man to see, and each man over him, or observing him to see exactly what has been done, — it has also an excellent effect upon the worker's mind.

Individuality Developed by Recording Output Separately

The spirit of individuality is brought out still more clearly by the fact that under Scientific Management, output is recorded separately. This recording of the outputs separately is, usually, and very successfully, one of the first features installed in Transitory Management, and a feature very seldom introduced, even unconscious of its worth, in day work under Traditional Management. It is one of the great disadvantages of many kinds of work, especially in this day, that the worker does only a small part of the finished article and that he has a feeling that what he does is not identified permanently with the success of the completed whole. We may note that one of the great unsatisfying features to such arts as acting and music, is that no matter how wonderful the performer's efforts, there was no permanent record of them; that the work of the day dies with the day. He can expect to live only in the minds and hearts of the hearers, in the accounts of spectators, or in histories of the stage.

It is, therefore, not strange that the world's best actors and singers are now grasping the opportunity to make their best efforts permanent through the instrumentality of the motion picture films and the talking machine records. This same feeling, minus the glow of enthusiasm that at least attends the actor during the work, is present in more or less degree in the mind of the worker.

Records Make Work Seem Worth While

With the feeling that his work is recorded comes the feeling that the work is really worth while, for even if the work itself does not last, the records of it are such as can go on.

Records Give Individuals a Feeling of Permanence

With recorded individual output comes also the feeling of permanence, of credit for good performance. This desire for permanence shows itself all through the work of men in Traditional Management, for example — in the stone cutter's art where the man who had successfully dressed the stone from the rough block was delighted to put his own individual mark on it, even though he knew that mark probably would seldom, if ever, be noticed again by anyone after the stone was set in the wall. It is an underlying trait of the human mind to desire this permanence of record of successful effort, and fulfilling and utilizing this desire is a great gain of Scientific Management.

Mental Development of Worker Through Records

It is not only for his satisfaction that the worker should see his records and realize that his work has permanence, but also for comparison of his work not only with his own record, but with the work of others. The value of these comparisons, not only to the management but to the worker himself, must not be underestimated. The worker gains mental development and physical skill by studying these comparisons.

Advantages to Worker of Making his Own Records

These possibilities of mental development are still further increased when the man makes his own records. This leads to closer attention, to more interest in the work, and to a realization of the man as to what the record really means, and what value it represents. Though even a record that is made for him and is posted where he can see it will probably result in a difference in his pay envelope, no such progress is likely to occur as when the man makes his own record, and must be conscious every moment of the time exactly where he stands.

Possibilities of Making Individual Records

Records of individual efficiency are comparatively easy to make when output is separated. But even when work must be done by gangs or teams of men, there is provision made in Scientific Management for recording this gang work in such a way that either the output or the efficiency, or both, of each man shows up separately. This may be done in several ways, such as, for example, by recording the total time of delays avoidable and unavoidable, caused by each man, and from this computing individual records. This method of recording is psychologically right, because the recording of the delay will serve as a warning to the man, and as a spur to him not to cause delay to others again.

The forcefulness of the "don't" and the "never" have been investigated by education. Undoubtedly the "do" is far stronger, but in this particular case the command deduced from the records of delay to others is, necessarily, in the negative form, and a study of the psychological results proves most instructive.

Benefits to Managers of Individual Records

The value of the training to the foremen, to the superintendents and to the managers higher up, who study these records, as well as to the timekeepers, recorders and clerks in the Time and Cost Department who make the records, is obvious. There is not only the possibility of appreciating and rewarding the worker, and thus stimulating him to further activity, there is also, especially in the Transitory stage, when men are to be chosen on whom to make Time Study observations, an excellent chance to compare various methods of doing work and their results.

Incentives with Individual Records

The greatest value of recorded outputs is in the appreciation of the work of the individual that becomes possible. First of all, appreciation by the management, which to the worker must be the most important of all, as it means to him a greater chance for promotion and for more pay. This promotion and additional pay are amply provided for by Scientific Management, as will be shown later in discussing Incentives and Welfare.

Not only is the work appreciated by the management and by the man himself, but also the work becomes possible of appreciation by others. The form of the record as used in Scientific Management, and as introduced early in the transitory stage, makes it possible for many beside those working on the job, if they take the pains to consult the records, which are best posted in a conspicuous place on the work, to know and appreciate what the worker is doing. This can be best illustrated, perhaps, by various methods of recording output on contracting work, — out-of-door work.

The flag flown by the successful contestants in the athletic contests, showing which gang or which individual has made the largest output during the day previous, allows everyone who passes to appreciate the attainment of that particular worker, or that group of workers. The photographs of the "high priced men," copies of which may be given to the workers themselves, allow the worker to carry home a record and thus impress his family with what he has done. Too often the family is unable by themselves to understand the value of the worker's work, or to appreciate the effect of his home life, food, and rest conditions upon his life work, and this entire strong element of interest of the worker's family in his work is often lost.

Relation of Individual Records to Scientific Management in General

Any study of Records of an individual's work again makes clear that no one topic of Scientific Management can be properly noted without a consideration of all other elements. The fact that under Scientific Management the record with which the man most surely and constantly competes is his own, as provided for by the individual instruction card and the individual task; the fact that under Scientific Management the man need be in no fear of losing his job if he does his best; the fact that Scientific Management is founded on the "square deal"; — all of these facts must be kept constantly in mind when considering the advantages of recording individual output, for they all have a strong psychological effect on the man's mind. It is important to remember that not only does Scientific Management provide for certain directions and thoughts entering the man's mind, but that it also eliminates other thoughts which would surely have a tendency to retard his work. The result is output far exceeding what is usually possible under Traditional Management, because drawbacks are removed and impetuses added.

The outcome of the records, and their related elements in other branches of Scientific Management, is to arouse interest. Interest arouses abnormally concentrated attention, and this in turn is the cause of genius. This again answers the argument of those who claim that Scientific Management kills individuality and turns the worker into a machine.

Individual Task Under Scientific Management

Individuality is also taken into consideration when preparing the task. This task would always be for an individual, even in the case of the gang instruction card. It usually recognizes individuality, in that, —

1. It is prepared for one individual only, when possible.
2. It is prepared for the particular individual who is to do it.

The working time, as will be shown later, is based upon time study observations on a standard man, but when a task is assigned for a certain individual, that proportion of the work of the standard or first class man is assigned to that particular given man who is actually to do it, which he is able to do. It is fundamental that the task must be such that the man who is actually put at it, when he obeys orders and works steadily, can do it; that is, the task must be achievable, and achievable without such effort as would do mental or physical injury to the worker. This not only gives the individual the proper amount of work to do, recognizes his particular capabilities and is particularly adapted to him, but it also eliminates all dread on the score of his not being appreciated, in that the worker knows that if he achieves or exceeds his task he will not only receive the wage for it, but will continue to receive that wage, or more, for like achievement. The rate is not cut. Under the "three-rate with increased rate system," which experience has shown to be a most advanced plan for compensating workmen, the worker receives one bonus for exactness as to methods, that is, he receives one bonus if he does the task exactly as he is instructed to do it as to methods; and a second bonus, or extra bonus, if he completes his task in the allotted time. This not only assures adequate pay to the man who is slow, but a good imitator, but also to the man who, perhaps, is not such a good imitator, and must put attention on the quality rather than the quantity of his performance.

Individuality Emphasized by Instruction Card

This individual task is embodied in an individual instruction card.

In all work where it is possible to do so, the worker is given an individual instruction card, even though his operations and rest periods are also determined by a gang instruction card. This card not only tells the man what he is to do, how he can best do it, and the time that it is supposed to take him to do it, — but it bears also the signature of the man who made it. This in order that if the worker cannot fulfil the requirements of the card he may lose no time in determining who is to give him the necessary instructions or help that will result in his earning his large wages. More than this, he must call for help from his assigned teachers, as is stated in large type on a typical Instruction Card as follows: "When instructions cannot be carried out, foreman must at once report to man who signed this card."

The signature of the man who made the card not only develops his sense of individuality and responsibility, but helps create a feeling of inter-responsibility between the workers in various parts of the organization.

The Gang Instruction Card

A gang instruction card is used for such work only as must be done by a group of men all engaged at the work at once, or who are working at a dependent sequence of operations, or both. This card contains but those portions of the instructions for each man which refer to those elements which must be completed before a following element, to be done by the next man in the sequence, can be completed.

Because of the nature of the work, the gang instruction card must be put in the hands of a leader, or foreman, whether or not it is also in the hands of each of the individuals. The amount of work which can be required as a set task for each individual member of the gang, the allowance for rest for overcoming fatigue, the time that the rest periods must occur, and the proper pay, are fully stated on the Individual Instruction Cards.

Methods of Teaching Foster Individuality

As will be shown at length in the Chapter on Teaching, under Scientific Management teaching is not only general, by "Systems," "Standing Orders," or "Standard Practice," but also specific. Specialized teachers, called, unfortunately for the emphasis desired to be put on teaching, "functional foremen," help the individual worker to overcome his peculiar difficulties.

This teaching not only allows every worker to supplement his deficiencies of disposition or experience, but the teachers' places give opportunities for those who have a talent for imparting knowledge to utilize and develop it.

Individual Incentive and Welfare

Finally, individual incentive and individual welfare are not only both present, but interdependent. Desire for individual success, which might lead a worker to respond to the incentive till he held back perhaps the work of others, is held in balance by interdependence of bonuses.

Summary

Result of Idea of Individuality upon Work

To recapitulate; — Under Traditional Management, because of its frequent neglect of the idea of individuality, work is often unsystematized, and high output is usually the result of "speeding up" only, with constant danger of a falling off in quality overbalancing men and injury to men and machinery. Under Transitory Management, as outputs are separated, separately recorded, and as the idea of Individuality is embodied in selecting men, setting tasks, the instruction cards, periods of rest, teaching, incentives and welfare, output increases without undue pressure on the worker. Under Scientific Management — with various elements which embody individuality fully developed, output increases, to the welfare of worker, manager, employer and consumer and with no falling off in quality.

Effect Upon the Worker

The question of the effect upon the worker of emphasis laid upon individuality, can perhaps best be answered by asking and answering the following questions: —

1. When, where, how, and how much is individuality considered?
2. What consideration is given to the relation of the mind to the body of the individual?
3. What is the relative emphasis on consideration of individual and class?
4. In how far is the individual the unit?
5. What consideration is given to idiosyncrasies?
6. What is the effect toward causing or bringing about development, that is, broadening, deepening and making the individual more progressive?

Extent of Consideration of Individuality

Under Traditional Management consideration of individuality is seldom present, but those best forms of Traditional Management that are successful are so because it is present. This is not usually recognized, but investigation shows that the successful manager, or foreman, or boss, or superintendent succeeds either because of his own individuality or because he brings out to good advantage the individual possibilities of his men.

The most successful workers under Traditional Management are those who are allowed to be individuals and to follow out their individual bents of greatest efficiency, instead of being crowded down to become mere members of gangs, with no chance to think, to do, or to be anything but parts of the gang.

Under Transitory Management, and most fully under Scientific Management, the spirit of individuality, far from being crowded out, is a basic principle, and everything possible is done to encourage the desire to be a personality.

Relation of Mind to Body

Under Traditional Management, where men worked in the same employ for a long time, much consideration was given to the relation of the mind to the body. It was realized that men must not be speeded up beyond what they could do healthfully; they must have good sleeping quarters and good, savory and appetizing food to eat and not be fatigued unnecessarily, if they were to become successful workers. More than this, philanthropic employers often attempted to supply many kinds of comfort and amusement.

Under Transitory Management the physical and mental welfare are provided for more systematically.

Under Scientific Management consideration of the mind and body of the workman, and his health, and all that includes, is a subject for scientific study and for scientific administration. As shown later, it eliminates all discussion and troubles of so-called "welfare work," because the interests of the employer and the worker become identical and everything that is done becomes the concern of both.

Scientific Management realizes that the condition of the body effects every possible mental process. It is one of the great advantages of a study of the psychology of management that the subject absolutely demands from the start, and insists in every stage of the work, on this relationship of the body to the mind, and of the surroundings, equipment, etc., of the worker to his work. It is almost impossible, in management, to separate the subject of the worker from that of his work, or to think of the worker as not working except in such a sense as "ceasing-from-work," "about-to-work," "resting to overcome fatigue of work," or "resting during periods of unavoidable delays." The relation of the worker to his work is constantly in the mind of the manager. It is for this reason that not only does management owe much to psychology, but that psychology, as applied to any line of study, will, ultimately, be recognized as owing much to the science of management.

Relative Emphasis on Individual and Class

Under Traditional Management the gang, or the class, usually receives the chief emphasis. If the individual developed, as he undoubtedly did, in many kinds of mechanical work, especially in small organizations, it was more or less because it was not possible for the managers to organize the various individuals into classes or gangs. In the transitory stage the emphasis is shifting. Under Scientific Management the emphasis is most decidedly and emphatically upon the individual as the unit to be managed, as has been shown.

Individual as the Unit

Under Traditional Management the individual was seldom the unit. Under Transitory Management the individual is the unit, but there is not much emphasis in the early stages placed upon his peculiarities and personalities. Under Scientific Management the unit is always the individual, and the utilizing and strengthening of his personal traits, special ability and skill is a dominating feature.

Emphasis on Idiosyncrasies

Under Traditional Management there is either no consideration given to idiosyncrasies, or too wide a latitude is allowed. In cases where no consideration is given, there is often either a pride in the managers in "treating all men alike," though they might respond better to different handling, or else the individual is undirected and his personality manifests itself in all sorts of unguided directions, many of which must necessarily be wasteful, unproductive, or incomplete in development. Under Scientific Management, functionalization, as will be shown, provides for the utilization of all idiosyncrasies and efficient deviations from class, and promotion is so planned that a man may develop along the line of his chief ability. Thus initiative is encouraged and developed constantly.

Development of Individuality

The development of individuality is more sure under Scientific Management than it is under either of the other two forms of management, (a) because this development is recognized to be a benefit to the worker and to the employer and (b) because this development as a part of a definite plan is provided for and perfected scientifically.

2

Functionalization

Definition of Functionalization

A function, says the Century Dictionary, is — "The fulfilment or discharge of a set duty or requirement, exercise of a faculty or office, or power of acting, faculty, — that power of acting in a specific way which appertains to a thing by virtue of its special constitution; that mode of action or operation which is proper to any organ, faculty, office structure, etc. (This is the most usual signification of the term)."

"Functionalization" is not given in the Century Dictionary. The nearest to it to be found there is "Functionality," which is defined as — "The state of having or being a function." Functionalization as here used means — the state of being divided into functions, or being functionalized. "Functionalize" is given in the Century Dictionary, defined as "to assign some office or function to" — the note being made that it is rare. "Functionalize" may not be the best word that could be used in this connection, but there seems to be no other word in the English language which contains its full meaning, therefore we will use the word here in the sense of assigning work according to capacity or faculty. A faculty means — "A specific power, mental or physical; a special capacity for any particular kind of action or affection; natural capability."

Psychological Use of Functionalization

The word "Function" is in constant use by modern psychologists, especially by those who believe that —

"Psychology is the science of the self in relation to environment," or that "Psychology is a scientific account of our mental processes." Sully defines a function as "a psychologically simple process," and compares its elementariness to a muscular contraction as an element of a step in walking.

In investigating the principle of Functionalization as embodied in various forms of Management, we must note that, while Management can, and does under Scientific Management, attempt to functionalize *work* as far as possible, it will be impossible to come to ultimate results until a psychological study of the requirement of the work *from* the worker, and results of the work *on* the worker is made.

Functionalization in Management

"Functional Management" consists, to quote Dr. Taylor, "in so directing the work of management that each man from the assistant superintendent down shall have as few functions as possible to perform. If practicable, the work of each man in the management should be confined to the performance of a single leading function."

A study of functionalization as applied to management must answer the following questions:

1. How is the work divided?
2. How are the workers assigned to the work?
3. What are the results to the work?
4. What are the results to the worker?

Traditional Management Seldom Functionalizes

Under Traditional Management the principle of Functionalization was seldom applied or understood. Even when the manager tried to separate planning from performing, or so to divide the work that each worker could utilize his special ability, there were no permanently beneficial results, because there was no standard method of division.

The Work of the Foreman Not Properly Divided

The work of a foreman was not divided, but the well rounded man, as Dr. Taylor says, was supposed to have

1. Brain

2. Education
3. Special or technical knowledge, manual dexterity or strength
4. Tact
5. Energy
6. Grit
7. Honesty
8. Judgment, or common sense
9. Good health.

Dr. Taylor says — "Plenty of men who possess only three of the above qualities can be hired at any time for labourer's wages. Add four of these qualities together, and you get a higher priced man. The man combining five of these qualities begins to be hard to find, and those with 6, 7 and 8 are almost impossible to get."

Yet, under Traditional Management these general qualities and many points of specific training were demanded of the foreman. Dr. Taylor has enumerated the qualifications or the duties of a gang boss in charge of lathes or planers. Careful reading of this enumeration will show most plainly that the demands made were almost impossible of fulfilment.

Another list which is interesting is found in "Cost Reducing System," a long list of the duties of the Ideal Superintendent or foreman in construction work.

Qualifications and Duties of First Class Foreman

A first class foreman must have:

- bodily
- strength
- brains
- common sense
- education
- energy
- good health
- good judgment
- grit

- manual dexterity
- special knowledge
- tact
- technical knowledge.

He must be:

- able to concentrate his mind upon small things
- able to read drawings readily
- able to visualize the work at every stage of its progress, and even before it begins
- a master of detail
- honest
- master of at least one trade.
- His duties consist of:
- considering broad policies.
- considering new applicants for important positions.
- considering the character and fitness of the men.
- determining a proper day's work.
- determining costs.
- determining the method of compensation.
- determining the sequence of events for the best results.
- disciplining the men.
- dividing the men into gangs for speed contests.
- fixing piece and day rates.
- getting rid of inferior men.
- handling relations with the unions.
- hiring good men.
- installing such methods and devices as will detect dishonesty.
- instructing the workman.
- keeping the time and disciplining those who are late or absent.
- laying out work.
- looking ahead to see that there are men enough for future work.

- looking ahead to see that there is enough future work for the men.
- making profits.
- measuring each man's effort fairly.
- obtaining good results in quality.
- paying the men on days when they are discharged.
- paying the men on pay day.
- preventing soldiering.
- readjusting wages.
- retaining good men.
- seeing that all men are honest.
- seeing that men are shifted promptly when breakdowns occur.
- seeing that repairs are made promptly before breakdowns occur,
- seeing that repairs are made promptly after breakdowns occur.
- seeing that the most suitable man is allotted to each part of the work.
- seeing that the work is not slighted.
- setting piece work prices.
- setting rates.
- setting tasks.
- supervising timekeeping.
- teaching the apprentices.
- teaching the improvers.
- teaching the learners.

In studying these lists we note —

1. That the position will be best filled by a very high and rare type of man.
2. That the man is forced to use every atom of all of his powers and at the same time to waste his energies in doing much unimportant pay reducing routine work, some of which could be done by clerks.

3. That in many cases the work assigned for him to do calls for qualifications which are diametrically opposed to each other.
4. That psychology tells us that a man fitted to perform some of these duties would probably be mentally ill fitted for performing others in the best possible way that they could be performed.

Work not Well Done

Not only does the foreman under Traditional Management do a great deal of work which can be done by cheaper men, but he also wastes his time on clerical work in which he is not a specialist, and, therefore, which he does not do as well as the work can be done by a cheaper man, and this takes more of his time than he ought to devote to it. The result is that the work is not done as well as it can and should be done. A most perfect illustration of a common form of Traditional Management is the old story of the foreman, who, in making his rounds of the various parts of the work, comes to the deep hole being excavated for a foundation pier and says hurriedly — "How many of yez is there in the hole?" "Seven." "The half of yez come up." The theoretical defects of the old type of management often seen before the advent of the trained engineer on the work include: —

1. lack of planning ahead.
2. an overworked foreman.
3. no functionalizing of the work.
4. no standards of individual efficiency.
5. unmeasured individual outputs.
6. no standard methods.
7. no attempt at teaching.
8. inaccurate directions.
9. lack of athletic contests.
10. no high pay for extra efficiency.
11. poor investigation of workers' special capabilities.

In spite of the fact that under unfunctionalized management the foreman has far more to do than he can expect to do well, the average foreman thinks that he belongs to a class above his position. This is partly because the position is so unstandardized that it arouses a sense of unrest, and partly because he has to spend much of his time at low priced functions.

Under the feeling of enmity, or at least, of opposition, which often exists, openly or secretly, between the average Traditional Management and men, the foreman must ally himself with one side or the other. If he joins with the men, he must countenance the soldiering, which they find necessary in order to maintain their rates of wages. Thus the output of the shop will seldom increase and his chance for appreciation and promotion by the management will probably be slight and slow. His position as boss, combined with that of ally of the men, is awkward.

If he allies himself to the management, he must usually become a driver of the men, if he wishes to increase output. This condition will never be agreeable to him unless he has an oversupply of brute instincts.

The Workers not best Utilized

Under the best types of Traditional Management we do find more or less spasmodic attempts at the functionalization of the worker. When there was any particular kind of work to be done, the worker who seemed to the manager to be the best fitted, was set at that kind of work. For example — if there was a particularly heavy piece of work he might say — "Let A do it because he is strong." If there was a particularly fine piece of work to be done he might say — "Let B do it because he is specially skilled." If there was a piece of work to be done which required originality, he might say — "Let C do it for the reason that he is inventive and resourceful;" but, in most cases, when the particular job on hand was finished, the worker selected to do it returned to other classes of work, and such special fitness or capability as he had, was seldom systematically utilized, or automatically assigned to his special function, neither was such experience as he had gained systematically conserved. Moreover, no such study of the work to be done had been made as would prove that the assignment of that particular worker to the work was right. The psychology of this was entirely wrong, — not only had no such study of the general and particular characteristics, traits, faculties, and talents of the man been made as would prove that he was the right man to be assigned, but the mere fact that he possessed one quality necessary for the work, if he really did possess it, was no sign that the other qualities which he possessed might not make him the wrong man to be chosen. Even if the man did happen to be assigned to work for which he was particularly suited, unless provision were made to keep him at such work only, to keep him well supplied with work, to allow time for rest, and to provide proper pay, he could not utilize his capabilities to the fullest extent.

Transitory Management Functionalizes

Under Transitory Management, management becomes gradually more and more functionalized. With separated outputs and separate records, the worker's capabilities become apparent, and he can be assigned to the standardized positions which gradually evolve. Every recognition of individuality carries with it a corresponding functionalization of men and work.

Functionalization a Fundamental of Scientific Management

With Scientific Management comes the realization that with close study and with functionalization only, can that provision and assignment of the work which is best for both work and worker be obtained. The principle is applied to every part of management, and results in

1. separating the planning from the performing.
2. functionalizing foremen.
3. functionalizing workers.
4. assigning competent workers to fitting work.

Separating the Planning from the Performing

The emphasis on separating the planning from the performing in Scientific Management cannot be over-estimated. It is a part of Dr. Taylor's fourth principle of Scientific Management, "Almost equal division of the work and the responsibility between the management and the workmen." The greatest outputs can be achieved to the greatest benefit to managers and men when the work is divided, the management undertaking that part of the work that it is best fitted to do, the workmen performing that part which they are best fitted to do.

The Work of the Planning Department

It has been determined by actual experience that the line of division most agreeable to the managers and the workmen and most productive of cooperation by both, as well as most efficient in producing low costs, is that which separates the planning from the performing. Under Scientific Management the Planning Department relieves the man of determining —

1. what work is to be done.
2. sequence in which it is to be done.
3. method by which it shall be done.
4. where it shall be done.
5. which men shall do it.
6. time that it shall take.
7. exact quality of product.
8. quantity of additional pay that shall be given for doing it.

Work of the Workers

The men are simply given standard tasks to do, with teachers to help them, and a standard wage according to performance as a reward. There are but three things expected of them: —

1. cooperation with the management in obtaining the prescribed work, method and quality.
2. the exercise of their ingenuity in making improvements after they have learned the standard prescribed practice.
3. the fitting of themselves for higher pay and promotion.

Functionalized Foremanship

The work that, under Scientific Management, is usually done by one man, the Foreman, is subdivided into eight or more functions. These functions are assigned to the following functional foremen: Planning Department

1. Order of work and route man
2. Instruction card man
3. Cost and time clerk
4. Disciplinarian.
5. Gang boss
6. Speed boss
7. Repair boss
8. Inspector.

Each of the above functions may be in charge of a separate man, or one man may be in charge of several functions, or several men may do the work of one function; the work being divided between them in some cases by further functionalizing it, — and in others by separating it into similar parts. Which of these conditions is most effective depends on the size of the job, or the nature of the job to be done.

The important question is, not the number of men doing the planning, but the fact that every foreman, so far as is possible, is assigned to the special kind of work that he is best fitted to do with the greatest elimination of unnecessary waste.

Changes in the Functions of the Foreman

A Foreman, under Scientific Management, must have three qualifications. He must be

1. a specialist at the work that he is to do.
2. a good observer, able to note minute variations of method, work, and efficiency.
3. a good teacher.

A comparison of these qualifications with those of the foreman under Traditional Management, will show as important changes, —

1. the particular place in the field of knowledge in which the foreman must specialize.
2. the change in the type of criticism expected from the foreman.
3. the far greater emphasis placed on duties as a teacher.

Importance of the Teaching Feature in Functional Foremanship

The teaching feature of management, — the most important feature of Scientific Management, — will be discussed in the Chapter on Teaching. Only so much is included here as shows its derivation from the principle of functionalization, and its underlying importance.

Functionalization means specialization. This results in cooperation between foremen, between foremen and workers, and between workers. By "cooperate" is here meant not only "to work together," but also "to work together to promote the object." This cooperation persists not only because it is demanded by the work, but also because it is insured by the inter-dependent bonuses.

Functionalization under Scientific Management separates planning from performing. This means that the specialists who plan must teach the specialist who performs, this being the way in which they cooperate to the greatest personal advantage to all.

Basis of Division into Functions

Under Scientific Management divisions are made on the basis of underlying ideas. Functions are not classified as they are embodied in particular men, but men are classified as they embody particular functions. This allows of standardization, through which alone can progress and evolution come quickest. It is comparatively easy and simple to standardize a function. Being a "set duty," it can be fixed, studied and simplified. It is extremely difficult and complex to standardize an individual. This standardizing of the function, however, in no wise stunts individuality. On the contrary, it gives each individual a chance to utilize his particular faculty for obtaining the greatest efficiency, pleasure and profit. This is well illustrated in the case of specialization in baseball, for excellence as a pitcher does not stunt the player as a catcher.

Functions may be subdivided as far as the nature of the work demands. Note here, again, that it is the relative complexity or simplicity of the nature of the work that is to be done that determines the degree of its functionalization, not the number of men employed at the work. Note, also, that with every subdivision of functions comes greater opportunity for specialization, hence for individual development.

Place of Operation of the Functions

Four functions of the eight find their place in the planning department. The other four are out on the work. That is to say,— the men who represent four functions work almost entirely in the planning room, while the men who represent the other four functions work mostly among the workers.

This division is, however, largely a matter of convenience. Three of the first four groups of men communicate with the workers mostly in writing and are seldom engaged as observers, except in obtaining data for the creation of standards, while the fourth is often in the planning room. The last four usually communicate with the men orally, and must observe and teach the worker constantly.

In the descriptions that follow, each function is represented as embodied in one man, this aiding simplicity and clearness in description.

The Order of Work and Route Clerk

The Order of Work and Route Clerk lays out the exact path of each piece of work, and determines the sequence of events of moving and a general outline of performance. With the requirements of the work in mind, the most efficient day's work for each worker is determined. The paths and sequences of transportation are outlined by means of route charts and route sheets showing graphical and detailed directions, which are the means by which the foremen of the other functions are enabled to cooperate with other foremen and with the workers.

The work of this function requires a practical man, of the successful foreman type, experienced in the class of work to be executed, who is also familiar with the theories of Scientific Management in general, and the work of the other foremen in particular, and who has the faculty of visualization and well developed constructive imagination. He must also have at his command in systematic form, and available for immediate use, records of previous experience.

The Instruction Card Clerk

The Instruction Card Clerk prepares written directions for the workers as to what methods should be used in doing the work, the sequence of performance of the elements of the method, the speeds and action of the accompanying machinery, the time that each element should take for its performance, the time allowed for rest for overcoming fatigue caused by its performance, and the total elapsed time allowed for performing all of the work on the instruction card in order to obtain the unusually high additional wages as a reward for his skill and cooperation.

The work of this function requires the best available (but not necessarily the fastest), practical experienced man in the trade described, who also has had sufficient experience in motion study and time study to enable him to write down the best known method for doing the work described, and also prophesying the correct time that the work and rest from its resulting fatigue will take. He must supplement the instruction card with such sketches, drawings and photographs as will best assist the worker to visualize his work before and during its performance.

Function of Time and Cost Clerk

The work done by the Time and Cost Clerk calls for accuracy and a love of statistical detail. It will help him if he knows the trades with which he is cooperating, but such knowledge is not absolutely essential. He will be promoted fastest who has a knowledge of the theory of management, coupled with the theory and practice of statistics and accountancy, for the true costs must include knowledge of costs of materials, and the distribution of the overhead burden of running expenses and selling.

Function of the Disciplinarian

The function of the Disciplinarian must be discussed at length, both because of the psychological effect upon the men of the manner of the discipline and of the disciplinarian, and because of the fact that the disciplinarian is the functional foreman of the four in the planning department who comes in most personal contact with the workers, as well as all of the other foremen, and the Superintendent. It is important to note, in the discussion that is to follow, not only how disciplining is transformed as management develops progressively, but also that the intimate acquaintance of discipliner with disciplined is not done away with, but rather supplemented by the standardizing which is the outcome of Scientific Management.

The defects of methods of disciplining under Traditional Management are remedied, but here, as always, Scientific Management retains and develops that which is good. This because the good in the older forms conformed, unconsciously, to the underlying laws.

Defects of Disciplining Under Traditional Management

Under Traditional Management, the disciplining is done by the foreman; that is, the punishment is meted out by the man who has charge of all activities of the men under him. This is actually, in practice and in theory, psychologically wrong. If there is one man who should be in a state of mind that would enable him to judge dispassionately, it is the disciplinarian. The man to be disciplined is usually guilty of one of six offenses:

1. an offense against an employe of a grade above him.
2. an offense against an employe of the same grade.
3. an offense against an employe of a grade below him.
4. falling short in the quality of his work.
5. falling short in the quantity of his work.
6. an offense against the system (disobeying orders), falling down on schedule, or intentionally not cooperating.

The employe over him, or the foreman, to whom he is supposed to have done some injustice, would be in no state of mind to judge as to the man's culpability. In the case of an offense against an employe of the same grade, the best that the injured employe could do would be to appeal to his foreman, who oftentimes is not an unprejudiced judge, and the multiplicity of whose duties give him little time to give attention to the subject of disciplining.

If the offense is against quantity or quality of work, again the old fashioned foreman, for lack of time, and for lack of training and proper standards of measurement, will find it almost impossible to know how guilty the man is, and what form of punishment and what amount of punishment or loss of opportunity for progress will be appropriate.

Changes in Disciplinarian's Function Under Scientific Management

All this is changed under Scientific Management. The disciplinarian is a specially appointed functional foreman, and has few other duties except those that are directly or indirectly connected with disciplining. He is in touch with the requirements of the work, because he is in the Planning Department; he is in touch with the employment bureau, and knows which men should be employed; he has a determining voice in deciding elementary rate fixing and should always be consulted before wages are changed or a reassignment of duties is determined. All of these are great advantages to him in deciding justly and appropriately punishments and promotion, not for the workers alone but also for the foremen and the managers.

Duties of the Disciplinarian

The Disciplinarian keeps a record of each man's virtues and defects; he is in position to know all about the man; where he comes from; what his natural and acquired qualifications are; what his good points, possibilities and special fitness are; what his wages are, and his need for them. All that it is possible for the managers to know of the men is to be concentrated in this disciplinarian. He is, in practice, more the counsel and advocate of the worker than an unsympathetic judge, as is indicated by the fact that his chief function is that of "diplomat" and "peacemaker." His greatest duty is to see that the "square deal" is meted out without fear or favour to employer or to employee.

Importance of Psychology in Disciplining

Not only does the position of disciplinarian under Scientific Management answer the psychological requirements for such a function, but also the holder of the position of disciplinarian must understand psychology and apply, at least unconsciously, and preferably consciously, the known laws of psychology, if he wishes to be successful. The disciplinarian must consider not only what the man has done and the relation of this act of his to his other acts; he must also investigate the cause and the motive of the act, for on the cause and motive, in reality, depends more than on the act itself. He must probe into the physical condition of the man, as related to his mental acts. He must note the effect of the same kind of discipline under different conditions; for example, he must note that, on certain types of people, disciplining in the presence of other people has a most derogatory effect, just as rewards before people may have a most advantageous effect. Upon others, discipline that is meted out in the presence of other people is the only sort of discipline which has the desired effect. The sensitiveness of the person to be disciplined, the necessity for sharp discipline, and for that particular sort of discipline which may require the element of shame in it, must all be considered. He must be able to discover and note whether the discipline should be meted out to a ringleader, and whether the other employees, supposed to be blameworthy, are really only guilty in acquiescing, or in failing to report one who has really furnished the initiative. He must differentiate acts which are the result of following a ringleader blindly from the concerted acts of disobedience of a crowd, for the "mob spirit" is always an element to be estimated and separately handled.

Inadequacy of Terms in Disciplining

The words "disciplinarian" and "punishment" are most unfortunate. The "Disciplinarian" would be far better called the "peacemaker," and the "punishment" by some such word as the "adjustment." It is *not* the duty of the disciplinarian to "take out anybody's grudge" against a man; it *is* his duty to adjust disagreements. He must remember constantly that his discipline must be of such a nature that the result will be for the permanent best interests of the one disciplined, his co-workers, his assoᵓiates and his family.

The aim is, not to put the man down, but to keep him up to his standard, as will be shown later in a chapter on Incentives. If the punishment is in the form of a fine, it must not in any way return to the coffers of the management. The fines collected— even those fines collected from the individuals composing the management, should go in some form to the benefit of the men themselves, such, for example, as contributions to a workman's sick benefit fund or to general entertainment at the annual outing of employees. In practice, the disciplinarian is rather the friend of the worker than of the employer, if the two interests can possibly be separated. Again "penalty" is a bad word to use. Any words used in this connection should preferably have had taken from them any feeling that personal prejudice affects the discipline. It is the nature of the offense itself which should prescribe what the outcome of it shall be.

The position of disciplinarian requires a man who has a keen sense of justice, who has had such experience as to enable him to smooth out difficulties until all are in a frame of mind where they can look upon their own acts and the acts of others calmly. He must be able so to administer his duties that each decision inspires the realization that he acted to the best of his knowledge and belief. He must be one who is fearless, and has no tendency to have favourites. He must have a clear knowledge of the theories and principles of Scientific Management, in order that he can fill the position of enforcer of its laws.

The Gang Boss

The duties of The Gang Boss are to see that the worker has plenty of work ahead, to see that everything that he will need with which to do the work is at hand, and to see that the work is actually "set," or placed and performed correctly. This position calls for a practical demonstrator, who must himself be able and willing actually to prepare and help on the work. It calls particularly for a man with teaching ability, with special emphasis on ability to teach, with great exactness, the prescribed method and to follow the orders of the planning department implicitly.

The Speed Boss

The speed boss is responsible for the methods of doing work with machinery. He has charge of overseeing the work, and teaching the worker, during the entire time that the work is being done. He must be prepared constantly to demonstrate at any time not only *how* the work is done, but also that it can be done in the specified time called for in order to earn the bonus. This position calls for a man who is able, personally, to carry out the detailed written orders of the instruction card in regard to speeds, feeds, cuts, methods of operation, quality and quantity.

He must be proficient at the art of imparting his knowledge to other workmen, and at the same time be able to secure the prescribed outputs and quantities. He need not be the fastest worker in the shop, but he should be one of the most intelligent workers and best teachers, with a keen desire to cooperate, both with the workers and with the other foremen.

The Repair Boss

The repair boss has charge of the plant and its maintenance. He must have a natural love of order and of cleanliness, and a systematic type of mind. This position calls for a man with an experience that will enable him to detect liability of breakdowns before they actually occur. He must be resourceful in repairing unexpected breakdowns in an emergency, and be able at all times to carry out literally the directions given on the instruction cards of the Planning Department for cleaning, maintaining, and repairing the machines.

The Inspector

The function of inspector under scientific or the Taylor plan of management is most important, especially in connection with the "first inspection." During the manufacture of the first piece and after it is finished the inspector passes and reports upon it before the worker proceeds with the other pieces. Here the worker gets a return in person for each successive act on the first piece he makes under a new instruction card, or, if he is a new worker, under an old instruction card. Ambiguity of instructions, if present, is thus eliminated, and wrong actions or results are corrected before much damage to material has been done and before much time and effort are wasted. The first erroneous cycles of work are not repeated, and the worker is promptly shown exactly how efficiently he has succeeded in determining the requirements of his instructions.

The inspector is responsible for the quality of the work. He fulfills the requirements of Schloss, who says, in speaking of the danger, under some managements, that the foreman will sacrifice quality to speed, if he gets a bonus for quantity of output, — "The best safeguard against this serious danger would be found in the appointment of a distinct staff of inspectors whose duty it should be to ascertain, as the work proceeds, that the stipulated standards of excellence are at all times scrupulously maintained." This position of inspector requires an observant man who naturally is inclined to give constructive rather than destructive-criticism. He should be a man who can cooperate with the workman and foreman to rescue condemned or damaged material with the least expenditure of time, effort and expense.

Functionalizing the Worker

Under Scientific Management, the worker as well as the foreman, is a specialist. This he becomes by being relieved of everything that he is not best fitted to do, and allowed to concentrate upon doing, according to exact and scientifically derived methods, that work at which he is an expert.

Relieving the Worker of the Planning

The planning is taken away from the worker, not because it is something too choice, sacred or entertaining for him to do, or something which the managers desire to do themselves, but because it is best, for the workers themselves as well as the work, that the planning be done by specialists at planning. If he is expert enough to plan, the worker will be promoted to the planning department. In the meantime, he is working under the best plan that experts can devise.

Master Planning a Life Study

The best planner is he who, — other things being equal,— is the most ingenious, the most experienced and the best observer. It is an art to observe; it requires persistent attention. The longer and the more the observer observes, the more details, and variables affecting details, he observes. The untrained observer could not expect to compete with one of special natural talent who has also been trained. It is not every man who is fitted by nature to observe closely, hence to plan. To observe is a condition precedent to visualizing. Practice in visualizing makes for increasing the faculty of constructive imagination. He with the best constructive imagination is the master planner.

The art of observing is founded on a study of fundamental elements. In order that planning may be done best, previous to starting work, the entire sequence of operations must be laid out, so that the ideas of value of every element of every subdivision of the process of working may be corrected to act most efficiently in relation with each and all of the subsequent parts and events that are to follow. This planning forwards and backwards demands an equipment of time study, motion study and micro-motion study records such as can be used economically only when all the planning is done in one place, with one set of records. The planner must be able to see and control the whole problem in all of its aspects.

For example, — the use that is to be made of the work after it is completed may entirely change the methods best used in doing it. Thus, the face of a brick wall that is to be plastered does not require and should not have the usual excellence of nicely ruled joints required on a face that is not to be plastered. In fact, the roughest, raggedest joints will be that quality of wall that will make the plaster adhere the best.

As an example of professional observation and investigation with which no untrained observer could compete, we cite the epoch making work of Dr. Taylor in determining the most efficient speeds, feeds, cuts and shape of tools to use for the least wastefulness in cutting metals.

Dr. Taylor, an unusually brilliant man, at the end of twenty-six years, working with the best scientists, engineers, experimenters, and workmen, after an expenditure of literally hundreds of thousands of dollars, was able to determine and write down a method for cutting metals many times less wasteful in time than was ever known before; but the data from the experiments was so complex and involved that a considerable knowledge of higher mathematics had to be used to apply the data. Furthermore, the data was in such form that it took longer to use the knowledge contained therein than it did to do the work on any given piece of metal cutting. After gathering this knowledge, Dr. Taylor, with his assistants, first Mr. Gantt and finally Mr. Barth, reduced it to such a form that now it can be used in a matter of a few seconds or minutes. This was done by making slide rules. Today workers have this knowledge in a form that any machinist can use with a little instruction. As a result, Dr. Taylor's observations have revolutionized the design of metal cutting machinery and the metal cutting industry, and the data he collected is used in every metal cutting planning department.

Furthermore, as a by-product to his observations and investigations, he discovered the Taylor-White process of making high speed steel, which revolutionized the steel tool industry. No untrained workman could expect ever to compete with such work as this in obtaining results for most efficient planning and at the same time perform his ordinary work.

Wastefulness of Individual Planning

Even if it were possible so to arrange the work of every worker that he could be in close proximity to the equipment for planning and could be given the training needed, individual planning for "small lots" with no systematized standardization of planning-results would be an economic waste that would cause an unnecessary hardship on the worker, the employer and the ultimate consumer. Individual planning could not fit the broad scheme of planning, and at best would cause delays and confusion, and make an incentive to plan for the individual self, instead of planning for the greatest good of the greatest number.

Again, even if it were possible to plan best by individual planning, there is a further waste in changing from one kind of work to another. This waste is so great and so obvious that it was noticed and recognized by the earliest manufacturers and economists.

Hardship to the Worker of Individual Planning

To obtain the most wages and profits there must be the most savings to divide. These cannot be obtained when each man plans for himself (except in the home trades), because all large modern operations have the quantity of output dependent upon the amount of blockades, stoppages and interferences caused by dependent sequences. It is not, therefore, possible to obtain the most profit or most wages by individual planning. Planning is a general function, and the only way to obtain the best results is by organized planning, and by seeing that no planning is done for one worker without proper consideration of its bearing and effect upon any or all the other men's outputs.

The Man Who Desires to be a Planner can be One

If the worker is the sort of a man who can observe and plan, or who desires to plan, even though he is not at first employed in the planning department, he is sure to get there finally, as the system provides that each man shall go where he is best fitted. Positions in planning departments are hard to fill, because of the scarcity of men equipped to do this work. The difficulty of teaching men to become highly efficient planners is one of the reasons for the slow advance of the general adoption of Scientific Management.

The Man Who Dislikes Planning can be Relieved

It must not be forgotten that many people dislike the planning responsibility in connection with their work. For such, relief from planning makes the performance of the planned work more interesting and desirable.

Provision for Planning by all Under Scientific Management

Much has been said about the worker's "God-given rights to think," and about the necessity for providing every worker with an opportunity to think.

Scientific Management provides the fullest opportunities for every man to think, to exercise his mental faculties, and to plan

1. in doing the work itself, as will be shown at length in chapters that follow.
2. outside of the regular working hours, but in connection with promotion in his regular work.

Scientific Management provides always, and most emphatically, that the man shall have hours free from his work in such a state that he will not be too fatigued to do anything. Furthermore, if he work as directed, his number of working hours per day will be so reduced that he will have more time each day for his chosen form of mental stimulus and improvement.

Our friend John Brashear is a most excellent example of what one can do in after hours away from his work. He was a labourer in a steel mill. His duties were not such as resemble in any way planning or research work, yet he became one of the world's most prominent astronomical thinkers and an Honorary member of the American Society of Mechanical Engineers, because he had the desire to be a student. Under Scientific Management such a desire receives added impetus from the method of attack provided for through its teaching.

Functionalizing the Work Itself

The work of each part of the planning and performing departments may be functionalized, or subdivided, as the result of motion study and time study. The elementary timed units are combined or synthesized into tasks, made to fit the capabilities of specialized workers. It is then necessary to: —

1. List the duties and requirements of the work.
2. Decide whether the place can be best handled as one, or subdivided into several further subdivisions, or functions, or even sub-functions, for two or more function specialists.

For the sake of analysis, all work may be considered as of one of two classes: —

1. the short time job.
2. the long time job.

These two divisions are handled differently, as follows:

The Short Time Job

On the short time job that probably will never be repeated, there is little opportunity and no economic reason for specially training a man for its performance. The available man best suited to do the work with little or no help should be chosen to do it. The suitability of the man for the work should be determined only by applying simple tests, or, if even these will cause costly delay or more expense than the work warrants, the man who appears suitable and who most desires the opportunity to do the work can be assigned to it. If the job is connected with a new art, a man whose habits will help him can be chosen.

For example: — in selecting a man to fly, it has been found advantageous to give a trick bicycle rider the preference.

There is no other reason why the man for the short job should not be fitted as well to his work as the man for the long job, except the all-important reason of cost for special preparation. Any expense for study of the workers must be borne ultimately both by worker and management, and it is undesirable to both that expense should be incurred which will not be ultimately repaid.

The Long Time Job

The long time job allows of teaching, therefore applicants for it may be carefully studied. Usually that man should be chosen who, with all the natural qualifications and capabilities for the job, except practical skill, requires the most teaching to raise him from the lower plane to that highest mental and manual plane which he is able to fill successfully continuously. In this way each man will be developed into a worker of great value to the management and to himself.

The man who is capable and already skilled at some work is thus available for a still higher job, for which he can be taught. Thus the long job affords the greatest opportunity for promotion. The long job justifies the expenditure of money, effort and time by management and men, and is the ideal field for the application of scientific selection and functionalization.

Summary

Effect of Functionalization upon the Work

Under Traditional Management, there was little or no definite functionalization. If the quantity of output did increase, as the result of putting a man at that work for which he seemed best fitted, there was seldom provision made for seeing that the quality of product was maintained by a method of constructive inspection that prevented downward deviations from standard quality, instead of condemning large quantities of the finished product.

Under Transitory Management, the Department of Inspection is one of the first Functions installed. This assures maintained quality, and provides that all increase in output shall be actual gain. Under Scientific Management, functionalization results in increased quantity of output, with maintained and usually increased quality. This results in decreased cost. The cost is sufficiently lower to allow of increased wages to the employees, a further profit to the employer, and a maintained, or lowered, selling price. This means a benefit to the consumer.

It may be objected that costs cannot be lowered, because of the number of so-called "non-producers" provided for by Scientific Management. In answer to this it may be said that there are no non-producers under Scientific Management. Corresponding work that, under Scientific Management, is done in the planning department must all be done somewhere, in a less systematic manner, even under Traditional Management. The planning department, simply does this work more efficiently, — with less waste. Moreover, much work of the planning department, being founded on elementary units, is available for constant use. Here results an enormous saving by the conservation and utilization of planning effort. Also, standard methods are more apt to result in standard quality, and with less occasion for rejecting output that is below the requisite standards than is the case under Traditional Management.

Effect of Functionalization upon the Worker

Under Traditional Management, even if the worker often becomes functionalized, he seldom has assurance that he will be able to reap the harvest from remaining so, and even so, neither data nor teaching are provided to enable him to fulfil his function most successfully. Under Transitory Management the worker becomes more and more functionalized, as the results of motion study and time study make clear the advantages of specializing the worker.

Effects upon the Scientifically Managed Worker

Under Scientific Management the effects of Functionalization are so universal and so far reaching that it is necessary to enumerate them in detail.

Worker Relieved of Everything but His Special Functions

Functionalization, in providing that every man is assigned a special function, also provides that he be called upon to do work in that function only, relieving him of all other work and responsibility. Realization of this elimination has a psychological effect on action and habits of thinking. Places are Provided for Specialists

Functionalization utilizes men with decided bents, and allows each man to occupy that place for which he is fitted. Assignment to functions is done according to the capabilities and desires of those who are to fill them.

Specializing is Encouraged

It is most important to remember that the man with any special talent or talents, individuality or special fitness is much more likely, under Scientific Management, to obtain and retain the place that he is fitted for than he ever could have been under Traditional Management, for, while many fairly efficient men can be found who can fill a general position, a man with the marked desirable trait necessary to fill a distinct position requiring that trait, will be one of few, and will have his place waiting for him.

One-Talent Men Utilized —.With Functionalization, men who lack qualifications for the position which they may, at the start, endeavour to fill, may be transferred to other positions, where the qualities they lack are not required. If a man has one talent, Scientific Management provides a place where that can be utilized.

For example: —

Men who cannot produce the prescribed output constantly, are placed on other work. The slow, unskilled worker who has difficulty to learn, may be put upon work requiring less skill, or where speed is not required so much as watchfulness and faithfulness. The worker who is slow, but exceptionally skilled, has the opportunity to rise to the position of the functional foreman, especially in the planning department, where knowledge, experience and resourcefulness, and especially ability to teach, are much more desired than speed and endurance. Thus there are places provided, below and above, that can utilize all kinds of abilities.

"All Round" Men are Utilized

The exceptional man who possesses executive ability in all lines, and balance between them all, is the ideal man for a manager, and his special "all round" ability would be wasted in any position below that of a manager.

Stability Provided For

Every man is maintained in his place by his interresponsibility with other men. If he is a worker, every man's work is held to standard quality by the inspector, while the requirements and rewards of his function are kept before him by the instruction card man, rate fixer and the disciplinarian.

Promotion and Development Provided For

Functionalization provides for promotion by showing every man not only the clearly circumscribed place where he is to work, but also by showing him the definite place above him to which he may be promoted and its path, and by teaching him how he can fill it. This allows him to develop the possibilities of his best self by using and specially training those talents which are most marked in him.

Functional Foremanship allows many more people, to become foremen, and to develop the will and judgment which foremanship implies.

Men in the Organization Preferred to Outsiders

Men in the organization are preferable to outsiders as functional foremen and for promotion. Not only does a worker's knowledge of his work help him to become more efficient when he is promoted to the position of foreman, — but his efficiency as a teacher is also increased by the fact that he knows and understands the workers whom he is there to teach.

All Men are Pushed Up

Scientific Management raises every man as high as he is capable of being raised. It does not speed him up, but pushes him up to the highest notch which he can fill. Actual practice has shown that there is a greater demand for efficient men in the planning department than there is supply; also, that men in the planning department who fit themselves for higher work can be readily promoted to positions of greater responsibility, either inside or outside the organization.

Years of Productivity Prolonged

Under Functionalization the number of years of productivity of all, workers and foremen alike, are increased. The specialty to which the man is assigned is his natural specialty, thus his possible and profitable working years are prolonged, because he is at that work for which he is naturally fitted.

Moreover, the work of teaching is one at which the teacher becomes more clever and more valuable as time goes on, the functional foreman has that much more chance to become valuable as years go by.

Change in the Worker's Mental Attitude

The work under functionalization is such as to arouse the worker's attention and to hold his interest. But the most important and valuable change in the worker's feelings is the change in his attitude towards the foremen and the employer. From "natural enemies" as sometimes considered under typical Traditional Management, these all now become friends, with the common aim, cooperation, for the purpose of increasing output and wages, and lowering costs. This change of feeling results in an appreciation of the value of teaching, and also in promoting industrial peace.

3

Measurement in Management

Definition of Measurement

"Measurement," according to the Century Dictionary, — "is the act of measuring," and to measure is — "to ascertain the length, extent, dimensions, quantity or capacity of, by comparison with a standard; ascertain or determine a quantity by exact observation," or, again, "to estimate or determine the relative extent, greatness or value of, appraise by comparison with something else."

Measurement Important in Psychology

Measurement has always been of importance in psychology; but it is only with the development of experimental psychology and its special apparatus, that methods of accurate measurements are available which make possible the measurement of extremely short periods of time, or measurements "quick as thought," These enable us to measure the variations of different workers as to their abilities and their mental and physical fatigue; to study mental processes at different stages of mental and physical growth; to compare different people under the same conditions, and the same person under different conditions; to determine the personal coefficient of different workers, specialists and foremen, and to formulate resultant standards.

As in all other branches of science, the progress comes with the development of measurement.

Methods of Measurement in Psychology

No student of management, and of measurement in the field of management, can afford not to study, carefully and at length, methods of measurement under psychology. This, for at least two most important reasons, which will actually improve him as a measurer, i.e

1. The student will discover, in the books on experimental psychology and in the "Psychological Review," a marvellous array of results of scientific labouratory experiments in psychology, which will be of immediate use to him in his work.
2. He will receive priceless instruction in methods of measuring. No where better than in the field of psychology, can one learn to realize the importance of measurements, the necessity for determination of elements for study, and the necessity for accurate apparatus and accuracy in observation.

Prof. George M. Stratton, in his book "Experimental Psychology and Culture," — says "In mental measurements, therefore, there is no pretense of taking the mind's measure as a whole, nor is there usually any immediate intention of testing even some special faculty or capacity of the individual. What is aimed at is the measurement of a limited event in consciousness, such as a particular perception or feeling. The experiments are addressed, of course, not to the weight or size of such phenomena, but usually to their duration and intensity."

The emphasis laid on a study of elements is further shown in the same book by the following, — "The actual labouratory work in time-measurement, however, has been narrowed down to determining, not the time in general that is occupied by some mental action, but rather the shortest possible time in which a particular operation, like discrimination or choice or association or recognition, can be performed under the simplest and most favorable circumstances.

The experimental results here are something like speed or racing records, made under the best conditions of track and training. A delicate chronograph or chronoscope is used, which marks the time in thousandths of a second."

Measurement in Psychology Related to Measurement in Management

Measurement in psychology is of importance to measurement in management not only as a source of information and instruction, but also as a justification and support. Scientific Management has suffered from being called absurd, impractical, impossible, over-exact, because of the emphasis which it lays on measurement. Yet, to the psychologist, all present measurement in Scientific Management must appear coarse, inaccurate and of immediate and passing value only. With the knowledge that psychologists endorse accurate measurement, and will cooperate in discovering elements for study, instruments of precision and methods of investigation, the investigator in industrial fields must persist in his work with a new interest and confidence.

Scientific Management cannot hope to furnish psychology with either data or methods of measurement. It can and does, however, open a new field for study to experimental psychology, and shows itself willing to furnish the actual working difficulties or problems, to do the preliminary investigation, and to utilize results as fast as they can be obtained.

Psychologists Appreciate Scientific Management

The appreciation which psychologists have shown of work done by Scientific Management must be not only a matter of gratification, but of inspiration to all workers in Scientific Management.

So, also, must the new divisions of the Index to the Psychological Review relating to Activity and Fatigue, and the work being so extensively done in these lines by French, German, Italian and other nations, as well as by English and American psychologists.

Measurement Important in Management

The study of individuality and of functionalization have made plain the necessity of measurement for successful management. Measurement furnishes the means for obtaining that accurate knowledge upon which the science of management rests, as do all sciences — exact and inexact. Through measurement, methods of less waste are determined, standards are made possible, and management becomes a science, as it derives standards, and progressively makes and improves them, and the comparisons from them, accurate.

Problem of Measurement in Management — One of the important problems of measurement in management is determining how many hours should constitute the working day in each different kind of work and at what gait the men can work for greatest output and continuously thrive. The solution of this problem involves the study of the men, the work, and the methods, which study must become more and more specialized; but the underlying aim is to determine standards and individual capacity as exactly as is possible.

Capacity

There are at least four views of a worker's capacity.

1. What he thinks his capacity is.
2. What his associates think his capacity is.
3. What those over him think his capacity is.
4. What accurate measurement determines his actual capacity to be.

Ignorance of Real Capacity

Dr. Taylor has emphasized the fact that the average workman does not know either his true efficiency or his true capacity. The experience of others has also gone to show that even the skilled workman has little or inaccurate knowledge of the amount of output that a good worker can achieve at his chosen vocation in a given time.

For example, — until a bricklayer has seen his output counted for several days, he has little idea of how many bricks he can lay, or has laid, in a day. The average manager is usually even more ignorant of the capacity of the workers than are the men themselves. This is because of the prevalence of, and the actual necessity for the worker's best interest, under some forms of management, of "soldiering." Even when the manager realizes that soldiering is going on, he has no way, especially under ordinary management, of determining its extent.

Little Measurement in Traditional Management

Under Traditional Management there was little measurement of a man's capacity. The emphasis was entirely on the results. There was, it is true, in everything beyond the most elementary of Traditional Management, a measurement of the result. The manager did know, at the end of certain periods of time, how much work had been done, and how much it had cost him. This was a very important thing for him to know. If his cost ran too high, and his output fell too low, he investigated. If he found a defect, he tried to remedy it; but much time had to be wasted in this investigation, because often he had no idea where to start in to look for the defects. The result of the defects was usually the cause for the inquiry as to their presence.

He might investigate the men, he might investigate the methods, he might investigate the equipment, he might investigate the surroundings, and so on, — and very often in the mind of the Traditional manager, there was not even this most elementary division. If things went wrong he simply knew, — "Something is wrong somewhere," and it was the work of the foremen to find out where the place was, or so to speed up the men that the output should be increased and the cost lowered. Whether the defects were really remedied, or simply concealed by temporarily speeding up, was not seriously questioned.

Moreover, until measuring devices are secured, the only standard is what someone thinks about things, and the pity of it is that even this condition does not remain staple.

Transitory Management Realizes Value of Measurement

One of the first improvements introduced when Traditional Management gives place to the Transitory stage is the measurement of the separated output of individual workers. These outputs are measured and recorded. The records for extra high outputs are presented to the worker promptly, so that he may have a keen idea constantly of the relation of effort to output, while the fatigue and the effort of doing the work is still fresh in his mind.

The psychology of the prompt reward will be considered later at length, but it cannot be emphasized too often that the prompter the reward, the greater the stimulus. The reward will become associated with the fatigue in such a way that the worker will really get, at the time, more satisfaction out of his fatigue than he will discomfort; at the least, any dissatisfaction over his fatigue will be eliminated, by the constant and first thought of the reward which he has gotten through his efforts.

This record of efficiency is often so presented to the workers that they get an excellent idea of the numerical measure of their efficiency and its trend. This is best done by a graphical chart.

The records of the outputs of others on the same kind of work done concurrently, or a corresponding record on work done previously, will show the relative efficiency of any worker as compared with the rest. These standards of comparison are a strong incentive and, if they are shown at the time that such work is done, they also become so closely associated not only with the mental but the bodily feeling of the man that the next time the work is repeated, the thoughts that the same effort will probably bring greater results, and that it has done so in the past with others, will be immediately present in the mind.

Measurement is Basic Under Scientific Management

Under Scientific Management measurement is basic. Measurement is of the work, of outputs, of the methods, the tools, and of the worker, with the individual as a unit, and motion study, time study and micro-motion study and the chrono-cyclegraph as the methods of measurement.

Measurement is a most necessary adjunct to selecting the workers and the managers and to assigning them to the proper functions and work. They cannot be selected to the greatest advantage and set to functionalized work until —

(a) the unit of measurement that will of itself tend to reduce costs has been determined.

(b) methods of measurement have been determined.

(c) measurement has been applied.

(d) standards for measurement have been derived.

(e) devices for cheapening the cost of measuring have been installed.

Under Scientific Management Measurement Determines the Task

An important aim of measurement under Scientific Management is to determine the Task, or the standard amount of any kind of work that a first class man can do in a certain period of time. The "standard amount" is the largest amount that a first class man can do and continuously thrive.

The "first-class" man is the man who can eventually become best fitted, by means of natural and acquired capabilities, to do the work. The "certain period of time" is that which best suits the work and the man's thriving under the work. The amount of time allowed for a task consists of three parts —

1. time actually spent at work.
2. time for rest for overcoming fatigue.
3. time for overcoming delays.

Measurement must determine what percentage of the task time is to be spent at work and what at rest, and must also determine whether the rest period should all follow the completed work, or should be divided into parts, these parts to follow certain cycles through the entire work period.

The method of constructing the task is discussed under two chapters that follow, Analysis and Synthesis, and Standardization. Here we note only that the task is built up of elementary units measured by motion study, time study, and micro-motion study.

When this standard task has been determined the worker's efficiency can be measured by his performance of, or by the amount that he exceeds, the task.

Qualifications of the Observer or Measurer

The position of observer, or as he has well been called, "trade revolutionizer," should be filled by a man specially selected for the position on account of his special natural fitness and previous experience. He also should be specially trained for his work. As in all other classes of work, the original selection of the man is of vital importance. The natural qualities of the successful hunter, fisherman, detective, reporter and woodsman for observation of minute details are extremely desirable. It is only by having intimate knowledge of such experiences as Agassiz had with his pupils, or with untrained "observers" of the trade, that one can realize the lack of powers of observation of detail in the average human being. Other natural qualifications required to an efficient observer are that of being:

(a) an "eye worker";

(b) able to concentrate attention for unusually long periods;

(c) able to get every thought out of a simple written sentence;

(d) keenly interested in his work;

(e) accurate;

(f) possessed of infinite patience;

(g) an enthusiastic photographer.

The measurer or observer should, preferably, have the intimate knowledge that comes from personal experience of the work to be observed, although such a man is often difficult if not impossible to obtain. The position of observer illustrates another of the many opportunities of the workmen for promotion from the ranks to higher positions when they are capable of holding the promotion. Naturally, other things being equal, no man is so well acquainted with the work to be observed as he who has actually done it himself, and if he have also the qualifications of the worker at the work, which should, in the future, surely be determined by study of him and by vocational guidance, he will be able to go at once from his position in the ranks to that of observer, or time study man.

The observer must also familiarize himself with the literature regarding motion study and time study, and must form the habit of recording systematically the minutest details observable.

The effect upon the man making the observation of knowing that his data, even though at the time they may seem unimportant, can be used for the deduction of vital laws, is plain. He naturally feels that he is a part of a permanent scheme, and is ready and willing to put his best activity into the work. The benefits accruing from this fact have been so well recognized in making United States surveys and charts, that the practice has been to have the name of the man in charge of the work printed on them.

Anyone Interested May Become an Observer

A review of the mental equipment needed by a measurer, or observer, will show that much may be done toward training oneself for such a position by practice. Much pleasure as well as profit can be obtained by acquiring the habit of observation, both in the regular working and in the non-working hours. Vocational Guidance Bureaus should see that this habit of observation is cultivated, not only for the aesthetic pleasure which it gives, but also for its permanent usefulness.

Unbiased Observation Necessary

In order to take observations properly, the investigator should be absolutely impartial, unprejudiced, and unbiased by any preconceived notions. Otherwise, he will be likely to think that a certain thing ought to happen. Or he may have a keen desire to obtain a certain result to conform to a pet theory. In other words, the observer must be of a very stable disposition. He must not be carried away by his observations. The elimination of any charting by the man who makes the observations, or at least its postponement until all observations are made, will tend to decrease the dangers of unconscious effect of what he considers the probable curve of the observations should be. As has been well said, watching the curve to be charted before all of the data have been obtained develops a distinct theory in the mind of the investigator and is apt to "bend the curve" or, at least, to develop a feeling that if any new, or special, data do not agree with the tendency of the curve — so much the worse for the reputation of the data for reliability.

Observed Worker Should Realize the Purpose of the Measurement

The observed worker should be made to realize the purpose and importance of the measurement. The observing should always be done with his full knowledge and hearty cooperation.

He will attain much improvement by intelligent cooperation with the observer, and may, in turn, be able to be promoted to observing if he is interested enough to study and prepare himself after hours.

Worker Should Never be Observed Surreptitiously

No worker should ever be observed, timed and studied surreptitiously. In the first place, if the worker does not know that he is being observed, he cannot cooperate with the observer to see that the methods observed are methods of least waste. Therefore the motion study and time study records that result will not be fundamental standards in any case and will probably be worthless.

In the second place, if the worker discovers that he is being observed secretly, he will feel that he is being spied upon and is not being treated fairly. The stop watch has too long been associated with the idea of "taking the last drop of blood from the worker." Secret observations will tend strongly to lend credence to this idea. Even should the worker thus observed not think that he was being watched in order to force him, at a later time, to make higher outputs, after he has once learned that he is being watched secretly, his attention will constantly be distracted by the thought that perhaps he is being studied and timed again. He will be constantly on the alert to see possible observers. This may result in "speeding him up," but the speed will not be a legitimate speed, that results to his good as well as to that of his employer.

Worst of all, he will lose confidence in the "squareness" of his employer. Hence he will fail to cooperate, and one of the greatest advantages of Scientific Management will thus be lost.

It is a great advantage of micro-motion study that it demands cooperation of the man studied, and that its results are open to study by all.

An Expert best Worker to Observe

The best worker to observe for time study is he who is so skilled that he can perform a cycle of prescribed standard motions automatically, without mental concentration. This enables him to devote his entire mental activity to deviating the one desired variable from the accepted cycle of motions.

The difficulty in motion study and time study is not so often to vary the variable being observed and studied, as it is to maintain the other variables constant. Neither skill nor appreciation of what is wanted is enough alone. The worker who is to be measured successfully must

1. have the required skill.
2. understand the theory of what is being done.
3. be willing to cooperate.

Everyone Should be Trained in Being Measured

Accurate measurement of individuals, in actual practice, brings out the fact that lamentably few persons are accustomed to be, or can readily be, measured. It has been a great drawback to the advance of Scientific Management that the moment a measurer of any kind is put on the work, either a device to measure output or a man to measure or to time reactions, motions, or output, the majority of the workers become suspicious. Being unaccustomed to being measured, they think, as is usually the case with things to which we are unaccustomed, that there is something harmful to them in it. This feeling makes necessary much explanation which in reality should not be needed.

The remedy for this condition is a proper training in youth. A boy brought up with the fundamental idea of the importance of measurement to all modern science, for all progress, accustomed to being measured, understanding the "why" of the measuring, and the results from it, will not hesitate or object, when he comes to the work, to being measured in order that he may be put where it is best for himself, as well as for the work, that he be put.

The importance of human measurement to vocational guidance and to the training of the young for life work has never been properly realized. Few people understand the importance of psychological experiment as a factor in scientific vocational guidance. For this alone, it will probably in time be a general custom to record and keep as close track as possible of the psychological measurements of the child during the period of education, vocational guidance and apprenticeship. Not only this, but he also should be accustomed to being measured, physically and psychologically, from his first years, just as he is now accustomed to being weighed.

The child should be taught to measure himself, his faculties, his reactions, his capabilities as compared with his former self and as compared with the capabilities of others. It is most important that the child should form a habit not only of measuring, but of being measured.

Motion Study and Time Study Are the Method of Measurement Under Scientific Management

Under Scientific Management, much measuring is done by motion study and time study, which measure the relative efficiency of various men, of various methods, or of various kinds of equipment, surroundings, tools, etc. Their most important use is as measuring devices of the men. They have great psychological value in that they are founded on the "square deal" and the men know this from the start. Being operated under laws, they are used the same way on all sorts of work and on all men. As soon as the men really understand this fact, and realize

1. that the results are applied to all men equally;
2. that all get an ample compensation for what they do;
3. that under them general welfare is considered; the objections to such study will vanish.

Motion Study Is Determining Methods of Least Waste

Motion Study is the dividing of the elements of the work into the most fundamental subdivisions possible; studying these fundamental units separately and in relation to one another; and from these studied, chosen units, when timed, building up methods of least waste.

Time Study is Determining Standard Unit Times

Time study consists of timing the elements of the best method known, and, from these elementary unit times, synthesizing a standard time in which a standard man can do a certain piece of work in accordance with the finally accepted method. Micro-motion study is timing sub-divisions, or elements of motions by carrying out the principles of motion study to a greater degree of accuracy by means of a motion picture camera, a clock that will record different times of day in each picture of a moving picture film together with a cross sectioned background and other devices for assisting in measuring the relative efficiency and wastefulness of motions. It also is the cheapest, quickest and more accurate method of recording indisputable time study records. It has the further advantage of being most useful in assisting the instruction card man to devise methods of least waste. Motion Study and Time Study Measure Individual Efficiency

Motion Study and Time Study measure individual capacity or efficiency by providing data from which standards can be made. These standards made, the degree to which the individual approaches or exceeds the standard can be determined.

Motion Study and Time Study Measure Methods

Motion Study and Time Study are devices for measuring methods. By their use, old methods are "tried out," once and for all, and their relative value in efficiency, determined. By their use, also, new methods are "tried out." This is most important under Scientific Management.

Any new method suggested can be tested in a short time. Such elements of it as have already been tested, can be valued at the start, the new elements introduced can be motion studied and time studied, and waste eliminated to as great an extent as possible, with no loss of time or thought.

Under Scientific Management, the men who understand what motion study and time study mean, know that their suggested methods will be tested, not only fairly, but so effectively that they, and everyone else, can know at once exactly the worth of their suggestions.

Comparison of Methods Fosters Invention

The value of such comparative study can be seen at a glance. When one such method after another is tried out, not only can one tell quickly what a new method is worth, but can also determine what it is worth compared to all others which have been considered. This is because the study is a study of elements, primarily, and not of methods as a whole. Not only can suggested methods be estimated, but also new methods which have never been suggested will become apparent themselves through this study. Common elements, being at once classified and set aside, the new ones will make themselves prominent, and better methods for doing work will suggest themselves, especially to the inventive mind.

Books of Preliminary Data Needed

In order that this investigation may be best fostered, not only must books of standards be published, but also books of preliminary data, which other workers may attack if they desire, and where they can find common elements. Such books of preliminary data are needed on all subjects.

Motion Study and Time Study Measure Equipment and Tools

Time and motion study are measuring devices for ascertaining relative merits of different kinds of equipment, surroundings and tools. Through them, the exact capacities of equipment or of a tool or machine can be discovered at once, and also the relative value in efficiency. Also motion study and time study determine exactly how a tool or a piece of equipment can best be used.

In "On The Art of Cutting Metals" Dr. Taylor explains the effect of such study on determining the amount of time that tools should be used, the speed at which they should be used, the feed, and so on. This paper exemplifies more thoroughly than does anything else ever written the value of Time Study, and the scientific manner in which it is applied.

The Scope of Time and Motion Study Is Unlimited

It is a great misfortune that the worker does not understand, as he should, that motion study and time study apply not only to his work, but also to the work of the managers. In order to get results from the start, and paying results, it often happens that the work of the worker is the first to be so studied, but when Scientific Management is in full operation, the work of the managers is studied exactly to the same extent, and set down exactly as accurately, as the work of the worker himself. The worker should understand this from the start, that he may become ready and willing to cooperate.

Detailed Records Necessary

Motion study and time study records must go into the greatest detail possible. If the observations are hasty, misdirected or incomplete they may be quite unusable and necessitate going through the expensive process of observation all over again.

Dr. Taylor has stated that during his earlier experiences he was obliged to throw away a large quantity of time study data, because they were not in sufficient detail and not recorded completely enough to enable him to use them after a lapse of a long period from the time of their first use. No system of time study, and no individual piece of time study, can be considered a success unless by its use at any time, when new, or after a lapse of years, an accurate prediction of the amount of work a man can do can be made.

All results attained should invariably be preserved, whether they appear at the moment to be useful or valuable or not. In time study in the past it has been found, as in the investigations of all other sciences, that apparently unimportant details of today are of vital importance years after, as a necessary step to attain, or further proof of a discovery.

This was exemplified in the case of the shoveling experiment of Dr. Taylor. The laws came from what was considered the unimportant portion of the data. There is little so unimportant that time and motion study would not be valuable. Just as it is a great help to the teacher to know the family history of the student, so it is to the one who has to use time and motion study data to know all possible of the hereditary traits, environment and habits of the worker who was observed.

Specialized Study Imperative

As an illustration of the field for specialized investigation which motion study and time study present, we may take the subject of fatigue. Motion Study and Time Study aim to show,

1. the least fatiguing method of getting least waste.
2. the length of time required for a worker to do a certain thing.
3. the amount of rest and the time of rest required to overcome fatigue.

Dr. Taylor spent years in determining the percentage of rest that should be allowed in several of the trades, beginning with those where the making of output demands weight hanging on the arms; but there is still a great amount of investigation that could be done to advantage to determine the most advisable percentage of rest in the working day of different lengths of hours. Such investigation would probably show that many of our trades could do the same amount of work in fewer hours, if the quantity and time of rest periods were scientifically determined.

Again, there is a question of the length of each rest period. It has been proven that in many classes of work, and especially in those where the work is interrupted periodically by reason of its peculiar nature, or by reason of inefficient performance in one of the same sequence of dependent operations, alternate working and resting periods are best. There is to be considered in this connection, however, the recognized disadvantage of reconcentrating the attention after these rest periods. Another thing to be considered is that the rate of output does not decline from the beginning of the day, but rather the high point of the curve representing rate of production is at a time somewhat later than at the starting point. The period before the point of maximum efficiency is known as "warming up" among ball players, and is well recognized in all athletic sports.

As for the point of minimum efficiency, or of greatest fatigue, this varies for "morning workers," and "night workers." This exemplifies yet another variable.

The minuteness of the sub-fields that demand observation, is shown by an entry in the Psychological Index: "1202. Benedict, F.G. "Studies in Body — Temperature." 1. Influence of the Inversion of the Daily Routine; the Temperature of Night Workers."

Selection of best Unit of Measurement Necessary and Important

Selecting the unit of measurement that will of itself reduce costs is a most important element in obtaining maximum efficiency. This is seldom realized. Where possible, several units of measurements should be used to check each other. One alone may be misleading, or put an incentive on the workers to give an undesirable result. The rule is, — always select that unit of output that will, of itself, cause a reduction in costs.

For example: — In measuring the output of a concrete gang, counting cement bags provides an incentive to use more cement than the instruction card calls for. Counting the batches of concrete dumped out of the mixer, provides an incentive to use rather smaller quantities of broken stone and sand than the proportions call for, — and, furthermore, does not put the incentive on the men to spill no concrete in transportation, neither does it put an incentive to use more lumps for Cyclopean concrete. Measuring the quantity actually placed in the forms puts no incentive to watch bulging forms closely.

While measuring outputs by all these different units of measurements would be valuable to check up accuracy of proportions, accuracy of stores account, and output records, the most important unit of measurement for selection would be, "cubic feet of forms filled," the general dimensions to be taken from the latest revised engineer's drawings.

Necessity for Checking Errors

Dr. Stratton says, — "No measurements, whether they be psychic or physical, are exact beyond a certain point, and the art of using them consists largely in checks and counter checks, and in knowing how far the measurement is reliable and where the doubtful zone begins."

Capt. Metcalfe says, — "Errors of observation may be divided into two general classes; the instrumental and those due to the personal bias of the observer; the former referring to the standard itself, and the latter to the application of the standard and the record of the measurement."

The concrete illustration given above is an example of careful checking up. Under Scientific Management so many, and such careful records are kept that detecting errors becomes part of the daily routine.

Summary

Results of Measurement to the Work

Under Traditional Management, even the crudest measurement of output and cost usually resulted in an increase in output. But there was no accuracy of measurement of individual efficiency, nor was there provision made to conserve results and make them permanently useful. Under Transitory Management and measurement of individual output, output increased and rewards for the higher output kept up the standard.

Under Scientific Management Better Methods and Better Work Results

Under Scientific Measurement, measurement of the work itself determines

1. what kind of workers are needed.
2. how many workers are needed.
3. how best to use them.

Motion Study and Time Study measurement, —

1. divide the work into units.
2. measure each unit.
3. study the variables, or elements, one at a time.
4. furnish resulting timed elements to the synthesizer of methods of least waste.

Accurate Measuring Devices Prevent Breakdowns and Accidents

The accurate measuring devices which accomplish measurement under Scientific Management prevent breakdowns and accidents to life and limb.

For example;

1. The maintained tension on a belt bears a close relation to its delay periods.
2. The speed of a buzz planer determines its liability to shoot out pieces of wood to the injury of its operator, or to injure bystanders.

Scientific Management, by determining and standardizing methods and equipment both, provides for uninterrupted output.

Effect on the Worker

Under Traditional Management there is not enough accurate

measurement done to make its effect on the worker of much value.

Under Transitory Management, as soon as individual outputs are measured, the worker takes more interest in his work, and endeavors to increase his output.

Under Scientific Management measurement of the worker tells

1. what the workers are capable of doing.
2. what function it will be best to assign them to and to cultivate in them.

Waste Eliminated by Accurate Measurement

This accurate measurement increases the worker's efficiency in that it enables him to eliminate waste. "Cut and try" methods are eliminated. There is no need to test a dozen methods, a dozen men, a dozen systems of routing, or various kinds of equipment more than once, — that one time when they are scientifically tried out and measured. This accurate measurement also eliminates disputes between manager and worker as to what the latter's efficiency is.

Efficiency Measured by Time and Motion Study

Time and Motion Study.

(a) measure the man by his work; that is, by the results of his activities;

(b) measure him by his methods;

(c) measure him by his capacity to learn;

(d) measure him by his capacity to teach.

Now measurement by result alone is very stimulating to increasing activities, especially when it shows, as it does under Scientific Management, the relative results of various people doing the same kind of work. But it does not, itself, show the worker *how* to obtain greater results without putting on more speed or using up more activities. But when the worker's methods are measured, he begins to see, for himself, exactly why and where he has failed.

Scientific Management provides for him to be taught, and the fact that he sees through the measurements exactly what he needs to be taught will make him glad to have the teacher come and show him how to do better. Through this teaching, its results, and the speed with which the results come, the workers and the managers can see how fast the worker is capable of learning, and, at the same time, the worker, the teacher and the managers can see in how far the foreman is capable of instructing.

Final Outcome Beneficial to Managers and Men

Through measurement in Scientific Management, managers acquire —

1. ability to select men, methods, equipment, etc.;
2. ability to assign men to the work which they should do, to prescribe the method which they shall use, and to reward them for their output suitably;
3. ability to predict. On this ability to predict rests the possibility of making calendars, chronological charts and schedules, and of planning determining sequence of events, etc., which will be discussed at length later.

Ability to predict allows the managers to state "premature truths," which the records show to be truths when the work has been done.

It must not be forgotten that the managers are enabled not only to predict what the men, equipment, machinery, etc., will do, but what they can do themselves.

The Effect on the Men is that the Worker Cooperates

1. The worker's interest is held. The men know that the methods they are using are the best. The exact measurements of efficiency of the learner, — and under Scientific Management a man never ceases to be a learner, — give him a continued interest in his work. It is impossible to hold the attention of the intelligent worker to a method or process that he does not believe to> be the most efficient and least wasteful.

   Motion study and time study are the most efficient measuring device of the relative qualities of differing methods. They furnish definite and exact proof to the worker as to the excellence of the method that he is told to use. When he is convinced, lack of interest due to his doubts and dissatisfaction is removed.

2. The worker's judgment is appealed to. The method that he uses is the outcome of cooperation between him and the management. His own judgment assures him that it is the best, up to that time, that they, working together, have been able to discover.
3. The worker's reasoning powers are developed. Continuous judging of records of efficiency develops high class, well developed reasoning powers.
4. The worker fits his task, therefore there is no need of adjustment, and his attitude toward his work is right.
5. There is elimination of soldiering, both natural and systematic.

All Knowledge Becomes the Knowledge of All

Two outcomes may be confidently expected in the future, as they are already becoming apparent where-ever Scientific Management is being introduced:

1. The worker will become more and more willing to impart his knowledge to others. When the worker realizes that passing on his trade secrets will not cause him to lose his position or, by raising up a crowd of competitors, lower his wages, but will, on the contrary, increase his wages and chances of promotion, he is ready and willing to have his excellent methods standardized.

   Desire to keep one's own secret, or one's own method a secret is a very natural one. It stimulates interest, it stimulates pride. It is only when, as in Scientific Management, the possessor of such a secret may receive just compensation, recognition and honor for his skill, and receive a position where he can become an appreciated teacher of others that he is, or should be, willing to give up this secret. Scientific Management, however, provides this opportunity for him to teach, provides that he receives credit for what he has done, and receive that publicity and fame which is his due, and which will give him the same stimulus to work which the knowledge that he had a secret skill gave him in the past.

One method of securing this publicity is by naming the device or method after its inventor. This has been found to be successful not only in satisfying the inventor, but in stimulating others to invent.

Measurement of Individual Efficiency will be Endorsed by All

2. The worker will, ultimately, realize that it is for the good of all, as well as for himself, that individual efficiency be measured and rewarded.

   It has been advanced as an argument against measurement that it discriminates against the "weaker brother," who should have a right to obtain the same pay as the stronger, for the reason that he has equal needs for this pay to maintain life and for the support of his family.

Putting aside at the moment the emotional side of this argument, which is undoubtedly a strong side and a side worthy of consideration, with much truth in it, and looking solely at the logical side, — it cannot do the "weaker" brother any good in the long run, and it does the world much harm, to have his work overestimated. The day is coming, when the world will demand that the quantity of the day's work shall be measured as accurately where one sells labour, as where one sells sugar or flour. Then, pretending that one's output is greater than it really is will be classed with "divers weights and divers measures," with their false standards. The day will come when the public will insist that the "weaker brother's" output be measured to determine just how weak he is, and whether it is weakness, unfitness for that particular job, or laziness that is the cause of his output being low. When he reaches a certain degree of weakness, he will be assisted with a definite measured quantity of assistance. Thus the "weaker brother" may be readily distinguished from the lazy, strong brother, and the brother who is working at the wrong job. Measurement should certainly be insisted on, in order to determine whether these strong brothers are doing their full share, or whether they are causing the weaker brothers to over-exert themselves.

No one who has investigated the subject properly can doubt that it will be better for the world in general to have each man's output, weak and strong, properly measured and estimated regardless of whether the weak and strong are or are not paid the same wages. The reason why the unions have had to insist that the work shall not be measured and that the weaker brother's weakness shall not be realized is, that in the industrial world the only brotherhood that was recognized was the brotherhood between the workers, there being a distinct antagonism between the worker and the manager and little or no brotherhood of the public at large. When Scientific Management does away, as it surely will, with this antagonism, by reason of the cooperation which is its fundamental idea, then the workers will show themselves glad to be measured.

As for the "weaker" brother idea, it is a natural result of such ill treatment. It has become such a far-reaching emotion that even Scientific Management, with its remedy for many ills, cannot expect in a moment, or in a few years, to alter the emotional bias of the multitudes of people who have held it for good and sufficient reasons for generations.

The Government Should Conserve Measurement Data

The one thing which can permanently alter this feeling forms the natural conclusion to this chapter. That is, measurements in general and motion study and time study in particular must become a matter of government investigation. When the government has taken over the investigation and established a bureau where such data as Scientific Management discovers is collected and kept on file for all who will to use, then the possessor of the secret will feel that it can safely place the welfare of its "weaker brothers" in the hands of a body which is founded and operates on the idea of the "square deal."

Appreciation of Time Study by Workers the First Step

The first step of the workers in this direction must be the appreciation of time study, for on time study hangs the entire subject of Scientific Management. It is this great discovery by Dr. Taylor that makes the elimination of waste possible. It has come to stay. Many labour leaders are opposed to it, but the wise thing for them to do is to study, foster and cultivate it. They cannot stop its progress. There is no thing that can stop it. The modern managers will obtain it, and the only way to prevent it from being used by unscrupulous managers is for the workman also to learn the facts of time study. It is of the utmost importance to the workers of the country, for their own protection, that they be as familiar with time study data as the managers are. Time study is the foundation and frame work of rate setting and fixing, and certainly the subject of rate fixing is the most important subject there is to the workmen, whether they are working on day work, piece work, premium, differential rate piece, task with bonus, or three-rate system.

Dr. Taylor has proved by time study that many of the customary working days are too long, that the same amount of output can be achieved in fewer hours per day. Time study affords the means for the only scientific proof that many trades fatigue the workers beyond their endurance and strength. Time study is the one means by which the workers can prove the real facts of their unfortunate condition under the Traditional plan of management.

The workers of the country should be the very ones that should insist upon the government taking the matter in hand for scientific investigation. Knowledge is power, — a rule with no exception, and the knowledge of scientific time study would prepare the workers of any trade, and would provide their intelligent leaders with data for accurate decisions for legislation and other steps for their best interests. The national bodies should hire experts to represent them and to cooperate with the government bureau in applying science to their life work.

The day is fast approaching when makers of machinery will have the best method of operating their machines micro-motion studied and cyclegraphed and description of methods of operation in accordance with such records will be everywhere considered as a part of the "makers' directions for using."

Furthermore associations of manufacturers will establish labouratories for determining methods of least waste by means of motion study, time study and micro-motion study, and the findings of such labouratories will be put in standardized shape for use by all its members. The trend today shows that soon there will be hundreds of books of time study tables. The government must sooner or later save the waste resulting from this useless duplication of efforts.

4

Analysis and Synthesis

Definition of Analysis

"Analysis," says the Century Dictionary is "the resolution or separation of anything which is compound, as a conception, a sentence, a material substance or an event, into its constituent elements or into its causes;" that is to say, analysis is the division of the thing under consideration into its definite cause, and into its definite parts or elements, and the explanation of the principle upon which such division is made.

Definition of Synthesis

"Synthesis" is, "a putting of two or more things together; composition; specifically, the combination of separate elements of objects of thought into a whole, as of simple into compound or complex conceptions, and individual propositions into a system."

Use of Analysis and Synthesis by Psychology

Analysis is defined by Sully as follows: "Analysis" is "taking apart more complex processes in order to single out for special inspection their several constituent processes."

He divides elements of thought activity into two

(a) analysis: abstraction

(b) synthesis: comparison.

Speaking of the latter, he says, "The clear explicit detachment in thought of the common elements which comparison secures allows of a new reconstructive synthesis of things as made up of particular groupings of a number of general qualities."

Place of Analysis and Synthesis in Management

Any study of management which aims to prove that management may be, and under Scientific Management is, a science, must investigate its use of analysis and of synthesis. Upon the degree and perfection of the analysis depends the permanent value and usefulness of the knowledge gained. Upon the synthesis, and what it includes and excludes, depends the efficiency of the results deduced.

Little Analysis or Synthesis Under Traditional Management

Under Traditional Management analysis and synthesis are so seldom present as to be negligible. Success or failure are seldom if ever so studied and measured that the causes are well understood.

Therefore, no standards for future work that are of any value can be established. It need only be added that one reason why Traditional Management makes so little progress is because it makes no analyses that are of permanent value. What data it has are available for immediate use only. Practically every man who does the work must "start at the beginning," for himself.

If this is often true of entire methods, it is even more true of elements of methods. As elements are not studied and recorded separately, they are not recognized when they appear again, and the resultant waste is appalling. This waste is inevitable with the lack of cooperation under Traditional Management and the fact that each worker plans the greater part of his work for himself.

Analysis and Synthesis Appear Late in Transitory Management

Division of output appears early in Transitory Management, but it is usually not until a late stage that motion study and time study are conducted so successfully that scientifically determined and timed elements can be constructed into standards. As everything that is attempted in the line of analysis and synthesis under Transitory Management is done scientifically under Scientific Management, we may avoid repetition by considering Scientific Management at once.

Relation of Analysis and Synthesis in Scientific Management to Measurement and Standardization

Analysis considers the subject that is to be measured, – be it individual action or output of any kind, — and divides it into such a number of parts, and parts of such a nature, as will best suit the purpose for which the measurement is taken. When these subdivisions have been measured, synthesis combines them into a whole.

Under Scientific Management, through the measurements used, synthesis is a combination of those elements which are necessary only, and which have been proven to be most efficient. The result of the synthesis is standardized, and used until a more accurate standard displaces it. Under Scientific Management analysis and synthesis are methods of determining standards from available knowledge. Measurement furnishes the means.

Analyst's Work is Division

It is the duty of the analyst to divide the work that he is set to study into the minutest divisions possible. What is possible is determined by the time and money that can be set aside for the investigation.

The Nature of the Work Must Determine the Amount of Analysis Practicable

In determining the amount of time and money required, it is necessary to consider —

1. the cost of the work if done with no special study.
2. how many times the work is likely to be repeated.
3. how many elements that it contains are likely to be similar to elements in work that has already been studied.
4. how many new elements that it contains are likely to be available in subsequent work.

5. the probable cost of the work after it has been studied—
   (a) the cost of doing it.
   (b) the cost of the investigation.
6. The loss, if any, from delaying the work until after it has been studied.
7. the availability of trained observers and measurers, analysts and synthesists.
8. the available money for carrying on the investigations.

These questions at least must be answered before it is possible to decide whether study shall be made or not, and to what degree it can be carried.

Cost the Determining Factor

It is obvious that in all observation in the industrial world cost must be the principal determining feature. Once the cost can be estimated, and the amount of money that can be allowed for the investigation determined, it is possible at least to approximate satisfactory answers to the other questions. How closely the answers approximate depends largely on the skill and experience of the analyst.

The greater number of times the work is to be repeated, the less the ultimate cost. The more elements contained similar to elements already determined, the less the additional cost, and the less the time necessary. The more elements contained that can be used again, even in different work, the less the ultimate cost. The better trained the analyst, the less the immediate or additional cost and time.

Much depends on the amount of previous data at hand when the investigation is being made, and on the skill and speed of the analyst in using these data.

Process of Division Unending

In practice, the process of division continues as long as it can show itself to be a method for cost reducing. Work may be divided into processes: each process into subdivisions; each subdivision into cycles; each cycle into elements; each element into time units; each time unit into motions, — and so on, indefinitely, toward the "indivisible minimum.

"Measuring may take Place at any Stage

At any of these stages of division the results may be taken as final for the purpose of the study, — and the operations, or final divisions of the work at that stage, may be measured. To obtain results with the least expenditure of time, the operations must be subjected to motion study before they are timed as well as after. This motion study can be accurate and of permanent value only in so far as the divisions are final. The resulting improved operations are then ready to be timed.

Ultimate Analysis the Field of Psychology

When the analyst has proceeded as far as he can in dividing the work into prime factors the problem continues in the field of psychology. Here the opportunities for securing further data become almost limitless.

Ultimate Analysis Justifiable

It is the justification for analysis to approach the ultimate as nearly as possible, that the smaller and more difficult of measurement the division is, the more often it will appear in various combinations of elements. The permanence and exactness of the result vary with the effort for obtaining it.

Qualifications of an Analyst

To be most successful, an analyst should have ingenuity, patience, and that love of dividing a process into its component parts and studying each separate part that characterizes the analytic mind. The analyst must be capable of doing accurate work, and orderly work. To get the most pleasure and profit from his work he should realize that his great, underlying purpose is to relieve the worker of unnecessary fatigue, to shorten his work period per day, and to increase the number of his days and years of higher earning power. With this realization will come an added interest in his subject.

Worker Should Understand the Process of Analysis

It is not enough that the worker should understand the methods of measurement. He can get most from the resultant standards and will most efficiently cooperate if he understands the division into elements to be studied.

Schools Should Provide Training

Much of the training in analysis in the schools comes at such a late period of the course that the average industrial worker must miss a large part of it. This is a defect in school training that should be remedied. Even very young children soon are capable of, and greatly enjoy, dividing a process into elements.

If the worker be taught, in his preparations, and in the work itself, to divide what he does into its elements, he will not only enjoy analysis of his work, but will be able to follow the analysis in his own mind, and to cooperate better in the processes of measurement.

The Synthesist's Work is Selection and Addition

The synthesist studies the individual results of the analyst's work, and their inter-relation, and determines which of these should be combined, and in what manner, for the most economic result. His duty is to construct that combination of the elements which will be most efficient.

Importance of Selection must be Emphasized

If synthesis in Scientific Management were nothing more than combining all the elements that result from analysis into a whole, it would be valuable. Any process studied analytically will be performed more intelligently, even if there is no change in the method.

But the most important part of the synthesist's work is the actual elimination of elements which are useless, and the combination of the remaining elements in such a way, or sequence, or schedule, that a far better method than the one analysed will result.

We may take an example from Bricklaying. In "Stringing Mortar Method, on the Filling Tiers before the Days of the Pack-on-the-Wall-Method" — the division, which was into operations only, showed eighteen operations and eighteen motions for every brick that was laid. Study and synthesis of these elements resulted in a method that required only 1 3/4 motions to lay a brick. Over half the original motions were found to be useless, hence entirely omitted. In several other cases it was found possible to make one motion do work for two or four brick, with the same, or less, fatigue to the worker.

Result is the Basis for the Task

The result of synthesis is the basis for the task, — it becomes the standard that shows what has actually been done, and what can be expected to be repeated. It is important to note the relation between the task and synthesis. When it becomes generally understood that the "Task," under Scientific Management is neither an ideal which exists simply in the imagination, nor an impossibly high estimate of what can be expected, — but is actually the sum of observed and timed operations, plus a definite and sufficient percentage of allowance for overcoming the fatigue, — then much objection to it will cease.

General Lack of Knowledge the Chief Cause of Objection to the Task

As is the case with most objections to Scientific Management, or its elements, ignorance is the chief obstacle to the introduction and success of the Task Idea. This ignorance seems to be more or less prevalent everywhere among managers as well as workers.

Scientific Management can, and does, succeed even when the workers are ignorant of many of its fundamental principles, but it will never make the strides that it should until every man working under it, as well as all outside, understand *why* it is doing as it does, as well as *what* is done.

This educational campaign could find no better starting point than the word "task," and the "task idea."

The Name Task Is Unfortunate. — The Century Dictionary defines "Task" as follows:

1. "a tax, an assessment, an impost
2. "labour imposed, especially a definite quantity or amount of labour; work to be done; one's stint; that which duty or necessity imposes; duty or duties collectively
3. "a lesson to be learned; a portion of study imposed by a teacher

4. "work undertaken, — an undertaking
5. "burdensome employment; toil."

Only the fourth meaning, as here given, covers in any way what is meant by the task in Scientific Management. The ideas included in the other four definitions are most unpleasant.

The thought of labour; the thought that the labour is imposed; the thought that the imposition is definite; that duty makes it necessary that it be done; that it is burdensome; that it is toilsome: these are most unfortunate ideas and have been associated with the word so long in the human mind that it will be a matter of years before a new set of associations can be formed which will be pleasant, and which will render the word "task" attractive and agreeable to the worker and to the public in general.

No Other Adequate Word has been Suggested

However, there seems to be no better word forthcoming; therefore, one can but follow the example of the masters in management, who have accepted this word, and have done their best to make it attractive by the way they themselves have used it.

To the writer, the word "stint" is far more attractive and more truly descriptive than is "task." Perhaps because of the old-fashioned idea that a reward, usually immediate, followed the completion of the "stint."

Opinions as to a preferable word will doubtless vary, but it is self-evident that the word "task" has already become so firmly established in Scientific Management that any attempt to change it would result in a confusion. It is far better to concentrate on developing a new set of associations for it in as many minds as possible.

Decided Advantage to the Use of the Word Task

Perhaps in one way it is fortunate that the use of the word "task" does coincide more or less with the use of that word under Traditional Management. Under Traditional Management the task is the work to be done. It may be just as well that the same word should be used under Scientific Management, in order that both the worker and investigator may realize, that, after all *the work that is to be done* is, in its essentials, exactly the same. With this realization from the beginning, the mind of the worker or investigator may be the more predisposed to note the eliminations of waste and the cutting down of time, effort and fatigue under the scientifically derived methods.

Definition of Task as Used in Scientific Management

The task, under Scientific Management, differs from the task under Traditional Management in that —

1. The tools and surrounding conditions with which the work shall be done are standardized.
2. The method in which the work shall be done is prescribed.
3. The time that the work shall take is scientifically determined.
4. An allowance is made for rest from fatigue.
5. The quality of the output is prescribed.

When to this is added the fact that the method is taught, and that the reward is ample, fixed, prompt and assured, the attractive features of the task under Scientific Management have been made plain.

Task Idea Applies to Work of Everyone

Under Scientific Management there is a task for every member of the organization, from the head of the management to the worker at the most rudimentary work. This is too often not known, or not appreciated by the worker, who feels that what is deemed best for him should be good for everyone. The mental attitude will never be right till all understand that the task idea will increase efficiency when applied to any possible kind of work. With the application of the task idea to all, will come added cooperation.

Task Idea Applies to the Work of the Organization

The work which is to be done by the organization should be considered the task of the organization, and this organization task is studied before individual tasks are set. The methods used in determining this organization task are analysis and synthesis, just as in the case of the individual task.

Individual Tasks Are Elements of Organization Task

The individual tasks are considered as elements of the organization task. The problem is, to determine the best arrangement of these individual tasks, the best schedule, and routing. The individual task may be thought of as something moving, that must be gotten out of the way. Management has been called largely a matter of transportation. It may be "transportation" or moving of materials, revolution of parts of fixed machinery, or merely transportation of parts of one's body in manual movements; in any case, the laws governing transportation apply to all.

This view of management is most stimulating to the mind. A moving object attracts attention and holds interest. Work that is interesting can be accomplished with greater speed and less fatigue. Thinking in terms of the methods of Scientific Management as the most accurate and efficient in transporting the finished output and its "chips" will be a great aid towards attaining the best results possible by means of a new method of visualizing the problem.

Qualifications of the Synthesist

The synthesist must have a constructive mind, for he determines the sequence of events as well as the method of attack. He must have the ability to see the completed whole which he is trying to make, and to regard the elements with which he works not only as units, but in relation to each other. He must feel that any combination is influenced not only by the elements that go into it, but by the inter-relation between these elements. This differs for different combinations as in a kaleidoscope.

The Synthesist a Conserver

The Synthesist must never be thought of as a destructive critic. He is, in reality, a conserver of all that is valuable in old methods. Through his work and that of the analyst, the valuable elements of traditional methods are incorporated into standard methods. These standard methods will, doubtless, be improved as time goes on, but the valuable elements will be permanently conserved.

Synthesist an Inventor

The valuable inventions referred to as the result of measurement are the work of the synthetic mind. It discovers new, better methods of doing work, and this results in the invention of better means, such as tools or equipment.

For example, — in the field of Bricklaying, the Non-stooping Scaffold, the Packet and the Fountain Trowel were not invented until the analysis of bricklaying was made, and the synthesis of the chosen elements into standard methods made plain the need and specifications for new equipment.

Relation of Invention to Scientific Management Important

There has been much discussion as to the relation of Invention to Scientific Management. It has been claimed by many otherwise able authorities that many results claimed as due to Scientific Management are really the results of new machinery, tools or equipment that have been invented. Scientific Management certainly can lay no claim to credit for efficiency which comes through inventions neither suggested nor determined by it. But the inventions from the results of which Scientific Management is said to have borrowed credit are usually, like the bricklaying inventions cited, not only direct results of Scientific Management, but probably would not have sprung from any other source for years to come.

Synthesist a Discoverer of Laws

It is the synthetic type of mind that discovers the laws. For example — it was Dr. Taylor, with the aid of a few of his specially trained co-workers, who discovered the following governing laws:

1. law of no ratio between the foot-pounds of work done and the fatigue caused in different kinds of work.
2. law of percentage of rest for overcoming fatigue.
3. law of classification of work according to percentage of fatigue caused.

4. laws for making high-speed steel.
5. laws relating to cutting metals.
6. laws that will predict the right speed, feed and cut on metals for the greatest output.
7. laws for predicting maximum quantity of output that a man can achieve and thrive.
8. laws for determining the selection of the men best suited for the work.

Synthesist an Adviser on Introduction of New Methods

Having constructed the standard tasks or standard methods which are new, the synthesist must remember to introduce his new task or method with as few new variables as possible. He should so present it that all the old knowledge will come out to meet the new, that all the brain paths that have already been made will be utilized, and that the new path will lead out from paths which are well known and well travelled.

Introduce with as Few New Variables as Possible

The greatest speed in learning a new method will be attained by introducing it with as few new variables as possible.

For example, — learning to dictate to a dictaphone. The writer found it very difficult, at first, to dictate into the dictaphone,— the whirling of the cylinder distracted the eye, the buzzing of the motor distracted the ear, the rubber tube leading to the mouth-piece was constantly reminding the touch that something new was being attempted. At the suggestion of one well versed in Scientific Management, the mouth-piece of the dictaphone was propped on the desk telephone on a level with the mouth-piece of the latter. The writer then found that as soon as one became interested in the dictating and one's attention was concentrated on the thought, one was able absolutely to forget the new variable, because it is one which is kept constant, and to dictate fluently. The emphasis laid on the likeness in thus dictating to the old accustomed act of talking through the telephone, seemed to put all other differences into the background, and to allow of forming the new and desired habit very quickly.

Summary

Effect of Analysis and Synthesis on the Work

As the outcome of Analysis and Synthesis is Standardization, so the effect of them upon work is standard work. Quantity of output can be predicted, quality of output is assured.

Effect on the Worker

The effect of Analysis and Synthesis upon the worker is to make him feel that the methods which he is using are right, and that, because of this, his work must be of value. The more the worker is induced to cooperate in the determining and the combination of elements, the more will he share with the investigators the satisfaction in getting permanent results. The outcome of this cooperation will, again, result in more perfect future results, and so on, progressively.

5

Standardization

Definition of Standardization

Standardization is "the act of standardizing, or the state of being standardized." "A standard," according to the Century Dictionary, "is that which is set up as a unit of reference; a form, type, example, incidence, or combination of conditions accepted as correct and perfect and hence as a basis of comparison. A criterion established by custom, public opinion or general consent; a model."

We must note particularly that the standard is a "unit of reference," that it is a "basis of comparison," and that it is "a model." These three phrases describe the standard in management, and are particularly emphasized by the use of the standard in Scientific Management.

Standards Derived from Actual Practice

Management derives its standards not from theories as to best methods, but from scientific study of actual practice. As already shown, the method of deriving a standard is —

1. to analyse the best practice known into the smallest possible elements,
2. to measure these elements,
3. to adopt the least wasteful elements as standard elements,
4. to synthesize the necessary standard elements into the standard.

The Standard is Progressive

A standard remains fixed only until a more perfect standard displaces it. The data from which the standard was derived may be reviewed because of some error, because a further subdivision of the elements studied may prove possible, or because improvements in some factor of the work, i.e., the worker, material, tools, equipment, etc., may make a new standard desirable.

The fact that a standard is recognized as not being an ultimate standard in no wise detracts from its working value. As Captain Metcalfe has said: "Whatever be the standard of measurement, it suffices for comparison if it be generally accepted, if it be impartially applied, and if the results be fully recorded." Change in the Standard Demands Change in the Task and in the Incentive

Necessarily, with the change in the standard comes a change in the task and in the reward. All parts of Scientific Management are so closely related that it is impossible to make a successful progressive step in one branch without simultaneously making all the related progressions in other branches that go with it.

For example, — if the material upon which a standard was based caused more care or effort, a smaller task must be set, and wages must be proportionately lowered. *Proportionately*, note, for determining that change would necessitate a review and a redistribution of the cost involved.

In the same way, if an improvement in equipment necessitated a new method, as does the packet in laying brick, a new task would become imperative, and a reconsideration of the wage. The wage might remain the same, it might go down, it might go up. In actual practice, in the case of bricklayers, it has gone up. But the point is, it *must* be restudied. This provides effectually against cutting the rate or increasing the task in any unjust manner.

Similarity Between the Standard and the "Judgment" of Psychology

There are many points of similarity between the "Standard," of management, and the "judgment" of psychology. Sully says, in speaking of the judgment, — "This process of judging illustrates the two fundamental elements in thought activity, viz., analysis and synthesis." "To judge is clearly to discern and to mark off as a special object of thought some connecting relation."

"To begin with, before we can judge we must have the requisite materials for forming a judgment." "In the second place, to judge is to carry out a process of reflection on given material." "In addition to clearness and accuracy, our judgments may have other perfections. So far as our statements accord with known facts, they should be adhered to, — at least, till new evidence proves them untrue."

Psychology a Final Appeal as to Permanent Value of Any Standard

The standard under management, even under Scientific Management, can lay no claim to being perfect. It can never nearly approach perfection until the elements are so small that it is practicable to test them psychologically and physiologically. The time when this can be done in many lines, when the benefit that will directly accrue will justify the necessary expenditure, may seem far distant, but every analysis of operations, no matter how rudimentary, is hastening the day when the underlying, permanently valuable elements can be determined and their variations studied.

Cooperation Will Hasten the Day of Psychological and Physiological Study of Standards

Cooperation in collecting and comparing the results of motion study and time study everywhere will do much to assist toward more ultimate determination of elements. At the present time the problems that management submits to psychology are too indefinite and cover too large a field to be attacked successfully. Cooperation between management standardizers would mean —

1. that all management data would be available to psychologists and physiologists.
2. that such data, being available also to all standardizers, would prevent reduplication of results.
3. that savings would result.

4. that, from a study and comparison of the collected data a trained synthetic mind could build up better standards than could be built from any set of individual data.
5. Savings would result from this.
6. Inventions would also result.
7. Savings would again result from these.
8. All of these various savings could be invested in more intensive study of elements.
9. These more valuable results would again be available to psychologists and physiologists.

This cycle would go on indefinitely. Meantime, all would benefit with little added cost to any. For the results of the psychological and physiological study would be available to all, and investigators in those lines have shown themselves ready and glad to undertake investigations.

Purpose of Standardization

The purpose of standardizing is the same under all types of management; that is, it is the elimination of waste.

Standardization Frequently Attempted Under Traditional Management

In much progressive Traditional Management there is an appreciation of the necessity of standardizing tools and equipment, that is to say, of having these on the "duplicate part system," that assembling may be done quickly, and repairs made without delay. The manager notices some particularly successful man, or method, or arrangement of tools, equipment, or the surroundings, and decides to have a record made thereof that the success may be repeated. These records, if made in sufficient detail, are very valuable. The difficulty is that so often the man making the records does not observe all the variables. Hence the very elements which caused the success may be overlooked entirely.

Value of Standardization not Appreciated Under Traditional Management

It is surprising, under Traditional Management, to note, in many cases, the years that elapse before any need for standardization is felt. It is also surprising that, even when some standardization has been done, its importance is seldom realized. The new standard becomes a matter of course, and the management fails to be impressed enough with its benefits to apply the principle of standardization to other fields.

Under Transitory Management Standardization Becomes Constantly more Important

Not until Motion Study and Time Study have been introduced can the full benefits of standardization be attained. But as soon as the Transitory Stage of Management appears, the importance of standardization is realized. This is brought about largely through the records of individual outputs, which constantly call attention to the necessity of making available to all the methods, tools and equipment of the most successful workers.

Records of Successes Become more Profitable

An appreciation of what scientific motion study and time study will ultimately do affects the minds of the management until the workers are given directions as to methods to be used, and the incentive of extra pay for following directions.

"Systems" Show an Appreciation of Psychology

The "Systems," standing orders or collections of written directions, that are evolved at this stage have a permanent value. This is especially true when the directions, often called "rules," contain the reason for the rule. There is a decided awakening to the importance of Psychology in this appeal to the reason of the worker. He is not affronted by being forced to follow directions for which he is given no reason and which he has no reason to believe have been scientifically derived. These rules, in a certain typical case, are stated in simple language, some in the form of commands, some in the form of suggestions, and are obviously so prepared as to be understood and obeyed by the workers with the least possible amount of effort, opposition and time.

As ample opportunity is given for suggestions, the worker's attention and interest are held, and any craving he may have for self-expression is gratified.

Systems Permanently Useful

These systems, collections of rules, directions or standing orders are useful even when Ultimate Management is completely installed —

1. for use as records of successful methods which may be scientifically studied for elements.
2. for use by the instruction card clerk in explaining to the men why the rules on the instruction card are given.

Relation of Systems to Standards Should be Emphasized

The worker is too often not made to understand the relation of Systems to Standards.

The average worker does not object to Systems, because he realizes that the System is a collection of his best, least wasteful methods of doing work. When he can be convinced that standards are only efficient elements of his own methods scientifically studied and combined, any opposition to them will disappear.

The Personal note of the "System" Should be Preserved

Perhaps one thing that makes the typical "Systems" so attractive is the personal note that they contain. Illustrated with pictures of successful work that the workers themselves have done, often containing pictures of the men themselves that illustrate successful methods, with mention of the names of men who have offered valuable suggestions or inventions, they make the worker feel his part in successful results. They conserve the old spirit of cooperation between the master and his apprentices.

The conditions of modern industry make it extremely difficult to conserve this feeling. Scientific Management is successful not only because it makes possible a more effective cooperation than has ever existed since the old "master-and-apprentice" relation died out, but also because it conserves in the Systems the interim channel for personal communication between the various members of the organization.

Systems a Valuable Assistance in Transition to Scientific Management

One great problem which those introducing Scientific Management have to face is exactly how to make the worker understand the relation of the new type of management to the old. The usefulness of the written system in use in most places where it is planned to introduce Scientific Management as a means of making the worker understand the transition has, perhaps, not been appreciated.

The development of the standard from the system is easy to explain. This being done, all parts of Scientific Management are so closely related that their interrelation can be readily made apparent.

It is the worker's right as well as privilege to understand the management under which he works, and he only truly cooperates, with his will and judgment as well as with his hands, when he feels that his mind is a part of the directing mind.

Standardization Under Scientific Management Eliminates Waste Scientifically

Under Scientific Management the elimination of waste by the use of standards becomes a science. Standards are no longer based on opinions, as under Traditional Management, but are based upon scientific investigation of the elements of experience.

As James says, in the "Psychology, Briefer Course," page 156, paragraph 4, — "It is obvious and palpable that our state of mind is never precisely the same. Every thought we have of a given fact is, strictly speaking, unique and only bears a resemblance of kind with our other thoughts of the same facts. When the identical fact recurs we must think of it in a fresh manner, see it under a somewhat different angle, apprehend it in different relations from those in which it last appeared."

The Standard the Result of Measurement

It is obvious, therefore, that a scientifically derived standard can never be the outcome of an opinion. Whenever the opinion returns, the different thoughts with which it would be accompanied would so color it as to change it, and the standard with it. It is obvious, therefore, that a standard must be the result of definite mathematical and other measured proof, and not of an opinion, and that the standard must be in such physical shape that the subject-matter will always be clearly defined, otherwise the ultimate losses resulting from dependent sequences of the standard schedule and time-tables would be enormous.

Successful Standardization Demands Complete Conformity to Standards

The laws for establishment of standards; the laws of achieving them; the laws for preventing deviations from those paths that will permit of their achievement; the dependent sequences absolutely necessary to perform the complete whole; these have been worked out and given to the world by Dr. Taylor, who recognized, as James has said, page 157, that, "a permanently existing 'Idea' which makes its appearance before the footlights of consciousness at periodic intervals, is as mythological an entity as the Jack of Spades." The entire organization from the highest to the lowest must conform to these standards. It is out of the question to permit the deviations resulting from individual initiative. Individual initiative is quite as objectionable in obtaining the best results, — that is, high wages and low production cost, — as service would be on a railroad if each locomotive engineer were his own train despatcher, determining at what time and to what place he would go.

Initiative Provided For

There is a distinct place for initiative in Scientific Management, but that place is not outside of the planning department, until the planning department's method has been proved to be fully understood by achieving it. The standards must be made by the men to whom this work is assigned, and they must be followed absolutely by the worker. He is willing to follow them, under Scientific Management, because he realizes that a place for his suggestions is supplied, and that, if his suggestions are accepted, they will be incorporated into the new standards which must then be followed by all thereafter.

Standardization Applies to the Work of All

It is important to note that standardizing is applied to the work of all. This, if understood by all, will do away with all question of discrimination or the lack of a "square deal." It will make the worker feel ready to follow his standard exactly, just as he knows the manager is following his. So, also, the worker should be made to realize that the very fact that there is a standardization means, under Scientific Management, that that applies to every man, and that there is no discrimination against him in any possible way.

Standardization Conserves and Develops Individuality

Standardization conserves individual capacity by doing away with the wasteful process of trial and error of the individual workman. It develops individuality by allowing the worker to concentrate his initiative upon work that has not before been done, and by providing incentive and reward for inventions.

Waste Eliminated is Eliminated Permanently

Scientific Management not only eliminates waste, but provides that waste shall be eliminated for all time in the future.

The standard once written down, there can be no slipping back into the old methods based upon opinions of the facts.

Standardization under Scientific Management Resembles Standardization of Spelling

The need for standardization has already been emphasized, but might further be illustrated by the discussions, pro and con, of the question of simplified spelling. Before the days of dictionaries, our spelling was not standardized — it was the privilege of any good writer to spell much as he desired; but the creation of written standards of spelling, that is to say the making of dictionaries, fixed the forms of spelling at that time, that is, created standards. The Simplified Spelling Board is now endeavoring to make some new standards, their action being based upon sufficient reasons for making a change, and also for not changing the spelling of any word until it is determined that the suggested spelling is more advisable than the old spelling.

Just so, under Scientific Management, the best known standards are used continuously until better have been discovered.

The planning department, consisting of the best men available, whose special duty it is to create new standards, acts as does the Simplified Spelling Board, as a court of appeals for new standards, which must pass this court before they can hope to succeed the old, and which must, if they are to be accepted, possess many elements of the old and be changed only in such a way that the users can, without difficulty, shift to the new use.

Under Scientific Management Nomenclature is Standardized

Under Standardization in Scientific Management the standardization of the nomenclature, of the names and of the terms used must be noted. The effect of this upon the mind is excellent, because the use of a word very soon becomes a habit— its associations become fixed.

If different names are used for the same thing, — that is to say, if different names are used indiscriminately, the thing itself becomes hazy, in just such a degree as it possesses many names. The use of the fixed term, the fixed word, leads to definiteness always. Just so, also, the Mnemonic Symbol system in use by Scientific Management, leads to swift identification of the subdivision of the classification to which it is applied, and to elimination of waste in finding and remembering where to find any particular thing or piece of information desired. By it may be identified "the various articles of manufacture and papers relating to it as well as the operations to be performed on each piece and the various charges of the establishment."

Mnemonic Symbols Save Time and Effort

These Mnemonic Symbols save actual motions and time in speaking and writing, and save time in that they are so designed as to be readily remembered. They also save time and effort in that the mind accustomed to them works with them as collective groups of ideas, without stopping to elabourate them into their more detailed form.

Standard Phraseology Eliminates Waste

As typical of the savings effected by standardization, we may cite a lineman talking to the Central Telephone Office: —

"John Doe — 1234 L. Placing Extension Station," This signified — "My name is John Doe, I am telephoning from number 1234, party L. I have finished installing an extension station. Where shall I go next?"

In the same way standard signals are remembered best by the man who signals and are understood quickest by the man who receives them, with a direct increase in speed to the work done.

Standard Man is the Man upon Whom Studies are Made

The standard man is the ideal man to observe and with whom to obtain the best Motion Study and Time Study data. He is the fastest worker, working under the direction of the man best informed in the particular trade as to the motions of best present practice, and being timed by a Time Study Expert.

Relation Between the Standard Man, the First-Class Man, the Given Man and the Task

The "first-class man" under Scientific Management means the man who is best fitted by nature and by training to do the task permanently or until promoted.

The "given man" is the man who is actually put to work at the task, whether or not he is well fitted for its performance.

The "task" is that percentage of the standard man's achievement that the given man to whom the task is to be assigned can do continuously and thrive, that he can do easily enough to win his bonus without injuring himself, temporarily or permanently, in any way.

Writing the Standard Means for Conveying Information

Under Scientific Management, and even in the early stages of Transitory Management, writing is the standard means of conveying information.

All orders, without exception, should be in writing. This insures that the "eye workers" get their directions in the most impressive form; does away with the need of constant oral repetition; eliminates confusion; insures a clear impression in the mind of the giver as well as of the receiver of the order as to exactly what is wanted; and provides a record of all orders given. Putting the instructions in writing in no way precludes utilizing the worker's natural aptitude to learn by imitation, for he also always has the opportunity to watch and imitate the workings of the functional teachers as well as his scientifically taught fellow-workers.

The Instruction Card the Standard Method of Conveying Instructions as to the Task

The records of the work of the standard man are contained in data of the Motion Study and Time Study department. These records, in the form in which they are to be used by the man who is to perform the task, are, for the benefit of that man, incorporated in what is known as the instruction card.

Definition of the Instruction Card

The instruction card is a set of directions for the man, telling him what he is to do, how he is to do it, how long it should take him to do it, and what he will receive for doing it, and giving him an opportunity to call for, and obtain, assistance the instant that he finds he cannot do it, and to report back to the managers as to how he has succeeded in the performance.

The Instruction Card has been called "a self-producer of a predetermined product."

Comparative Definition of Instruction Cards, Under Scientific Management

There are three types of Instruction Cards, which may be described as follows:

Type One: — Largely geographical, telling

1. Where to Work.
2. From Whom to Take Orders.
3. What to Do.

Type Two: — Typical engineer's specification, — telling

1. Results desired.
2. Qualities of Products.

Type Three: — A list of elementary, step-by-step instructions, subdivided into their motions, with time allowed for each timable element, preferably for each motion, and a division between.

1. Getting ready.
2. Making or constructing.
3. Clearing up. This is the only type used by Scientific Management.

Directions, Pay Allowance and Time Allowance Essential

The Instruction Card under Scientific Management must contain directions, and state the pay allowance and time allowance.

Directions as to how the work shall be done eliminate waste by cutting out all wrong methods and prescribing the right method exactly.

The setting of a time in which the work is to be done is a great stimulus to the worker, and is also necessary, because upon the attainment of this set time depends the ability of the managers to pay the bonus to the worker, and also to maintain a schedule, or timetable, that will make possible the maintaining of necessary conditions for others, in turn, to earn their bonuses.

It cannot be too often emphasized that the extra wages are paid to the men out of the savings, and are absolutely dependent upon the fact of there being savings. It is only when the worker does the work within the time prescribed, that the managers do save enough to warrant the payment of the extra wages that compensate the man for doing the stipulated quantity of work.

The instruction card contains a statement of the wage or bonus that will be earned for the complete performance of the task set therein, thus furnishing an incentive at the time that the work is done.

Standard Division of Instruction Card Necessary

There are many reasons for dividing an instruction card in the present standard way, namely, —

(a) to reduce the amount of time study observation necessary to be taken,

(b) to reduce the difficulties of synthesizing the time studied element,

(c) to locate quickly just where the worker needs help and instruction to enable him to achieve his task,

(d) to keep up the interest of the worker by having short time elements with which to measure his relative ability,

(e) to present the subject-matter of instruction in such natural subdivisions that resting places are automatically provided that allow the mind to recover from its absorption of each subdivision. This provides definite stopping places between co-related units of instruction holding the attention as a complete unit against distraction, and a complete resting place between subdivisions that permits the mind to relax and wander without losing complete grasp of each unit as a whole.

Detailed Instruction Educative

The greater the perfection of the detail of the instruction card, the greater the educative value of this plan of management. The educative value of the instruction card will be discussed at length under Teaching.

Those inexperienced in Scientific Management have complained that the detail of Instruction Cards and other parts of Scientific Management is tiresome. Dr. Taylor has answered such objectors in Discussions, and also in his own directions for planning the Instruction Card, which are to be found in "Shop Management."

The advantages of the detailed instruction card are more than might appear on the surface. Not only does the man whose attention is easily distracted keep to his work better if he is told every possible detail, but also the cards when filed can be taken out again, and every detail and item of the method reviewed at length and revised if necessary. The experienced worker who gets to know the instruction by rote is not bothered by extreme detail. On the contrary, he grasps it at a glance, and focuses his mind upon any new feature and upon the speed and exactness of muscular action needed for compliance with the card.

Language of Instruction Card Important

The language in which instructions and commands are transmitted on the instruction card is of sufficient importance to warrant careful consideration. It would be helpful if the instruction card clerk and the man who is to use the instruction cards were both masters of English, but this is hardly to be expected. The best substitute for such special English training is a "System" for the use of the instruction card clerk that will give him some outline of English that will by degrees make his wording terse, simple and unambiguous.

He should be impressed with the value of short sentences, and of sentences that will require no punctuation other than a period at the end. The short sentence is the most important step toward brevity, terseness, conciseness and clear thinking.

The second most important feature is that the instruction card clerk always uses the same standard wording for the same instructions. Repetition of phrasing is a virtue, and the use of the same word for the same thing and the same meaning repeatedly is very desirable. The wording, phrasing and sentencing should be standard wherever possible.

Standard Phrasing Desirable

After a short time a phrase or sentence that is often repeated will be recognized as quickly as will a word or a letter. Men who cannot read and write at all are comparatively few. Men who can read and write but little are many. It is entirely possible to teach such men standard groupings, which they can recognize on the Instruction Card and use in a very short time.

For example, — labourers who do not even know their alphabets will learn quickly to read setting marks on cut stone.

Just as mnemonic symbols save time and effort, so standard phrasing aids toward finding out what is to be done, and remembering how it is to be done. Both of these can be accomplished if the standardization is so complete that directions can be read and remembered almost at a glance. Specific Terms Helpful

To be most effective, directions should be in the imperative form, and in specific terms.

The history and growth of language shows that the language of the savage consisted of vague general terms as compared to the specific individual terms of the modern language of civilized man. There are examples to be seen on every hand today where the oral language of instructions and orders to proceed, that are given to the worker, are still more vague, comparatively, than the language between savages.

Similarity of Form and Shape Advisable

As for the form and shape, as Dr. Taylor says, "anything that will transmit ideas by sketch or wording will serve as an instruction card." He advises, however, taking advantage of the saving in time to be gained by having the instruction cards as nearly alike as possible. They may, for convenience' sake, vary as to length, but in width, ruling, spacing and wording they should be as nearly alike as possible.

Standard Surroundings Valuable

Standard environment, or surroundings, of the worker are valuable for two reasons:

1. Because they directly increase output by eliminating everything which might distract attention or cause needless fatigue, and by assisting in the attainment of more output by having the best possible surroundings for greater output.
2. Because all surroundings suggest an easy achievement. Knowing that everything has been done to make his work possible and easy, the worker feels this atmosphere of possibility and ease around him, and the suggestive power of this is strong.

Unnecessary Fatigue Should be Eliminated

The walls, appliances and furniture, and the clothing of the worker should be of that color which will rest his eyes from the fatigue of the work. All unnecessary noise should be eliminated, and provision should be made, where possible, that the workers may enjoy their sleep or their rest hours in perfect quiet.

Records show the value of having quiet reign in and near the camp, that the workers may not be disturbed. Even though they are not disturbed enough to be waked up, every noise that is registered in the brain affects the body, for it is now conceded that the body reflects every phase of mental activity.

All Mental States Affect Bodily States — Dr. Stratton says: "It is now generally accepted that the body reflects every shade of psychic operations; that in all manner of mental action there is some physical expression." All consciousness is motor "is the brief expression of this important truth; every mental state somehow runs over into a corresponding bodily state."

Elimination of Worry Assists in Concentrating Attention

The more fireproof the building, and the more stable the other conditions, the greater the efficiency of the inmate. Burglar-proof buildings not only actually induce better sleep, in that possible intrusions are eliminated, but give a state of mental peace by the removal of apprehension. So also, a "germ proof" house is not only really more healthful for an inmate, but eliminates worry over possible danger of ill health. The mental health of the worker not only controls, in a measure, his physical health, but also his desire to work. Having no distractions, he can put his mind upon that which is given him to do.

Distracted Attention Causes Fatigue

The attention of the worker is apt to be distracted not only by recognized dangers, such as burglars, fires, and disease, but also by other transitory things that, involuntarily on his part, take his mind from the work in hand. A flickering light distracts the attention and causes fatigue, whether we have consciously noticed it or not. Many things are recorded by the senses without one's being conscious of them.

For example, the ceasing of a clock to tick, although we have not noticed that it was ticking. Another example is the effect upon the pulse or the brain of being spoken to when asleep. The flickering lamp of the chronocyclegraph device is much more fatiguing than the steady lamp of plain cyclegraphs.

Proper Placing of Workers Eliminates Distracted Attention

Workers must be placed so that they do not see intermittently moving objects out of the corners of their eyes. In the early history of man it was continuously necessary to watch for first evidence of things behind one, or at a distance, in order to be safe from an enemy. From generations of survival of the most fit there have developed human eyes most sensitive to moving objects that are seen out of the corner of the eye. Even civilized man has his attention distracted quickest, and most, by those moving objects that he sees the least distinctly, and furthest to one side from the direction in which he is looking.

The leaf that moves or the grass that trembles may attract the attention where seen "out of the corner of the eye" to a point where it will even cause a start and a great fear.

As an example of the distracting effect of moving objects seen "out of the corner of the eye," try reading a book facing a window in a car where the moving scenery can be seen on each side of the book. The flitting object will interrupt one, one cannot get the full meaning out of what one is reading — yet if one lays down the book and looks directly at the scenery, the mind can concentrate to a point where one does not see that moving scenery which is directly in front of the eyes.

There is a great difference in this power of sensitiveness of the corners of some workers' eyes from that of others. The first move of Scientific Management is to place and arrange all workers, as far as is possible, in such a position that nothing to distract them will be behind them, and later to see that the eyes of workers are tested, that those whose eyes are most sensitive may be placed accordingly.

This Elimination May Take Place in all Kinds of Work

The necessity of removing all things which will distract the attention is as great for the brain worker as for the shop or construction worker. All papers that attract the eye, and hence the attention, should be cleaned from the desk, everything except that on which the worker is working. The capability of being distracted by the presence of other things varies in all workers.

In using the dictaphone, one can do much better work if one is in a room where there is little or nothing to distract attention. An outline of work ahead, may tempt to study and planning of what is ahead, rather than to carrying out the task scheduled for immediate performance. The presence of a paper with an outline merely of what is being done is found to be a great help, as the eye can rest on that, and after a few moments, will become so accustomed to it that the whole attention will be given to the dictating.

Benefits of Eliminating "Decision of Choice." — There is always time lost by "decision of choice." The elimination of this is well illustrated by the bricks that are piled on the packet, which decides for the bricklayer which brick is next, making an obvious sequence, hence the saving of time of decision regarding motions, also the saving coming from the play for position. Oftentimes a handicap of slow mental action can be compensated for, in a measure, by planning ahead in great detail. In this way, if the plan is made sufficiently in detail, there is absolutely no time possible left to be wasted in "decision of choice." The worker goes from one step to another, and as these steps are arranged logically, his mind does not tend to wander away, but to keep on in an uninterrupted sequence to the goal.

Standard Equipment Important

As for equipment, the phenomena of habit are among the most important features of the psychology of management and the possibilities of the elimination of unnecessary waste resulting from taking advantage of this feature is possible only when the equipment, surroundings and methods of the worker are standardized. Therefore the insistence upon standardization, even down to the smallest things, is vital for achieving the greatest output.

For example, — suppose the keys of the monotype machine, piano or typewriter were not located permanently in the same relative position. Consider the loss of time in not being able to use habits in finding each key. Such an arrangement sounds ridiculous on the face of it, yet it is a common practice for many operators, especially of monotype machines, to make a complete mental decision as to the muscles and fingers with which they will strike the desired key.

Imagine the records of output of a typist who was using a different keyboard every day, if there were that many kinds of keyboards. It is easy for anyone to conceive the great advantages of standard keyboards for such machines, but only those who have made a study of output of all kinds of workers can fully realize that similar differences in sizes of output are being produced by the workers of the country for lack of similar standardization of working conditions and equipment.

Utmost Standardization does not Make "Machines" of the Workers Operating Under It

The attention of those who believe that standardization makes machines out of the workers themselves, is called to the absence of such effect upon the typist as compared with the scribe, the monotype and linotype operator as compared with the compositor, and the mechanical computing machine operator as compared with the arithmetician.

Standard Methods Demand Standard Tools and Devices

Habits cannot be standardized until the devices and tools used are of standard pattern. It is not nearly so essential to have the best tools as it is to have standard tools. Experience in the hospitals points to the importance of this fact in surgery. Tools once adopted as standard should not be changed until the improvement or greater efficiency from their use will compensate for the loss during the period of "breaking in" the user, that is, of forming new habits in order to handle strange tools. As will be brought out more fully under "Teaching," good habits are as difficult to break as bad ones, the only difference being that one does not usually desire to break good ones. Naturally, if a new device is introduced, what was an excellent habit for the old device becomes, perhaps, a very bad habit for the new device. There must come a time before the manipulation of the new device has become a habit when output will go down and costs will go up. It is necessary, before introducing this device, to investigate whether the ultimate reduction of costs will be sufficient to allow for this period of lower production. It is not fair, however, to the new device or method really to consider its record until the use of it has become such a habit with the workers as was the use of the old device.

No one who has not made a study of cutting tools can realize the crying need for standardizing in that field. Dr. Taylor says, writing in the Revised "Shop Management" of 1911, — "Hardly a shop can be found in which tools made from a dozen different qualities of steel are not used side by side, in many cases with little or no means of telling one make from another." The effect of the slightest variation in the shape or the method of handling the tool upon the three dimensions of the work that the tool can do in a given time, is astounding. More important, from the psychological point of view, is the effect upon the mind of the worker of seeing such unstandardized equipment; of having to stop to select the particular tool that he desires, and thus having his attention distracted from his work; and of knowing that his act of judgment in so selecting is of no permanent value, as the next time he needs a similar tool he will probably have to reselect.

Standard Clothing a Crying Need

There is a great need today for standardization in the field of clothing. The idea prevalent that wearing apparel is attractive only when it is "different" is unfortunate in its influence upon the cost of living. How much more unfortunate is it, when it affects the mind of the worker, and leads him to look upon standard working clothes with distaste.

To a careful observer, there is nothing more disheartening than a study of workers' clothes, especially the clothes of women workers. Too warm clothes where work requiring high temperature is done, with no provision for adding needed wraps for the trip home; high-heeled shoes where the worker must stand at her task for hours at a time; tight waists and ill fitting skirts, where every muscle should have free play, — these are but examples of hundreds of places where reforms are needed.

Little or no blame attaches to the worker for this state of affairs. Seldom, if ever, does the management attempt to standardize working clothes. Moreover, the underlying idea is not made clear that such clothes bear no resemblance to the meaningless uniforms which are badge and symbol of service. They resemble rather the blouse or pinafore of the artist, the outfit of the submarine diver or the fireman.

The Sports Present a Fine Example of This

The greatest advance toward standardizing clothing has come in the sports, which, in many respects, present admirable object-lessons. In the tennis court, on the links, on the gridiron, the diamond, or track, the garment worn of itself does not increase fatigue. On the contrary, it is so designed as not to interfere with the efficiency of the wearer.

Management Should Provide Clothing Standards

Under Ultimate Management the most efficient clothing for any kind of work will be standardized. The expense of such articles of clothing as will add to the quantity or quality of output will, directly or indirectly, be borne by the management, just as it now bears the expense for equipment and tools. These essentials being supplied, and the underlying dignity and importance of standardization understood, the worker will gladly conform, and supply the minor accessories.

Such Standards must Apply to All

It is of the utmost importance that such standardization, when adopted, should apply to the clothing of all, managers as well as employees. When the old pride in the "crafts" returns, or when efficiency is as universal in the industrial world as it is in the world of sport, — then one may look for results.

Effects of such Standards Enormous

The effect which such standardized clothing would have on the physical and mental well-being of the wearers can scarcely be overestimated. Fatigue would be eliminated, and the old "joy in working" might return. Not being based upon looks alone,— though the aesthetic appeal should not be neglected, — the worker's ability to work more and better with greater content of mind would be the criterion. The success of the clothing would be scientifically measured, the standards improved, and progress itself become standardized.

Standard Methods Eliminate Fatigue

There is no doubt in the minds of those who have made it a study, that the constant receipt of the same kind of impressions, caused by the same kind of stimulation of the same terminal sense organs, causes semi-automatic response with less resulting fatigue, corresponding to the lessened effort. All methods should, therefore, as far as possible, be made up of standard elements under standard conditions, with standard devices and appliances, and they should be standardized from the standpoint of all of our senses as to color, shape, size, weight, location, position and surface texture, that the worker may grasp at a single thought by means of each or all his senses, that no special muscles or other fatiguing processes need be operated to achieve the standard result desired.

Muscles that Tire Easily Should be Saved

It must be remembered that all work should be so arranged that the muscle that changes the position or shape of the eye or the size of its pupil should not be operated except when necessary. Care in planning can oftentimes standardize conditions so as to relieve these and other muscles, which grow tired easily, or transfer this work to other muscles which are not so easily tired.

Not only do the reactions from such standards require less bodily effort, but it also requires less mental effort to work under methods that are standardized. Therefore, both directly and indirectly, the worker benefits by the standardization.

Rest from Fatigue is Provided for Scientifically

Scientific Management provides and prescribes rest for overcoming fatigue of the worker more scientifically and economically than he could possibly provide it for himself. Weber's law is that "our power of detecting differences between sensations does not depend on the absolute amount of difference in the stimuli, but on the relative amount." The additional fatigue from handling additional weights causes fatigue to increase with the weight, but not in direct proportion to the extra weight handled. When the correct weight of the unit to be handled has been determined, the additional weight will cause fatigue in quantities greater in proportion than the extra weight handled.

Rest Periods Arranged for best Good of Work and Worker

If possible, rest from fatigue is so arranged as to interfere with work the least. The necessary rest periods of the individuals of a gang should come at that period of the cycle that does not cause any allowance to be made for rest in between the performance of the dependent operations of different members of the gang. Such an arrangement will enable the worker to keep a sustained interest in the work.

Work with Animals Should be Standardized

The necessity for standardizing work with animals has been greatly underestimated, although it has been done more or less successfully in systems for construction work. For work with horses and carts, the harnesses and the carts should be standardized and standards only should be used. The instruction card dealing with the action, motions and their sequence should be standard to save time in changing teams from the full to the empty cart and *vice versa*. While standardized action is necessary with men, it is even more necessary for men in connection with the work of animals, such as horses, mules and oxen. The instruction card for the act of changing of teams from an empty cart to a full cart should state the side that the driver gets down from his seat to the ground, the sequence in which he unhooks the harness and hooks it up again, and the side on which he gets up to his seat in the cart. Even the wording of his orders to his horse should be standardized.

While this book will deal with the human mind only, it is in order to state that a book could be written to advantage on training the horse by means of a standard man-horse language and a standard practice of their combined action.

Animals have not the capacity for forming new habits that they have for remembering the sequence of former acts. They have little ability to adapt themselves to a sequence of motions caused by unexpected conditions, unless those conditions suggest the opportunity of revenge, or the necessity of self-preservation, or immediate welfare. This is only touched upon here from the man side. Naturally, the output earning power of a man working with animals depends largely upon the handling of the animal, and the man can never attain his full output, or the managers get what they might expect to get from the man-horse combination, until the psychology of the horse, or mule, or elephant, or whatever animal is used, is also studied and combined with the other studies on Scientific Management.

An example of the benefits of standardized work with animals: — The standard fire signals in the Fire House cause such perfect horse action that fire horses always have a reputation for superior intelligence. An exaggerated case of the result of leaving the selection of the method to the worker is that of the West Indian negro who carried the wheelbarrow on his head. This well-known example, though it seems impossible and absurd, is no more inefficient than are hundreds of methods in use in the industrial world today.

Under Scientific Management Quality is Standardized

Scientific Management determines exactly what quality as well as what quantity of work is needed, and the method prescribed is that one not only of lower costs, but which fits the particular need of the particular occasion most accurately. Workers are kept under pressure for quality, yet the pressure is not irksome, because the worker understands exactly what quality is desired, and what variations from exactness are permitted.

Variations in Quality or Exactness Indicated by Standard Signs

All dimensions on the drawings of work have either a letter or symbol or plus or minus signs. There is much to be said about the effect this has on the worker.

1. It gives the worker immediate knowledge of the prescribed quality demanded.
2. He does not have to worry as to the maximum variation that he can make without interfering with his bonus.

3. There is no fear of criticism or discharge for using his own faulty judgment.

Scientific Management Has a Standard "Method of Attack."— We must note next the standard "method of attack" in Scientific Management. It is recognized that sensations are modified by those that come before, by those that come simultaneously, and by those that follow. The psychic effect of each and every kind of sensation depends upon what other sensations have been experienced, are being experienced at that time, or will presently be experienced. The scientific manager realizes this, and provides for the most desirable sequence of sensation; then, having seen, to the best of his ability, that the sensation occurs at the time which he desires it to occur, he provides for concentration upon that one sensation and elimination of all other thoughts or desires.

Professor Faraday says: "That part of self-education which consists in teaching the mind to resist the desires and inclinations until they are proved to be right is the most important of all." How this is shown under Scientific Management will be shown in "Teaching." It is sufficient to say here that the method of attack of Scientific Management is to eliminate all possible bodily as well as mental exertion, — to cut down motions, to cut down even sensations and such mental acts as visualizing. The object is, not so much to eliminate these motions and these sensations, and this visualizing from the life of the worker, as simply to use up less energy in producing the output. This allows the worker an extra supply of energy upon which to fall back to produce greater output and to get greater wages. If his energy is not all utilized in his working hours, then, as will be shown more clearly under "Welfare," there is that much more left for him to enjoy in his own leisure time.

Summary

Result to the Work

Under Traditional Management, where standards are not established, the worker is constantly delayed by the necessity for decision of choice, by the lack of knowing what should be chosen, and by a dearth of standard equipment, materials and tools from which to choose.

Under Transitory Management, with the introduction of standards, the elimination of delays and the provision for standard surroundings and supplies of all kinds, comes increased output of the desired quality.

Under Scientific Management, not only is output increased and quality assured, but results of work can be predicted.

Results to the Worker

Results from standardization to the worker under Traditional and Transitory Management are the same as, and are included in, results under Scientific Management.

State of Worker's Feelings Improved

Under Scientific Management the state of the employe's feelings is improved by the standardization. It is a recognized fact that mental disturbance from such causes as fear of losing his job will sometimes have the same ill effect upon a workman as does overwork, or insufficient rest for overcoming fatigue. It will occasionally wear upon the nervous system and the digestive organs. Now Scientific Management by standardization removes from the workman this fear of losing his job, for the worker knows that if he conforms to the standard instructions he certainly will not lose his position unless the business as a whole is unsuccessful.

On the other hand, feelings, such as happiness and contentment, and even hearing rhythmic sounds, music, etc., are an aid toward increasing output. For the best results, therefore, under Scientific Management the worker is furnished with standard conditions; his train of ideas is held upon the work in hand without interruption, and the working conditions are such that the managers furnish the worker with inducements to conform to the standard conditions happily.

Worker's Retentive Power Increased

We note in the second place, the increased retentive power of anyone who is working with standards. There is great difference between different people of the same degree of intelligence as to their ability to memorize certain things, especially such as sequences of the elements of a process. This lack of retentive power is illustrated particularly well in the cases often found where the student has difficulty in learning to spell. It is here that the standard instruction card comes into play to good effect. Its great detail remedies the defect in memorizing of certain otherwise brilliant workers, and its standard form and repetition of standard phrases aid the retentive power of the man who has a good memory.

Standard Elements Serve as Memory Drills

This use of standardized elements makes the time elapsing between repetitions shorter, for, while it may be a long time before the worker again encounters the identical work or method, still, the fact that elements are standard means that he will have occasion to repeat elements frequently, and that his memory will each time be further drilled by these repetitions.

Gang Instruction Card an Aid to Memory

The gang instruction card has been used with good effect at the beginning of unfamiliar repetitive cycles of work to train the memory of whole gangs of men at once, and to cut down the elapsed time from the time when one man's operation is sufficiently completed to permit the next man to commence his. It has been found, in the case of setting timbers in mill construction for example, that to have one man call out the next act in the sequence as fast as the preceding one is finished, until all have committed the sequence to memory, will materially decrease the time necessary for the entire sequence of elements in a cycle of work.

Individual Instruction Card an Inanimate Memory

The instruction card supplies a most accurate memory in inanimate form, that neither blurs nor distorts with age.

The ranter against this standard memory is no more sensible than a man who would advocate the worker's forgetting the result of his best experience, that his mind might be periodically exercised by rediscovering the method of least waste anew with each problem.

Other things being equal, that worker has the longest number of years of earning power who remembers the largest number of right methods; or at least remembers where to find them described in detail; and, conversely, those who have no memory, and know not where to look for or to lay their hand on the method of least waste, remain at the beginning of their industrial education. "Experience," from an earning standpoint, does not exist when the mind does not retain a memory of the method. The instruction card, then, acts as a form of transferable memory — it conserves memory. Once it is made, it furnishes the earning power without the necessity of the former experience having been had more than once.

Plans, details, free-hand sketches, and two-dimension photographs surpass the highest form of mental imagery, and such cultivated imagery is undoubtedly a high achievement. There is no kind of memory, visualization, nor constructive imagination that can equal the stereoscopic or three-dimension photographs that may accompany the instruction card for enabling the worker to "see the completed work before it is begun." Probably the greatest hindrance to development of lower forms of animal life is their inability to picture past experiences, and the reason for the intellectual strides made by the worker under Scientific Management is the development of this faculty.

A Conserver of Individual Memories

Many people believe that the memory of a person ceases at his death. Whether this is so or not, the loss to the world, and particularly the industrial world, of not having the instruction card for the passing on of the worker's experience to the workers who follow is stupendous and incalculable, and this loss, like so many other losses, can be eliminated by the process of making written standards.

Motor Memory Improved by Standardization

Not only are the retentive powers of the brain improved, but also the brain centers, and the muscles, etc., become trained through standardization. With standardization a long sequence of muscular motions or operations can be noted at a glance, and can be remembered without difficulty.

Standards Prevent Men from Becoming Machines

Those who object to the worker taking advantage of these scientifically derived standards which aid the memory, can only be compared to such people as desire the workers to turn into unthinking animals. Psychologists believe that some of the lower animals have no memory. Turning the workers into machines which do not in any way utilize thought-saving devices is simply putting them but little above the class of these lower, memory-less, animals.

Through Standards the Worker's Attention is Gained at the Start

The general act of attention plays an important part in Scientific Management. The insistence upon standardized performance requires the utmost attention at the beginning of learning a new method of performance. This extra output of mental activity, which is always required for accomplishing new methods of work, could not be continuously maintained, but after the new method has once been learned, its repetition requires less attention, consequently less fatigue. The attention of the worker is, therefore, strongly demanded at the beginning and when, later, it is not needed except for new and unfamiliar work, an opportunity arises for invention and mental advancement.

Attention Allowed to Lapse and Then Recalled

Standardization shifts the objects of attention and eliminates the need for constant concentration. The standardization of processes relieves the worker to a marked extent from the extremely fatiguing mental effort of unproductive fixed, valueless, and unnecessary attention on the stream of consciousness. The repeated elements which form a part of all standards reconcentrates the attention if it is allowed to lapse.

Standardization Eliminates the Shifting Viewpoint

Under old-time Traditional Management the way that the man happened to feel at the particular time made a great difference, not only in his work, but in his relations with other men. The standardization not only of the relationship between the men, but of the relationships between the foreman, the manager, and the worker, the fact that the disciplining is put in the hands of a man who is not biased by his personal feelings in his dealings with the men; — all of these things mean that the viewpoint of the men as to their work and their relationship remains fixed. This standardizing of the viewpoint is an enormous help toward increasing output.

The Common Viewpoint is an Impetus

There are those who believe that the concerted standard process of thought of the many minds assists the operation of any one mind. However this may be, there is no doubt that the fact that the standard thought is present in all minds at one time at least eliminates some cause for discussion and leads to unity and consequent success in the work.

Invention is Stimulated

Chances for invention and construction are provided by standardization. By having a scientifically derived standard method as a starter, the worker can exert much of his mental power toward improvement from that point upward, instead of being occupied with methods below it and in wasting, perhaps, a lifetime in striving to get up to it, this in distinction to the old plan, where a worker knew only what he could personally remember of what had been handed down by tradition, tradition being the memory of society. Under Scientific Management a worker has many repetitions of experience, some of which he does not always recognize as such. When he does recognize them, he has the power and daring for rapid construction that come to those only who "know that they know."

Standardization of ultimate subdivisions, as such, brings that power to the worker sooner. The conscious knowledge of familiarity of process is an essential for attaining the complete benefits of experience.

Far from making machines out of the men, standardization causes a mental state that leads to invention, for the reason that the worker's brain is in most intimate contact with the work, and yet has not been unnecessarily fatigued by the work itself. No more monotonous work could be cited than that of that boy whose sole duty was to operate by hand the valve to the engine, yet he invented the automatic control of the slide valve used throughout the world today.

Standardization Prevents Accidents

The results of standardization so far given, concern changes in the worker's mental capacity, or attitude. Such changes, and other changes, will be discussed from a different viewpoint under "Teaching." As for results to the worker's body, one of the most important is the elimination of causes for accidents.

The rigid inspection, testing, and repairing provided for by Scientific Management provides against accidents from defects in equipment, tools, or material. The fact that instructions are written, provides against wrong methods of handling work. The concentrated attention caused by standardization, is a safeguard against accidents that occur from the worker's carelessness. The proper allowance of rest for overcoming fatigue, insures that the worker's mind is fresh enough to enable him to comply with standards, and, finally, the spirit of cooperation that underlies Scientific Management is an added check against accidents, in that everyone is guarding his fellows as well as himself.

Progress of Standardization Assured

As Scientific Management becomes older, progress will be faster, because up to this time there has been a hindrance standing in the way of rapid advancement of the best standards. This hindrance has been the tendency of habits of thought coinciding with former practice. For example, the design of concrete building for years followed the habit of thinking in terms of brick, or wood, or steel, and then attempting to design and construct in reinforced concrete. Again, in the case of the motor car, habits of thinking in vehicles drawn by animals for years kept the design unnecessarily leaning toward that of horse vehicles. As soon as thought was in terms of power vehicles, the efficient motor truck of today was made, using the power also for power loading and power hoisting, as is now done in motor trucks specially designed for transporting and handling pianos and safes. So, also, while the thought was of traditional practice, standard practice was held back. Now that the theories of standardization are well understood, standardization and standards in general can advance with great rapidity.

6

Records and Programmes

Definition of Record

A record is, according to the Century Dictionary — "something set down in writing or delineated for the purpose of preserving memory; specifically a register; an authentic or official copy of any writing, or an account of any fact and proceedings, whether public or private, usually entered in a book for preservation; also the book containing such copy or account." The synonyms given are "note, chronicle, account, minute, memorandum."

Few Written Records Under Traditional Management

For the purposes of this preliminary study of records, emphasis will be laid on the fact that the record is written. Under Traditional Management there are practically no such labour records. What records are kept are more in the nature of "bookkeeping records," as Gillette and Dana call them, records "showing debits and credits between different accounts." In many cases, under Traditional Management, not even such records of profit or loss from an individual piece of work were kept, the manager, in extreme cases, oftentimes "keeping his books in his head" and having only the vaguest idea of the state of his finances.

Importance of Records Realized Under Transitory Management

As has been amply demonstrated in discussing Individuality and Standardization, the recognition of the value of records is one of the first indications of Transitory Management. Since this stage of management has Scientific Management in view as “a mark to come to,” the records evolved and used are not discarded by Scientific Management, but are simply perfected. Therefore, there is no need to discuss these transitory records, except to say that, from the start, *quality* of records is insisted upon before quantity of records.

No “Bookkeeping” Records Under Scientific Management

Under Scientific Management there are no “bookkeeping records” kept of costs as such. Instead, there are “time and cost records,” so called, of the time and efficiency of performance. From these, costs can be deduced at any time. Items of cost without relation to their causes, on work that is not to be repeated, have little value.

Cost records, as such, usually represent a needless, useless expenditure of time and money. It must be emphasized that Scientific Management can in no way be identified with “cost keeping,” in the sense that is understood to mean aimlessly recording unrelated costs. Under Scientific Management costs are an ever-present by-product of the system, not a direct product.

Records Must Lower Costs and Simplify Work

The quantity of records that should be made depends on the amount, diversity and state of development of the work done. No record should be made, which does not, directly or indirectly, actually reduce costs or in some way increase efficiency.

The purpose of the records, as of Scientific Management in general, is to simplify work. Only when this is recognized, can the records made be properly judged. Numerous as they may at times seem to be, their number is determined absolutely by the satisfactory manner in which they —

1. Reduce costs.
2. Simplify work.
3. Increase efficiency.

Records of Work and Workers

Records may be of the work or of the worker — that is to say, of material used, tools used, output produced, etc., or of individual efficiency, in one form or another. Records of efficiency may be of workers, of foremen, and of managers, and a record may be made of any man in several capacities; for example, a record is kept of a functional foreman in the form of the work of the men who are under him, while another record might be kept of him as a worker himself; for example, the time being taken that it took him to teach others their duties, the time to learn what was to be done on any new work, etc.

Records of Initiative

Records of initiative are embodied in the Suggestion Card. Even under advanced Traditional Management the cards are furnished to the men upon which to write any ideas as to improvements. These suggestions are received, and, if accepted, are rewarded.

Under Scientific Management such suggestions become more valuable, for, as has been shown, they are based upon standards; thus if accepted, they signify not only a real, but a permanent improvement. Their greatest value, however, is in the stimulus that they furnish to the worker, in the information that they furnish the management as to which workers are interested, and in the spirit of cooperation that they foster.

The worker receives not only a money-reward, but also publicity, for it is made known which worker has made a valuable suggestion. This indicates that the worker has shown good judgment. His interest is thus stimulated, his attention is held to his work, and the habit of initiative comes to him. That this habit of initiative can be fostered, is shown by the actual fact that in many sorts of work the same man constantly makes suggestions. It becomes a habit with him to look for the new way, and as he is constantly rewarded, the interest is not allowed to diminish.

Records of Good Behaviour

Records of good behaviour are incorporated in the White List File. The White List File contains the names of all men who have ever been employed who merit a recommendation, if they should go to work for others, and would deserve to be given work as soon as possible, if they came back. This White List File should be filled out with many details, but even if it contains nothing but a record of the names, and the addresses where the men can be reached when new work starts up, it has a stimulating effect upon the worker. He feels, again, the element of permanence; there is a place for individuality, and not only does the manager have the satisfaction of actually having this list, and of using it, but a feeling that his men know that he is in some way recognizing them, and endeavoring to make them and their good work permanent.

Records of Achievement

Records of achievement vary with the amount and nature of the work done. Such records are, as far as possible, marked upon programmes.

Records made by Worker where Possible

Wherever possible the worker makes his own records. Even when this is not advisable he is informed of his record at as short intervals as are practicable.

Records Made on the "Exception Principle." — Much time is saved by separating records for the inspection of the man above, simply having him examine the exceptions to some desired condition, — the records which are exceptionally good, the records which are exceptionally bad. This not only serves as a reward to the man who has a good record, and a punishment for the man who has had a bad record, but it also enables the manager to discover at once what is wrong and where it is wrong, and to remedy it.

The value of the exception principle can hardly be overestimated. It would be of some value to know of exceptionally good or poor work, even if the cause were not known. At least one would be made to observe the signpost of success or of danger. But, under Scientific Management, the cause appears simultaneously with the fact on the record, — thus not only indicating the proper method of repeating success, or avoiding failure, in the future, but also showing, and making clear, the direct relation of cause to effect, to the worker himself.

This Discussion Necessarily Incomplete

The records mentioned above are only a few of the types of records under Scientific Management. Discussion has been confined to these, because they have the most direct effect upon the mind of the worker and the manager. Possible records are too numerous, and too diverse, to be described and discussed in detail. They constitute a part of the "how" of Scientific Management, — the manner in which it operates. This is covered completely in the literature of Scientific Management, written by men who have made Scientific Management and its installation a life study. We need only further discuss the posting of records, and their effect.

Posting of Records Beneficial

As has been already noted under Individuality, and must be again noted under Incentives, much benefit is derived from posting records, especially when these are of such a character, or are so posted, that the worker may see at a glance the comparative excellence of his results.

Summary

Results of Records to the Work. — The results of recording are the same under all forms of management, if the records are correct.

Output increases where records are kept. Under Traditional Management there is the danger that pressure for quantity will affect quality, especially if insufficient records of the resultant quality are kept. Under Transitory and Scientific Management, quality is maintained or improved, both because previous records set the standard, and because following records exhibit the quality.

Results to the Worker

James says, "A man's social use is the recognition which he gets from his mates. We are not only gregarious animals, liking to be liked in sight of our fellow, but we have an innate propensity to get ourselves noticed, and noticed favourably, by our kind. No more fiendish punishment could be devised, were such a thing physically possible, than that one should be turned loose in society and remain absolutely unnoticed by all the members thereof. If no one turned around when we entered, answered when we spoke or minded what we did, but if every person we met 'cut us dead' and acted as if we were non-existing things, a kind of rage and impotent despair would ere long well up in us, from which the cruelest bodily tortures would be a relief; for these would make us feel that, however bad might be our plight, we had not sunk to such a depth as to be unworthy of attention at all."

This recognition the worker gets partly through the records which are made of him.

Self-Knowledge Attained through Records

Through records of output, and especially through charts of such records, and timed motion-picture films, or micro-motion study pictures the worker may, if he be naturally observant, or if he be taught to observe, gain a fine knowledge of himself.

The constant exhibit of cause and effect of the relation of output to, for example, — drink of alcoholic beverages; to smoking; to food values; to nutrition; to family worries; and to other outside influences; — in fact, the effects of numerous different modes of living, are shown promptly to the worker in the form of records.

Two things should here be noted:

1. The necessity of having more accurate records of the worker and the work, that the relation of cause to effect may be more precise and authentic.
2. The necessity for so training the worker, before, as well as after, he enters the industrial world, that he can better understand and utilize the lesson taught by his own records and those of others.

Educative Value of Worker Making his own Record

Under Scientific Management in its most highly developed form, the worker makes his own records on his return cards and hands them in. The worker thus not only comes to realize, by seeing them and by writing them down, what his records are, but he also realizes his individual position today compared to what it was yesterday, and compared to that of his fellows in the same line of work. Further, he gains accuracy, he gains judgment, he gains a method of attack. He realizes that, as the managers are more or less recorders, so also he, in recording himself, is vitally connected with the management. It is, after all, more or less an attitude of mind which he gains by making out these records himself.

It is because of this attitude of mind, and of the value which it is to him, that he is made to make out his own record under the ultimate form of management, even though at times this may involve a sacrifice of the time in which he must do it, and although he may work slower than could a specialist at recording, who perhaps would, in spite of that, be paid less for doing the work.

Exact Knowledge Valuable

We cannot emphasize too often in this connection the far-reaching psychological effect upon the worker of exact knowledge of the comparative efficiency of methods. The value of this is seldom fully appreciated; for example, we are familiar with the many examples where the worker has been flattered until he believes that he cannot make mistakes or do inefficient work.

This is most often found where the glowing compliments to the manufacturing department, found in the advertising pages of the magazine and in the praises sung in print by the publicity department, oftentimes ends in an individual overconfidence. This unjustified self-esteem is soon shattered by accurate comparative records.

On the other hand, hazing of the new worker and the sneers of the jealous, accompanied by such trite expressions as — "You can't teach an old dog new tricks," have often destroyed self-confidence in a worker, who, in the absence of accurate records of his efficiency, is trying to judge himself at new methods. The jibes and jokes at the new man at the new work, and especially at the experienced, efficient man at unfamiliar work cease, or at least are wholly impotent, so far as discouraging the man is concerned, provided the worker sees by the records of a true measuring device, or method, that his work compares favourably with others of the same experience, made under the same conditions.

Definition of Programme

The word "programme" is defined by the Century Dictionary as "a method of operation or line of procedure prepared or announced beforehand. An outline or abstract of something to be done or carried out."

Two Meanings of "Programme" in Management

The word "programme" has two meanings in management.

1. the work, as it comes to the management to be done
2. the work as it is planned out by the managers, and handed over to the worker to be done.

Programme as here used is a plan for doing work, the plan which the planning department lays out and hands over for the performers, or the workers, to do.

Under Traditional Management no Accurate Programme is Possible

Under Traditional Management the plan is at best a repetition of records of unscientifically planned work. The most that the managers can hope to do is to lay out the time in which they expect, after consulting previous elapsed time records, the work to be done. Methods are not prescribed, so there is no assurance that the calendar will be followed, for the times are set by guess, or at best by referring to old unscientifically made records.

Under Transitory Management Calendars can be Designed

Under Transitory Management, with the introduction of systems, that is, records of how the work has been done best at various times, come methods and a possibility of a more exact calendar. There is some likelihood under Transitory System of the work being done on time, as the method has been considered and, in many cases, is specified.

Under Scientific Management Accurate Calendars Possible

Under Scientific Management programmes are based on accurate records scientifically made and standardized, and a calendar may be made that can be conformed to with exactness.

Programmes a Matter of Routing

The problems of a programme under Scientific Management are two, both problems of routing: —

1. to route materials to the work place.
2. to route the worker to the placed materials.

At first glance it might seem simpler to consider the worker as static and the materials as in motion. The "routing" of the worker is really often not a question of motion at all, as the worker, if he were operating a machine, for example, would not change his position between various pieces of work — except to rest from fatigue — enough to be considered. The word "routing" is used figuratively as regards the worker. He is considered as transported by the management through the day's work.

But, whether the work move, or the worker, or both, programmes must so plan out the progress of each, in detail, for as many days ahead as possible, that the most efficient outcome will ensue.

Routing of Work

The work is routed through schedules of materials to buy, schedules of material to handle, and schedules of labour to be performed. The skilled worker finds all the materials for his work ready and waiting for him when he arrives at the task, this being provided for by programmes made out many tasks ahead.

Routing of Workers

The workers themselves are routed by means of the route sheet, route chart, pin plan and bulletin board.

The devices for laying out the work of the workers appeal to the imagination as well as the reason. The route chart is a graphical representation of a large river, starting with the small stream, — the first operation, gathering to itself as the tributaries, the various other operations, — till it reaches its full growth, the completed work.

The pin plan, with each pin or flag representing a worker, or work place, and following his progress on a plan of the work, presents a bird's-eye view in miniature of the entire working force; and the bulletin board, with its cards that represent work ahead, not only eliminates actual delay of shifting from one task to another, but permits studying out one task while doing another, and also destroys all fear of delay between jobs.

Impossibility of Describing Routing Devices Accurately

These routing devices might all be described at length, but no description could do them justice. A visit to a shop, or factory, or other industrial organization operating under Scientific Management is necessary, in order to appreciate not only their utility, but the interest that they arouse. These programmes are no dead, static things. They are alive, pulsing, moving, progressing with the progress of the work.

Prophecy Becomes Possible Under Scientific Management

The calendar, or chronological chart, becomes a true prophecy of what will take place. This is based on the standardized elementary units, and the variations from it will be so slight as to allow of being disregarded.

7

Teaching in Organization

Definition of Teaching

The Century Dictionary defines "teaching" as "the act or business of instructing," with synonyms: "training" and "education;" and "to teach" is defined: —

1. "to point out, direct, show;" "to tell, inform, instruct, explain;"
2. "to show how (to do something); hence, to train;"
3. "to impart knowledge or practical skill to;" "to guide in learning, educate."

"Educate," we find meaning "to instruct, to teach methodically, to prescribe to; to indoctrinate;" and by "indoctrinate" is meant "to cause to hold as a doctrine or belief." "To educate," says the same authority, "is to develop mentally or morally by instruction; to qualify by instruction and training for the business and duty of life."

Under Traditional Management no Definite Plan of Teaching

Under Traditional Management there is either no definite scheme of teaching by the management itself, or practically none; at least, this is usually the condition under the most elementary types of Traditional Management. In the very highest examples of the traditional plan the learner may be shown how, but this showing is not usually done in a systematic way, and under so-called Traditional Management is seldom in the form of written instructions.

No Specified Time for or Source of the Teaching

Under Traditional Management there is no particular time in which this teaching goes on, no particular time allowed for the worker to ask for the instruction, nor is there any particular source from which he obtains the instructions. There is, moreover, almost every hindrance against his getting any more instruction than he absolutely must have in order to get the work done.

The persons to whom he can possibly appeal for further information might discharge him for not already knowing. These persons are, if he is an apprentice, an older worker; if he is a journeyman, the worker next to him, or the foreman, or someone over him. An important fact bearing on this subject is that it is not to the pecuniary advantage of any particular person to give this teaching. In the first place, if the man be a fellow-worker, he will want to do his own work without interruption, he will not want to take the time off; moreover, he regards his particular skill as more or less of a trade secret, and desires to educate no more people than necessary, to be as clever as he is. In the third place, there is no possible reward for giving this instruction. Of course, the worker necessarily improves under any sort of teaching, and if he has a receptive mind, or an inventive mind, he must progress constantly, either by teaching himself or by the instruction, no matter how haphazard.

Great Variation Under Traditional Management

Only discussion of teaching under this type of management with many men who have learned under it, can sufficiently emphasize the variations to be found. But the consensus of opinion would seem to prove that an apprentice of only a generation ago was too often hazed, was discouraged from appealing for assistance or advice to the workers near him, or to his foreman; was unable to find valuable literature for home-study on the subject of his trade. The experience of many an apprentice was, doubtless, different from this, but surely the mental attitude of the journeymen who were the only teachers must have tended toward some such resulting attitude of doubt or hesitancy in the apprentice.

Mental Attitude of the Worker-Teacher

Under the old plan of management, the apprentice must appear to the journeyman more or less of a supplanter. From the employee's standpoint it was most desirable that the number of apprentices be kept down, as an oversupply of labour almost invariably resulted in a lowering of wages. The quicker and better the apprentice was taught, the sooner he became an active competitor. There seldom existed under this type of management many staff positions to which the workers could hope to be promoted, certainly none where they could utilize to the fullest extent their teaching ability. There was thus every reason for a journeyman to regard the teaching of apprentices as unremunerative, irksome, and annoying.

Worker Not to Blame for This

The worker is not to be blamed for this attitude. The conditions under which he worked made it almost inevitable. Not only could he gain little or nothing by being a successful teacher, but also the bullying instinct was appealed to constantly, and the desire of the upper classmen in hazing days to make the next class "pay up" for the hazing that they were obliged to endure in their Freshman year.

Attitude of the Learner

The attitude of the typical learner must frequently be one of hesitancy and self-distrust if not of fear, though conditions were so varied as almost to defy classification. One type of apprentice was expected to learn merely by observation and imitation. Another was practically the chore boy of the worker who was assigned to teach him. A third was under no direct supervision at all, but was expected to "keep busy," finding his work by himself. A fourth was put through a severe and valuable training by a martinet teacher, — and so on.

Teaching often Painstaking

It is greatly to the credit of the worker under this type of management that he was, in spite of all drawbacks, occasionally a painstaking teacher, to the best of his lights. He insisted on application, and especially on quality of work. He unselfishly gave of his own time and skill to help the apprentice under him.

Methods of Teaching Usually Wrong

Unfortunately, through no fault of the worker-teacher the teaching was usually done according to wrong methods. Quality of resulting output was so emphasized that neither speed nor correct motions were given proper consideration.

Teacher Not Trained to Teach

The reason for this was that the worker had no training to be a teacher. In the first place, he had no adequate idea of his own capabilities, and of which parts of his own method were fit to be taught. In the second place, he did not know that right motions must be insisted on first, speed next, and quality of output third; or in other words that if the motions were precise enough, the quality would be first. In the fourth place he had no pedagogical training.

Lack of Standards an Underlying Lack

All shortcoming in the old time teaching may be traced to lack of standards. The worker had never been measured, hence had no idea of his efficiency, or of possible efficiency. No standard methods made plain the manner in which the work should be done. Moreover, no standard division and assignment of work allowed of placing apprentices at such parts of the work that quality could be given third place. No standard requirements had determined his fitness as a teacher, nor the specialty that he should teach, and no incentive held his interest to the teaching. These standards the worker-teacher could not provide for himself, and the wonder is that the teaching was of such a high character as it was.

Very Little Teaching of Adults

Under Traditional Management, teaching of adults was slight, — there being little incentive either to teacher or to learner, and it being always difficult for an adult to change his method. Moreover, it would be difficult for a worker using one method to persuade one using another that his was the better, there being no standard. Even if the user of the better did persuade the other to follow his method, the final result might be the loss of some valuable elements of the poorer method that did not appear in the better.

Failure to Appreciate the Importance of Teaching

An underestimation of the importance of teaching lay at the root of the lack of progress. This is so directly connected with all the other lacks of Traditional Management, — provision for adequate promotion and pay, standards, and the other underlying principles of Scientific Management, especially the appreciation of cooperation, — that it is almost impossible to disentangle the reasons for it. Nor would it be profitable to attempt to do so here. In considering teaching under Scientific Management we shall show the influence of the appreciation of teaching, — and may deduce the lacks from its non-appreciation, from that discussion.

Under Transitory System Teaching Becomes more Important

Under Transitory Management the importance of teaching becomes at once more apparent. This, both by providing for the teaching of foremen and journeymen as well as apprentices, and by the providing of written systems of instructions as to best practice. The worker has access to all the sources of information of Traditional Management, and has, besides these, in effect, unsystematically derived standards to direct him.

Systems Make Instruction Always Available

The use of written systems enables every worker to receive instruction at any time, to feel free to ask it, and to follow it without feeling in any way humiliated.

The result of the teaching of these systems is a decided improvement in methods. If the written systems are used exclusively as a source of teaching, except for the indefinite teachers of the Traditional Management, the improvement becomes definitely proportioned to the time which the man spends upon the studying and to the amount of receptive power which he naturally has.

Incentives to Conform to System

The worker has incentives to follow the systems —

1. In that he is required to render reasons in writing for permanent filing, for every disobedience of system.

2. That, as soon as work is placed on the bonus basis, the first bonus that is given is for doing work in accordance with the prescribed method.

Even before the bonus is paid, the worker will not vary for any slight reasons, if he positively knows at the time that he must account for so doing, and that he will be considered to have "stacked his judgment" against that of the manager. Being called to account for deviations gives the man a feeling of responsibility for his act, and also makes him feel his close relationship with the managers.

No Set Time for Using Systems

There is, under this type of management, no set time for the study of the systems.

Systems Inelastic

Being written, these systems have all the disadvantages of anything that is written. That is to say, they require considerable adaptability on the part of the man who is using them. He must consider his own mind, and the amount of time which he must put on studying; he must consider his own work, and adapting that method to his work while still obeying instructions. In the case of the system being in great detail, he can usually find a fairly detailed description of what he is going to do, and can use that. In the case of the system being not so complete, if his work varies, he must show intelligence in varying the system, and this intelligence often demands a knowledge which he has not, and knows not where to obtain.

Waste of Time from Unstandardized Systems

The time necessitated by the worker's laying out details of his method is taken from the total time of his working day, hence in so far cuts down his total product. Moreover, if no record is kept of the details of his planning the next worker on the same kind of work must repeat the investigation.

Later Transitional Management Emphasizes Use of Standards

Later Transitional Management eliminates this waste of time by standardizing methods composed of standardized timed units, thus both rendering standards elastic, and furnishing details.

Teaching Most Important Under Scientific Management

Teaching is a most important element under Scientific Management not only because it increases industrial efficiency, but also because it fosters industrial peace. Importance Depends on Other Elements of Scientific Management

As we have seen, Scientific Management has as a basic idea the necessity of divided responsibility, or functionalization. This, when accompanied by the interdependent bonus, creates an incentive to teach and an incentive to learn. Scientific Management divides the planning from the performing in order to centralize and standardize knowledge in the planning department, thus making all knowledge of each available to all. This puts at the disposal of all more than any could have alone. The importance of having this collected and standardized knowledge conveyed best to the worker cannot be overestimated. Through this knowledge, the worker is able to increase his output, and thus insure the lowered costs, that provide the funds with which to pay his higher wages, — to increase his potential as well as actual efficiency, and best to cooperate with other workers and with the management.

Importance of Teaching Element Best Claim to Permanence of Scientific Management

Upon the emphasis which it places on teaching rests/a large part of the claim of Scientific Management for permanence. We have already shown the derivation of the standards which are taught. We have shown that the relation between the planning and performing departments is based largely on means and methods for teaching. We have only to show here that the teaching is done in accordance with those laws of Psychology that are the laws of Pedagogy.

Teaching in Scientific Management Not the Result of Theory Only

The methods of teaching under Scientific Management were not devised in response to theories of education. They are the result of actual experience in getting work done most successfully. The teachers, the methods, the devices for teaching, — all these grew up to meet needs, as did the other elements of Scientific Management.

Conformity of Teaching to Psychological Laws Proof of Worth of Scientific Management

The fact that teaching under Scientific Management does conform, as will be shown, to the laws of Psychology, is an added proof of the value of Scientific Management.

Change from Teaching Under Traditional Management

Mr. Gantt says, "The general policy of the past has been to drive; but the era of force must give way to that of knowledge, and the policy of the future will be to teach and to lead, to the advantage of all concerned." This "driving" element of Traditional Management is eliminated by Scientific Management.

Necessity for Personally Derived Judgment Eliminated

So also is eliminated the old belief that the worker must go through all possible experiences in order to acquire "judgment" as to best methods. If the worker must pass through all the stages of the training of the old-fashioned mechanic, and this is seriously advocated by some, he may fail to reach the higher planes of knowledge afforded by training under Scientific Management, by reason of sheer lack of time. If, therefore, by artificial conditions caused by united agreement and collective bargaining, workmen insist upon forcing upon the new learners the old-school training, they will lose just so much of the benefits of training under those carefully arranged and carefully safe-guarded processes of industrial investigation in which modern science has been successful.

To refuse to start in where others have left off, is really as wasteful as it would be to refuse to use mathematical formulas because they have been worked out by others. It might be advocated that the mind would grow by working out every possible mathematical formula before using it, but the result would be that the student would be held back from any further original investigation. Duplicating primary investigations might be original work for him, but it would be worthless as far as the world is concerned. The same is absolutely true in management. If the worker is held back by acquiring every bit of knowledge for himself instead of taking the work of others as the starting point, the most valuable initiative will be lost to the world.

Bad Habits the Result of Undirected Learning

Even worse than the waste of time would be the danger of acquiring habits of bad methods, habits of unnecessary motions, habits of inaccurate work; habits of inattention. Any or all of these might develop. These are all prevented under Scientific Management by the improved methods of teaching.

Valuable Elements of Traditional Management Conserved

There are, however, many valuable elements of the old Traditional system of teaching and of management which should be retained and not be lost in the new.

For example, — the greatest single cause of making men capable under the old plan was the foreman's unconscious ability to make his men believe, before they started a task, that they could achieve it.

It must not be thought that because of the aids to the teacher under Scientific Management the old thought of personality is lost. The old ability to convert a man to the belief that he could do a thing, to inspire him with confidence in his foreman, with confidence in himself, and a desire to do things, is by no means lost, on the contrary it is carefully preserved under Scientific Management.

Teaching of Transitory Management Supplemented

In the transforming of Transitory into Scientific Management, we note that the process is one of supplementing, not of discarding. Written system, which is the distinguishing characteristic of Transitory Management, is somewhat limited in its scope, but its usefulness is by no means impaired.

Scope of Teaching Under Scientific Management

Under Scientific Management teaching must cover;

1. Teaching of right methods of doing work,
2. Teaching of right habits of doing the right methods.

The teacher must so impart the knowledge that judgment can be acquired without the learner being obliged himself to experience all the elements of the judgment.

Needs for Teaching Under Scientific Management

The needs for this teaching have been stated, but may be recapitulated here.

1. Worker may not observe his own mistakes.
2. Worker has no opportunity under the old industrial conditions to standardize his own methods.
3. Worker must know standard practice.
4. Waste can be eliminated by the teaching.
5. Right habits can be instilled.

Methods of Teaching Under Scientific Management

The Methods of Teaching under Scientific Management are

1. Written, by means of
   (a) Instruction Cards telling *what* is to be done and *how*.
   (b) Systems, explaining the *why*.
   (c) Drawings, charts, plans, photographs, illustrating methods.
   (d) Records made by the worker himself.
2. Oral, the teaching of the Functional Foremen.
3. Object-lessons:
   (a) Exhibits.
   (b) Working models.
   (c) Demonstrations by the Teacher.
   (d) Demonstrations by the worker under Supervision.

Worker a Source of these Methods

It should be often stated that, ultimately, the elements of

all methods are derived from a study of workers, and that the worker should be enabled to realize this. Only when he feels that he is a part of what is taught, and that the teachers are a *means* of presenting to him the underlying principles of his own experience, will the worker be able to cooperate with all his energy.

Instruction Cards are Directions

Instruction Cards are direct instructions for each piece of work, giving, in most concise form, closely defined description of standard practice and directions as to how each element of the standardized task is to be performed. The makers know that they must make their directions clear ultimately, therefore they strive constantly for clearness.

Instruction Cards Teach Directly and Indirectly

These Instruction Cards not only teach the worker directly best to do his work, but also teach him indirectly how to become a leader, demonstrator, teacher and functional foreman. Study of them may lead to an interest in, and a study of, elements, and to preparation for becoming one of the planning department. The excellent method of attack of the Instruction Card cannot fail to have some good effect, even upon such workers as do not consciously note it.

Systems are Reasons and Explanations

"Systems" or standing orders are collections of detailed reasons for, and explanations of, the decisions embodied in the directions of the Instruction Cards. There is a system showing the standard practice of each kind of work.

They Enlist the Judgment of the Worker

Under really successful management, it is realized that the worker is of an inquiring mind, and that, unless this inquiring tendency of his is recognized, and his curiosity is satisfied, he can never do his best work. Unless the man knows why he is doing the thing, his judgment will never reënforce his work. He may conform to the method absolutely, but his work will not enlist his zeal unless he knows just exactly why he is made to work in the particular manner prescribed. This giving of the "why" to the worker through the system, and thus allowing his reason to follow through all the details, and his judgment to conform absolutely, should silence the objections of those who claim that the worker becomes a machine, and that he has no incentive to think at his work. On the contrary, it will be seen that this method furnishes him with more viewpoints from which he can consider his work.

Drawings, Charts, Plans and Photographs Means of Making Directions Clearer

The Instruction Cards are supplemented with drawings, charts, plans and stereoscopic and timed motion photographs,— any or all, — in order to make the directions of the Instruction Cards plainer.

Stereoscopic and Micro-Motion Study Photographs Particularly Useful

Stereoscopic photographs are especially useful in helping non-visualizers, and in presenting absolutely new work. The value as an educator of stereoscopic and synthesized micro-motion photographs of right methods is as yet but faintly appreciated. The "timed motion picture," or "micro-motion study photograph" as it is called, consists of rapidly photographing workers in action accompanied by a specially constructed chronometer that shows such minute divisions of time that motion pictures taken at a speed that will catch the most rapid of human motions without a blur, will show a different time of day in each photograph. The difference in the time in any two pictures gives the elapsed time of the desired motion operation or time unit.

Self-Made Records Educative

The educative value of the worker's making his own records has never been sufficiently appreciated. Dr. Taylor insists upon this procedure wherever possible. Not only does the worker learn from the actual marking in of the spaces reserved for him, but also he learns to feel himself a part of the record making division of the management. This proof of the "square deal," in recording his output, and of the confidence in him, cannot fail to enlist his cooperation.

Oral Instruction Comes from the Functional Foremen

The Functional Foremen are teachers whose business it is to explain, translate and supplement the various written instructions when the worker either does not understand them, does not know how to follow them, or makes a mistake in following them.

Oral Instruction has its Fitting Place Under Scientific Management

Oral instruction under Scientific Management has at least four advantages over such instruction under Traditional Management.

1. The Instructor is capable of giving instruction.
2. The Instructor's specialty is giving instruction.
3. The instruction is a supplement to written instructions.
4. The instruction comes at the exact time that the learner needs it.

Teacher, or Functional Foreman, Should Understand Psychology and Pedagogy

The successful teacher must understand the minds of his men, and must be able to present his information in such a way that it will be grasped readily. Such knowledge of psychology and pedagogy as he possesses he may acquire almost unconsciously

1. from the teaching of others,
2. from his study of Instruction Cards and Systems,
3. from actual practice in teaching.

The advantages of a study of psychology itself, as it applies to the field of teaching in general, and of teaching in the industries in particular, are apparent. Such study must, in the future, become more and more prevalent.

Advantage of Functional Foreman-Teacher over Teacher in the Schools

The Functional Foreman-teacher has an advantage over the teacher in the school in that the gap between him and those he teaches is not so great. He knows, because he remembers, exactly how the worker must have his information presented to him. This gap is narrowed by functionalizing the oral teaching, by using it merely as a supplement to the written teaching, and by supplementing it with object-lessons.

Teacher Must have Practical Knowledge of the Trade he is to Teach

The teacher must have an intimate practical knowledge of the art or trade that he is to teach. The most profound knowledge of Psychology will never be a substitute for the mastery of the trade, as a condition precedent to turning out the best craftsmen. This is provided for by securing teachers from the ranks of the workers.

He must have a Thorough Knowledge of the Standards

He must have more than the traditional knowledge of the trade that he is to teach; he must have also the knowledge that comes only from scientific investigation of his trade. This knowledge is ready and at hand, in the standards of Scientific Management that are available to all for study.

He must be Convinced of the Value of the Methods he Teaches

The teacher must also have an intimate acquaintance with the records of output of the method he is to teach as compared with those of methods held in high esteem by the believer in the old methods; for it is a law that no teacher can be efficient in teaching any method in which he does not believe, any more than a salesman can do his best work when he does not implicitly believe in the goods that he is selling.

He must be an Enthusiast

The best teacher is the one who is an enthusiast on the subject of the work itself, who can cause contagion or imitation of his state of mind, by love of the problems themselves.

Such Enthusiasm Contagious

It is the contagion of this enthusiasm that will always create a demand for teachers, no matter how perfect instruction cards may become. There is no form or device of management that does away with good men, and in the teacher, as here described, is conserved the personal element of the successful, popular Traditional foreman.

Valuable Teacher Interests Men in the Economic Value of Scientific Management

The most valuable teacher is one who can arouse his pupils to such a state of interest in the economic values of the methods of Scientific Management, that all other objects that would ordinarily distract or hold their attention will be banished from their minds. They will then remember each step as it is introduced, and they will be consumed with interest and curiosity to know what further steps can be introduced, that will still further eliminate waste. Object-lesson May Be "Working Models." — The object-lesson may be a "fixed exhibit" or a "working model," "a process in different stages," or "a micro-motion study film" of the work that is to be done. Successful and economical teaching may be done with such models, which are especially valuable where the workers do not speak the same language as the teacher, where many workers are to perform exactly similar work, or where the memory, the visualizing and the constructive imagination, are so poor that the models must be referred to constantly. Models naturally appeal best to those who take in information easiest through the eyes.

Object-lessons may be Demonstrations by the Teacher

The teacher may demonstrate the method manually to the worker, or by means of films showing synthesized right methods on the motion-picture screen. This, also, is a successful method of teaching those who speak a different language, or of explaining new work, — though it calls for a better memory than does the "working model," The model, however, shows desired results; the demonstration, desired methods.

Demonstration Method Chief Method of Teaching by Foremen

The manual demonstration method is the chief method of teaching the workmen by the foremen under Scientific Management, and no method is rated as standard that cannot be successfully demonstrated by the teacher, at any time, on request.

Worker may Demonstrate Under Supervision

If the worker is of that type that can learn only by actually doing the work himself, he is allowed to demonstrate the method under supervision of the teacher. Teaching Always Available Under Scientific Management

Under Scientific Management all of these forms of teaching are available constantly. The instruction card and accompanying illustrations are given to the worker before he starts to work, and are so placed that he can consult them easily at any time during the work. As, also, if object-lessons are used, they are given before work commences, and repeated when necessary.

The teacher is constantly available for oral instruction, and the systems are constantly available for consultation.

Methods of Teaching Under Scientific Management Psychologically Right

In order to prove that teaching under Scientific Management is most valuable, it is necessary to show that it is psychologically right, that it leads to mental development and improvement. Under Scientific Management, teaching, —

1. uses and trains the senses.
2. induces good habits of thinking and acting.
3. stimulates attention,
4. provides for valuable associations.
5. assists and strengthens the memory.
6. develops the imagination.
7. develops judgment.
8. utilizes suggestion.
9. utilizes "native reactions."
10. develops the will.

Teaching Under Scientific Management Trains the Senses

Scientific Management, in teaching the man, aims to train all of his senses possible. Not only does each man show an aptitude for some special sense training, but at certain times one sense may be stronger than another; for example, the sense of hearing, as is illustrated by the saying, "The patient in the hospital knoweth when his doctor cometh by the fall of his footsteps, yet when he recovereth he knoweth not even his face." At the time that a certain thing becomes of interest, and becomes particularly interesting to one sense, that sense is particularly keen and developed.

Scientific Management cannot expect, without more detailed psychological data than is as yet available, to utilize these periods of sense predominance adequately. It can, and does, aim to utilize such senses as are trained, and to supply defects of training of the other senses.

Such Training Partially Determines the Quality of the Work

The importance of sense training can scarcely be overestimated. Through his senses, the worker takes in the directions as to what he is to do, and on the accuracy with which his senses record the impressions made upon them, depends the mental model which he ultimately follows, and the accuracy of his criticism of the resulting physical object of his work. Through the senses, the worker sets his own task, and inspects his work.

Sense Training Influences Increase of Efficiency

With the training of the senses the possibility of increased efficiency increases. As any sense becomes trained, the minimum visable is reduced, and more accurate impressions become possible. They lead to more rapid work, by eliminating time necessary for judgment. The bricklayer develops a fineness of touch that allows him to dispense with sight in some parts of his work.

Selective Power of Senses Developed

James defines the sense organs as "organs of selection." Scientific Management so trains them that they can select what is of most value to the worker.

Methods of Sense Training Under Scientific Management

The senses are trained under Scientific Management by

means of the various sources of teaching. The instruction card, with its detailed descriptions of operations, and its accompanying illustrations, not only tends to increase powers of visualization, but also, by the close observation it demands, it reduces the minimum visible. The "visible instruction card," or working model, is an example of supplementing weak power of visualization. The most available simple, inexpensive and easily handled device to assist visualizing is the stereo or three-dimension photograph, which not only serves its purpose at the time of its use, but trains the eye to see the third dimension always.

Much training is given to the eye in Scientific Management by the constant insistence on inspection. This inspection is not confined to the inspector, but is the constant practice of worker and foremen, in order that work may be of such a quality as will merit a bonus.

Senses that are most Utilized best Trained

The relative training given to the various senses depends on the nature of the work. When the ear is the tester of efficiency, as it often is with an engineer watching machinery in action, emphasis is laid on training the hearing. In work where touch is important, emphasis is on such training as will develop that sense. Variations in Sense Power Should be Utilized

Investigations are constantly going to prove that each sense has a predominance at a different time in the age of the child or man. Dottoressa Montessori's experience with teaching very young children by touch shows that that sense is able to discriminate to an extraordinary extent for the first six years of life.

So, also, acute keenness of any sense, by reason of age or experience should be conserved. Such acuteness is often the result of some need, and, unless consciously preserved, will vanish with the need.

Progress in Such Training

The elementary sense experiences are defined and described by Calkins. Only through a psychological study can one realize the numerous elements and the possibility of study. As yet, doubtless, Scientific Management misses many opportunities for training and utilizing the senses. But the standardizing of elements, and the realization of the importance of more and more intensive study of the elements lends assurance that ultimately all possibilities will be utilized.

As Many Senses as Possible Appealed To

Scientific Management has made great progress in appealing to as many senses as possible in its teaching. The importance of the relation between the senses is brought out by Prof. Stratton.

In teaching, Scientific Management has, in its teachers, animate and inanimate, great possibilities of appealing to many senses simultaneously. The instruction card may be

1. read to oneself silently — eyes appealed to
2. read to oneself aloud — eyes and ears appealed to, also muscles used trained to repeat
3. read aloud to one — ears
4. read aloud to one and also read silently by one, — eyes and ears
5. read aloud, and at the same time copied — eyes, ears, muscles of mouth, muscles of hand
6. read to one, while process described is demonstrated
7. read to one while process is performed by oneself.

There are only a few of the possible combinations, any of which are used, as best suits the worker and the work.

Untrained Worker Requires Appeal to Most Senses

The value of appeal to many senses is best realized in teaching an inexperienced worker. His senses help to remind him what to do, and to "check up" his results.

At Times Appeal to but One Sense Preferable

In the case of work that must be watched constantly, and that involves continuous processes, it may prove best to have directions read to the worker. So also, the Gang Instruction Card may often be read to advantage to the gang, thus allowing the next member of a group of members to rest, or to observe, while directions are taken in through the ears only.

In this way time is allowed to overcome fatigue, yet the work is not halted.

At Times One Sense is best not Utilized

At times teaching may well omit one sense in its appeal, because that sense will tend to confuse the learning, and will, when the method is learned, be otherwise utilized than it could be during the learning process. In teaching the "touch system" of typewriting, the position of the keys is quickly remembered by having the key named aloud and at the same time struck with the assigned finger, the eyes being blindfolded. Thus hearing is utilized, also mouth muscles and finger muscles, but *not* sight.

Importance of Fatigue Recognized

A large part of the success of sense appeal and sense training of Scientific Management is in the appreciation of the importance of fatigue. This was early recognized by Dr. Taylor, and is constantly receiving study from all those interested in Scientific Management.

Psychology Already Aiding the Industries in such Study

Study of the *Psychological Review* will demonstrate the deep and increasing interest of psychclogists in the subject of fatigue. The importance of such stimulating and helpful work as that done by Doctor A. Imbert of the University of Montpellier, France, is great. Not only are the results of his investigations commercially valuable, but also they are valuable as indicating the close connection between Psychology and Industrial Efficiency.

Importance of Habits. — Prof. William James says "an acquired habit, from the psychological point of view, is nothing but a new pathway of discharge formed in the brain, by which certain incoming currents ever after tend to escape."

And again, — "First, habit simplifies our movements, makes them accurate, and diminishes fatigue," and habit diminishes the conscious attention with which our acts are performed. Again he says, page 144, "The great thing, then, in all education, is to make our nervous system our ally instead of an enemy;

as it is to fund and capitalize our acquisitions, and live at ease upon the interest of the fund. For this we must make automatic and habitual, as early as possible, as many useful actions as we can, and guard against the growing into ways that are likely to be disadvantageous to us, as we should guard against the plague."

These quotations demonstrate the importance of habit.

How deep these paths of discharge are, is illustrated by the fact that often a German, having spent the early years of his school life in Germany, will, even after learning to speak, read, write and think in English, find it difficult to figure in anything but German.

Habit Easily Becomes the Master

Another illustration of the power of habit is exhibited by the bricklayer, who has been trained under old-time methods, and who attempts to follow the packet method. The standard motions for picking up the upper row of bricks from the packet are entirely different from those for picking up the lower row. The bricklayers were taught this, yet invariably used the old-time motions for picking up the bricks, in spite of the waste involved.

Wrong Preconceived Ideas Hamper Development

Wrong habits or ideas often retard development. For example, it took centuries for artists to see the colours of shadows correctly, because they were sure that such shadows were a darker tone of the color itself.

Teaching Under Scientific Management Results in Good Habits

The aim of teaching under Scientific Management, as has been said, is to create good habits of thinking and good habits of doing.

Standards Lead to Right Methods of Thinking and Acting

The standards of Scientific Management, as presented to the worker in the instruction card, lead to good habits, in that they present the best known method of doing the work. They thus aid the beginner, in that he need waste no time searching for right methods, but can acquire right habits at once. They aid the worker trained under an older, supplanted method, in that they wage a winning war against old-time, worn-out methods and traditions. Old motor images, which tend to cause motions, are overcome by standard images, which suggest, and pass into, standard motions.

The spontaneous recurring of images under the old method is the familiar cause of inattention and being unable to get down to business, and the real cause of the expression, "You can't teach old dogs new tricks." On the other hand, the spontaneous recurrence of the images of the standard method is the cause of greater speed of movement of the experienced man, and these images of the standard methods do recur often enough to drive down the old images and to enable all men who desire, to settle down and concentrate upon what they are doing.

Through Standards Bad Habits are Quickest Broken

Through the standards the bad habit is broken by the abrupt acquisition of a new habit. This is at once practiced, is practiced without exception, and is continually practiced until the new habit is in control.

Through Standards New Habits are Quickest Formed

These same standards, as presented in teaching, allow of the speediest forming of habits, in that repetition is exact and frequent, and is kept so by the fact that the worker's judgment seconds that of the teacher.

Habits are Instilled by Teaching

The chief function of the teacher during the stage that habits are being formed is the instilling of good habits.

Methods of Instilling Good Habits

This he does by insisting on;

1. right motions first, that is to say, — the right number of right motions in the right sequence.
2. speed of motions second, that is to say, constantly increasing speed.

3. constantly improving quality. This Method is Contrary to Most Old-time Practice

Under most old-time practice the quality of the work was the first consideration, the quantity of work the second, and the methods of achieving the results the third.

Results of Old-time Practice

As a result, the mechanical reactions, which were expected constantly to follow the improved habits of work, were constantly hindered by an involuntary impulse of the muscles to follow the old methods. Waste time and low output followed.

Benefits of Teaching Right Motions First

Through teaching right motions first reactions to stimuli gain in speed. The right habit is formed at the outset. With the constant insistence on these right habits that result from right motions, will come, naturally, an increase in speed, which should be fostered until the desired ultimate speed is reached.

Ultimately, Standard Quality will Result

The result of absolute insistence on right motions will be prescribed quality, because the standard motions prescribed were chosen because they best produced the desired result.

Under Scientific Management no Loss from Quality During Learning

As will be shown later, Scientific Management provides that there shall be little or no loss from the quality of the work during the learning period. The delay in time before the learner can be said to produce such work as could a learner taught where quality was insisted upon first of all, is more than compensated for by the ultimate combination of speed and quality gained.

Results of Teaching the Right Motions First are Far-reaching

There is no more important subject in this book on the Psychology of Management than this of teaching right motions first. The most important results of Scientific Management can all, in the last analysis, be formulated in terms of habits, even to the underlying spirit of cooperation which, as we shall show in "Welfare," is one of the most important ideas of Scientific Management. These right habits of Scientific Management are the cause, as well as the result, of progress, and the right habits, which have such a tremendous psychological importance, are the result of insisting that right motions be used from the very beginning of the first day.

From Right Habits of Motion Comes Speed of Motions

Concentrating the mind on the next motion causes speed of motion. Under Scientific Management, the underlying thought of sequence of motions is so presented that the worker can remember them, and make them in the shortest time possible.

Response to Standards Becomes Almost Automatic

The standard methods, being associated from the start with right habits of motions only, cause an almost automatic response. There are no discarded habits to delay response.

Steady Nerves Result

Oftentimes the power to refrain from action is quite as much a sign of education and training as the power to react quickly from a sensation. Such conduct is called, in some cases, "steady nerves." The forming of right habits is a great aid toward these steady nerves. The man who knows that he is taught the right way, is able almost automatically to resist any suggestions which come to him to carry out wrong ways. So the man who is absolutely sure of his method, for example, in laying brick, will not be tempted to make those extra motions which, after all, are merely an exhibition in his hand of the vacillation that is going on in his brain, as to whether he really is handling that brick in exactly the most efficient manner, or not.

Reason and Will are Educated

"The education of hand and muscle implies a corresponding training of reasoning and will; and the coordination of movements accompanies the coordination of thoughts."

The standards of Scientific Management educate hand and muscle; the education of hand and muscle train the mind; the mind improves the standards. Thus we have a continuous cycle.

Judgment Results with No Waste of Time

Judgment is the outcome of learning the right way, and knowing that it is the right way. There is none of the lost time of "trying out" various methods that exists under Traditional Management.

This power of judgment will not only enable the possessor to decide correctly as to the relative merits of different methods, but also somewhat as to the past history and possibilities of different workers.

This, again, illustrates the wisdom of Scientific Management in promoting from the ranks, and thus providing that every member of the organization shall, ultimately, know from experience how to estimate and judge the work of others.

Habits of Attention Formed by Scientific Management

The good habits which result from teaching standard methods result in habits of attention. The standards aid the mind in holding a "selective attitude," by presenting events in an orderly sequence. The conditions under which the work is done, and the incentives for doing it, provide that the attention shall be "lively and prolonged."

Prescribed Motions Afford Rhythm and Aesthetic Pleasure

The prescribed motions that result from motion study and time study, and that are arranged in cycles, afford a rhythm that allows the attention to "glide over some beats and linger on others," as Prof. Stratton describes it, in a different connection. So also the "perfectly controlled" movements, which fall under the direction of a guiding law, and which "obey the will absolutely," give an aesthetic pleasure and afford less of a tax upon the attention.

Instruction Card Creates and Holds Attention

As has been already said in describing the instruction card under Standardization, it was designed as a result of investigations as to what would best secure output, — to attract and hold the attention. Providing, as it does, all directions that an experienced worker is likely to need, he can confine his attention solely to his work and his card; usually, after the card is once studied, to his work alone. The close relation of the elements of the instruction card affords a field for attention to lapse, and be recalled in the new elements that are constantly made apparent.

Oral Individual Teaching Fosters Concentrated Attention

The fact that under Scientific Management oral teaching is individual, not only directly concentrates the attention of the learner upon what he is being taught, but also indirectly prevents distraction from fear of ridicule of others over the question, or embarrassment in talking before a crowd.

The Bulletin Board Furnishes the Element of Change

In order that interest or attention may be held, there must be provision for allied subjects on which the mind is to wander. This, under Scientific Management, is constantly furnished by the collection of jobs ahead on the bulletin board.

The tasks piled up ahead upon this bulletin board provide a needed and ready change for the subject of attention or interest, which conserves the economic value of concentrated attention of the worker upon his work. Such future tasks furnish sufficient range of subject for wandering attention to rest the mind from the wearying effect of overconcentration or forced attention.

The assigned task of the future systematizes the "stream of attention," and an orderly scheme of habits of thought is installed. When the scheme is an orderly shifting of attention, the mind is doing its best work, for, while the standardized extreme subdivision of Taylor's plan, the comparison of the ultimate unit, and groupings of units of future tasks are often helps in achieving the present tasks, without such a definite orderly scheme for shifting the attention and interest, the attention will shift to useless subjects, and the result will be scattered.

Incentives Maintain Interest

The knowledge that a prompt reward will follow success stimulates interest. The knowledge that this reward is sure concentrates attention and thus maintains interest.

In the same way, the assurance of promotion, and the fact that the worker sees those of his own trade promoted, and knows it is to the advantage of the management, as well as to his advantage, that he also be promoted, — this also maintains interest in the work.

This Interest Extends to the Work of Others

The interest is extended to the work of others, not only by the interrelated bonuses, but also by the fact that every man is expected to train up a man to take his place, before he is promoted.

Close Relationship of all Parts of Scientific Management Holds Interest

The attention of the entire organization, as well as of the individual worker, is held by Scientific Management and its teaching, because all parts of Scientific Management are related, and because Scientific Management provides for scientifically directed progression.

Every member of the organization knows that the standards which are taught by Scientific Management contain the permanent elements of past successes, and provide for such development as will assure progress and success in the future. Every member of the organization realizes that upon his individual cooperation depends, in part, the stability of Scientific Management, because it is based on universal cooperation. This provides an intensity and a continuity of interest that would still hold, even though some particular element might lose its interest.

This Relationship also Provides for Associations

The close relationship of all parts of Scientific Management provides that all ideas are associated, and are so closely connected that they can act as a single group, or any selected number of elements can act as a group.

Scientific Management Establishes Brain Groups that Habitually Act in Unison

Professor Read, in describing the general mental principle of association says, "When any number of brain cells have been in action together, they form a habit of acting in unison, so that when one of them is stimulated in a certain way, the others will also behave in the way established by the habit."

This working of the brain is recognized in grouping of motions, such as "playing for position." Scientific Management provides the groups, the habit, and the stimulus, all according to standard methods, so that the result is largely predictable.

Method of Establishing Such Groups in the Worker's Brain

The standard elements of Scientific Management afford units for such groups. Eventually, with the use of such elements in instruction cards, would be formed, in the minds of the worker, such groups of units as would aid in foreseeing results, just as the foreseeing of groups of moves aids the expert chess or checker player. The size and number of such groups would indicate the skill of the worker.

That such skill may be gained quickest, Scientific Management synthesizes the units into definite groups, and teaches these to the workers as groups.

Teaching Done by Means of Motion Cycles

The best group is that which completes the simplest cycle of performance. This enables the worker to associate certain definite motions, to make these into a habit, and to concentrate his attention upon the cycle as a whole, and not upon the elementary motions of which it is composed.

For example — The cycle of the pick and dip process of bricklaying is to pick up a brick and a trowel full of mortar simultaneously and deposit them on the wall simultaneously. The string mortar method has two cycles, which are, first to pick a certain number of trowelfuls of mortar and deposit them on the wall, and then to pick up a corresponding number of bricks and deposit them on the wall. Each cycle of these two methods consists of an association of units that can be remembered as a group.

Such Cycles Induce Speed

The worker who has been taught thus to associate the units of attention and action into definite rhythmic cycles, is the one who is most efficient, and least fatigued by a given output. The nerves acquire the habit, as does the brain, and the resulting swift response to stimulus characterizes the efficiency of the specialist. Scientific Management Restricts Associations

By its teaching of standard methods, Scientific Management restricts association, and thus gains in the speed with which associated ideas arise. Insistence on causal sequence is a great aid. This is rendered by the Systems, which give the reasons, and make the standard method easy to remember.

Scientific Management Presents Scientifically Derived Knowledge to the Memory

Industrial memory is founded on experience, and that experience that is submitted by teaching under Scientific Management to the mind is in the form of scientifically derived standards. These furnish

(a) data that is correct.

(b) images that are an aid in acquiring new habits of forming efficient images.

(c) standards of comparison, and constant demands for comparison.

(d) such arrangement of elements that reasoning processes are stimulated.

(e) conscious, efficient grouping.

(f) logical association of ideas.

Provision for Repetition of Important Ideas

Professor Ebbinghaur says, "Associations that have equal reproductive power lapse the more slowly, the older they are, and the oftener they have been reviewed by renewed memorizing." Scientific Management provides for utilizing this law by teaching right motions first, and by so minutely dividing the elements of such motions that the smallest units discovered are found frequently, in similar and different operations.

Best Periods for Memorizing Utilized

As for education of the memory, there is a wide difference of opinion among leading psychologists in regard to whether or not the memorizing faculty, as the whole, can be improved by training; but all agree that those things which are specially desired to be memorized can be learned more easily, and more quickly, under some conditions than under others: For example, there is a certain time of day, for each person, when the memory is more efficient than at other times. This is usually in the morning, but is not always so. The period when memorizing is easiest is taken advantage of, and, as far as possible, new methods and new instruction cards are passed out at that time when the worker is naturally best fitted to remember what is to be done.

Individual Differences Respected

It is a question that varies with different conditions, whether the several instruction cards beyond the one he is working on shall be given to the worker ahead of time, that he may use his own judgment as to when is the best time to learn, or whether he shall have but one at a time, and concentrate on that. For certain dispositions, it is a great help to see a long line of work ahead. They enjoy getting the work done, and feeling that they are more or less ahead of record. Others become confused if they see too much ahead, and would rather attack but one problem at a time. This fundamental difference in types of mind should be taken advantage of when laying out material to be memorized.

Aid of Mnemonic Symbols to the Memory

The mnemonic classifications furnish a place where the worker who remembers but little of a method or process can go, and recover the full knowledge of that which he has forgotten. Better still, they furnish him the equivalent of memory of other experiences that he has never had, and that are in such form that he can connect this with his memory of his own personal experience. The ease with which a learner or skilled mechanic can associate new, scientifically derived data with his memory, because of the classifications of Scientific Management, is a most important cause of workers being taught quicker, and being more intelligent, under Scientific Management, than under any other type of management.

Proper Learning Insures Proper Remembering

Professor Read says, "Take care of the learning and the remembering will take care of itself." Scientific Management both provides proper knowledge, and provides that this shall be utilized in such a manner that proper remembering will ensue.

Better Habits of Remembering Result

The results of cultivating the memory under Scientific Management are cumulative. Ultimately, right habits of remembering result that aid the worker automatically so to arrange his memory material as to utilize it better.

"Imagination" Has Two Definitions

Professor Read gives definitions for two distinct means of Imagination.

1. "The general function of the having of images."
2. "The particular one of having images which are not consciously memories or the reproduction of the facts of experience as they were originally presented to consciousness." Scientific Management Provides Material for Images

As was shown under the discussion of the appeals of the various teaching devices of Scientific Management, — provision is made for the four classes of imagination of Calkins —

1. visual,
2. auditory,
3. tactual, and
4. mixed.

It also Realizes the Importance of Productive Imagination

Scientific Management realizes that one of the special functions of teaching the trades is systematic exercising and guiding of imaginations of apprentices and learners. As Professor Ennis says, — "Any kind of planning ahead will result in some good," but to plan ahead most effectively it is necessary to have a well-developed power of constructive imagination. This consists of being able to construct new mental images from old memory images; of being able to modify and group images of past experiences, or thoughts, in combination with new images based on imagination, and not on experience. The excellence of the image arrived at in the complete work is dependent wholly upon the training in image forming in the past. If there has not been a complete economic system of forming standard habits of thought, the worker may have difficulty in controlling the trend of associations of thought images, and difficulty in adding entirely new images to the groups of experienced images, and the problem to be thought out will suffer from wandering of the mind. The result will be more like a dream than a well balanced mental planning. It is well known that those apprentices, and journeymen as well, are the quickest to learn, and are better learners, who have the most vivid imagination. The best method of teaching the trade, therefore, is the one that also develops the power of imagination.

Scientific Management Assists Productive Imagination

Scientific Management assists productive, or constructive, imagination, not only by providing standard units, or images, from which the results may, be synthesized, but also, through the unity of the instruction card, allows of imagination of the outcome, from the start. For example, — in performing a prescribed cycle of motions, the worker has his memory images grouped in such a figure, form, or sequence— often geometrical— that each motion is a part of a growing, clearly imagined whole. The elements of the cycle may be utilized in other entirely new cycles, and are, as provided for in the opportunities for invention that are a part of Scientific Management.

Judgment the Result of Faithful Endeavour

Judgment, or the "mental process which ends in an affirmation or negation of something," comes as the result of experience, as is admirably expressed by Prof. James, — "Let no youth have any anxiety about the upshot of his education whatever the line of it may be. If he keeps faithfully busy each hour of the working day, he may safely leave the final result to itself. He can with perfect certainty count on waking up some fine morning, to find himself one of the competent ones of his generation, in whatever pursuit he may have singled out. Silently, between all the details of his business, the *power of judging* in all that class of matter will have built itself up within him as a possession that will never pass away. Young people should know this truth in advance. The ignorance of it has probably engendered more discouragement and faint-heartedness in youths embarking on arduous careers than all other causes put together." Teaching Supplies this Judgment Under Scientific Management

Under Scientific Management this judgment is the result of teaching of standards that are recognized as such by the learner. Thus, much time is eliminated, and the apprentice under Scientific Management can work with all the assurance as to the value of his methods that characterized the seasoned veterans of older types of management.

Teaching Also Utilizes the Judgment

The judgment that is supplied by Scientific Management is also used as a spring toward action. Scientific Management appeals to the reason, and workers perform work as they do because, through the Systems and otherwise, they are persuaded that the method they employ is the best.

The Power of Suggestion Is Also Utilized. — The dynamic power of ideas is recognized by Scientific Management, in that the instruction card is put in the form of direct commands, which, naturally, lead to immediate action. So, also, the teaching written, oral and object, as such, can be directly imitated by the learner. Imitation, which Dr. Stratton says "may well be counted a special form of suggestion," will be discussed later in this chapter at length.

Worker Always has Opportunity to Criticise the Suggestion

The worker is expected to follow the suggestion of Scientific Management without delay, because he believes in the standardization on which it is made, and in the management that makes it. But the Systems afford him an opportunity of reviewing the reasonableness of the suggestion at any time, and his constructive criticism is invited and rewarded.

Suggestion must be Followed at the Time

The suggestion must be followed at the time it is given, or its value as a suggestion is impaired. This is provided for by the underlying idea of cooperation on which Scientific Management rests, which molds the mental attitude of the worker into that form where suggestions are quickest grasped and followed. "Native Reactions" Enumerated by Prof. James

Prof. James enumerates the "native reactions" as (1) fear, (2) love, (3) curiosity, (4) imitation, (5) emulation, (6) ambition, (7) pugnacity, (8) pride, (9) ownership, (10) constructiveness. These are all considered by Scientific Management. Such as might have a harmful effect are supplanted, others are utilized.

Fear Utilized by Ancient Managers

The native reaction most utilized by the first managers of armies and ancient works of construction was that of fear. This is shown by the ancient rock carvings, which portray what happened to those who disobeyed.

Fear Still Used by Traditional Management

Fear of personal bodily injury is not usual under modern Traditional Management, but fear of less progress, less promotion, less remuneration, or of discharge, or of other penalties for inferior effort or efficiency is still prevalent.

Fear Transformed Under Scientific Management

Under Scientific Management the worker may still fear that he will incur a penalty, or fail to deserve a reward, but the honest, industrious worker experiences no such horror as the old-time fear included. This is removed by his knowledge

1. that his task is achievable.
2. that his work will not injure his health.
3. that he may be sure of advancement with age and experience.

4. that he is sure of the "square deal."

Thus such fear as he has, has a good and not an evil effect upon him. It is an incentive to cooperate willingly. Its immediate and ultimate effects are advantageous.

Love, or Loyalty, Fostered by Scientific Management

The worker's knowledge that the management plans to maintain such conditions as will enable him to have the four assurances enumerated above leads to love, or loyalty, between workers and employers.

Far from Scientific Management abolishing the old personal and sympathetic relations between employers and workers, it gives opportunities for such relations as have not existed since the days of the guilds, and the old apprenticeship.

The cooperation upon which Scientific Management rests does away with the traditional "warfare" between employer and workers that made permanent friendliness almost impossible. Cooperation induces friendliness and loyalty of each member in the organization to all the others.

Mr. Wilfred Lewis says, in describing the installation of Scientific Management in his plant, "We had, in effect, been installing at great expense a new and wonderful means for increasing the efficiency of labour, in the benefits of which the workman himself shared, and we have today an organization second, I believe, to none in its loyalty, efficiency and steadfastness of purpose." This same loyalty of the workers is plain in an article in *Industrial Engineering*, on "Scientific Management as Viewed from the Workman's Standpoint," where various men in a shop having Scientific Management were interviewed. After quoting various workers' opinions of Scientific Management and their own particular shop, the writer says: "Conversations with other men brought out practically the same facts. They are all contented. They took pride in their work, and seemed to be especially proud of the fact that they were employed in the Link-Belt shops." Teaching Under Scientific Management Develops Such Loyalty

The manner of teaching under Scientific Management fosters such loyalty. Only through friendly aid can both teacher and taught prosper. Also, the perfection of the actual workings of this plan of management inspires regard as well as respect for the employer.

Value of Personality Not Eliminated

It is a great mistake to think that Scientific Management underestimates the value of personality. Rather, Scientific Management enhances the value of an admirable personality. This is well exemplified in the Link-Belt Co., and in the Tabor Manufacturing Co. of Philadelphia, as well as on other work where Scientific Management has been installed a period of several years.

Curiosity Aroused by Scientific Management

Scientific Management arouses the curiosity of the worker, by showing, through its teaching, glimpses of the possibilities that exist for further scientific investigation. The insistence on standard methods of less waste arouses a curiosity as to whether still less wasteful methods cannot be found.

Curiosity Utilized by Scientific Management

This curiosity is very useful as a trait of the learner, the planner and the investigator. It can be well utilized by the teacher who recognizes it in the learner, by an adaptation of methods of interpreting the instruction card, that will allow of partially satisfying, and at the same time further exciting, the curiosity.

In selecting men for higher positions, and for special work, curiosity as to the work, with the interest that is its result, may serve as an admirable indication of one sort of fitness. This curiosity, or general interest, is usually associated with a personal interest that makes it more intense, and more easy to utilize.

Scientific Management Places a High Value on Imitation

It was a popular custom of the past to look down with scorn on the individual or organization that imitated others. Scientific Management believes that to imitate with great precision the best, is a work of high intelligence and industrial efficiency.

Scientific Management Uses Both Spontaneous and Deliberate Imitation

Teaching under Scientific Management induces both spontaneous and deliberate imitation. The standardization prevalent, and the conformity to standards exacted, provide that this imitation shall follow directed lines.

Spontaneous Imitation Under Scientific Management has Valuable Results

Under Scientific Management, the worker will spontaneously imitate the teacher, when the latter has been demonstrating. This leads to desired results. So, also, the worker imitates, more or less spontaneously, his own past methods of doing work. The right habits early formed by Scientific Management insure that the results of such imitation shall be profitable.

Deliberate Imitation Constantly Encouraged

Deliberate imitation is caused more than anything else by the fact that the man knows, if he does the thing in the way directed, his pay will be increased.

Such imitation is also encouraged by the fact that the worker is made to believe that he is capable, and has the will to overcome obstacles. He knows that the management believes he can do the work, or the instruction card would not have been issued to him. Moreover, he sees that the teacher and demonstrator is a man promoted from his rank, and he is convinced, therefore, that what the teacher can do he also can do. Scientific Management Provides Standards for Imitation

It is of immense value in obtaining valuable results from imitation, that Scientific Management provides standards. Under Traditional Management, it was almost impossible for a worker to decide which man he should imitate. Even though he might come to determine, by constant observation, after a time, which man he desired to imitate, he would not know in how far he would do well to copy any particular method. Recording individually measured output under Transitory Management allows of determining the man of high score, and either using him as a model, or formulating his method into rules. Under Scientific Management, the instruction card furnishes a method which the worker knows that he can imitate exactly, with predetermined results.

Imitation is Expected of All

As standardization applies to the work of all, so imitation of standards is expected of all. This fact the teacher under Scientific Management can use to advantage, as an added incentive to imitation. Any dislike of imitation is further decreased, by making clear to every worker that those who are under him are expected to imitate him, — and that he must, himself, imitate his teachers, in order to set a worthy example.

Imitation Leads to Emulation

Imitation, as provided for by teaching under Scientific Management, and admiration for the skilful teacher, or the standard imitated, naturally stimulate emulation. This emulation takes three forms:

1. Competition with the records of others.
2. Competition with one's own record.
3. Competition with the standard record.

No Hard Feeling Aroused

In the first sort of competition only is there a possibility of hard feeling being aroused, but danger of this is practically eliminated by the fact that rewards are provided for all who are successful. In the second sort of competition, the worker, by matching himself against what he has done, measures his own increased efficiency. In the third sort of competition, there is the added stimulus of surprising the management by exceeding the task expected. The incentive in all three cases is not only more pay and a chance for promotion, but also the opportunity to win appreciation and publicity for successful performance.

Ambition is Aroused

The outcome of emulation is ambition. This ambition is stimulated by the fact that promotion is so rapid, and so outlined before the worker, that he sees the chance for advancement himself, and not only advancement that means more pay, but advancement also that means a chance to specialize on that work which he particularly likes.

Pugnacity Utilized

Pugnacity can never be entirely absent where there is emulation. Under Scientific Management it is used to overcome not persons, but things. Pugnacity is a great driving force. It is a wonderful thing that under Scientific Management this force is aroused not against one's fellow-workers, but against one's work. The desire to win out, to fight it out, is aroused against a large task, which the man desires to put behind him. Moreover, there is nothing under Scientific Management which forbids an athletic contest. While the workers would not, under the ultimate form, be allowed to injure themselves by overspeeding, a friendly race with a demonstration of pugnacity which harms no one is not frowned upon.

Pride is Stimulated

Pride in one's work is aroused as soon as work is functionalized. The moment a man has something to do that he likes to do, and can do well, he takes pride in it. So, also, the fact that individuality, and personality, are recognized, and that his records are shown, makes pride serve as a stimulus. The outcome of the worker's pride in his work is pride in himself. He finds that he is part of a great whole, and he learns to take pride in the entire management, — in both himself and the managers, as well as in his own work.

Feeling of Ownership Provided For

It may seem at first glance that the instinct of ownership is neglected, and becomes stunted, under Scientific Management, in that all tools become more or less standardized, and the man is discouraged from having tools peculiar in shape, or size, for whose use he has no warrant except long time of use.

Careful consideration shows that Scientific Management provides two opportunities for the worker to conserve his instinct for ownership, —

1. During working hours, where the recognition of his personality allows the worker to identify himself with

his work, and where his cooperation with the management makes him identified with its activities.

2. Outside the work. He has, under Scientific Management, more hours away from work to enjoy ownership, and more money with which to acquire those things that he desires to own.

The teacher must make clear to him both these opportunities, as he readily can, since the instinct of ownership is conserved in him in an identical manner.

Constructiveness a Part of Scientific Management

Every act that the worker performs is constructive, because waste has been eliminated, and everything that is done is upbuilding. Teaching makes this clear to the worker. Constructiveness is also utilized in that exercise of initiative is provided for. Thus the instinct, instead of being weakened, is strengthened and directed.

Progress in Utilizing Instincts Demands Psychological Study

Teaching under Scientific Management can never hope fully to understand and utilize native reactions, until more assistance has been given by psychology. At the present time, Scientific Management labours under disadvantages that must, ultimately, be removed. Psychologists must, by experiments, determine more accurately the reactions and their controlability. More thorough study must be made of children that Scientific Management may understand more of the nature of the reactions of the young workers who come for industrial training. Psychology must give its help in this training. Then only, can teaching under Scientific Management become truly efficient.

Scientific Management Realizes the Importance of Training the Will

The most necessary, and most complex and difficult part of Scientific Management, is the training of the will of all members of the organization. Prof. Read states in his "Psychology" five means of training or influencing the will. These are:

"1. The first important feature in training the will is the help furnished by supplying the mind with a useful body of ideas.

"2. The second great feature of the training of the will is the building up in the mind of the proper interests, and the habit of giving the attention to useful and worthy purposes.

"3. Another important feature of the training of the will is the establishing of a firm association between ideas and actions, or, in other words, the forming of a good set of habits.

"4. Another very important feature of the training of the will has reference to its strength of purpose or power of imitation.

"5. The matter of discipline."

Teaching under Scientific Management does supply these five functions, and thus provide for the strengthening and development of the will.

Variations in Teaching of Apprentices and Journeymen

Scientific Management must not only be prepared to teach apprentices, as must all types of management, it must also teach journeymen who have not acquired standard methods.

Apprentices are Easily Handled

Teaching apprentices is a comparatively simple proposition, far simpler than under any other type of management. Standard methods enable the apprentice to become proficient long before his brother could, under the old type of teaching. The length of training required depends largely on how fingerwise the apprentice is.

Older Workers must be Handled with Tact

With adult workers, the problem is not so simple. Old wrong habits, such as the use of ineffective motions, must be eliminated. Physically, it is difficult for the adult worker to alter his methods. Moreover, it may be most difficult to change his mental attitude, to convince him that the methods of

Scientific Management are correct. A successful worker under Traditional Management, who is proud of his work, will often be extremely sensitive to what he is prone to regard as the "criticism" of Scientific Management with regard to him.

Appreciation of Varying Viewpoints Necessary

No management can consider itself adequate that does not try to enter into the mental attitude of its workers. Actual practice shows that, with time and tact, almost any worker can be convinced that all criticism of him is constructive, and thac for him to conform to the new standards is a mark of added proficiency, not an acknowledgment of ill-preparedness. The "Systems" do much toward this work of reconciling the older workers to the new methods, but most of all can be done by such teachers as can demonstrate their own change from old to standard methods, and the consequent promotion and success. This is, again, an opportunity for the exercise of personality.

Scientific Management Provides Places for such Teaching

Under the methods of teaching employed by Scientific Management, — right motions first, next speed, with quality as a resultant product, — it is most necessary to provide a place where learners can work. The standard planning of quality provides such a place. The plus and minus signs automatically divide labour so that the worker can be taught by degrees, being set at first where great accuracy is not demanded by the work, and being shifted to work requiring more accuracy as he becomes more proficient. In this way even the most untrained worker becomes efficient, and is engaged in actual productive work.

Measurement of Teaching and Learning

Under Scientific Management the results of teaching and learning become apparent automatically in records of output. The learner's record of output of proper prescribed quality determines what pay he shall receive, and also has a proportionate effect on the teacher's pay. Such a system of measurement may not be accurate as a report of the learner's gain, — for he doubtless gains mental results that cannot be seen in his output, — but it certainly does serve as an incentive to teaching and to learning.

Relation of Teaching in Scientific Management to Academic Training and Vocational Guidance. — Teaching under Scientific Management can never be most efficient until the field of such teaching is restricted to training learners who are properly prepared to receive industrial training. This preparedness implies fitting school and academic training, and Vocational Guidance.

Learner Should be Manually Adept

The learner should, before entering the industrial world, be taught to be manually adept, or fingerwise, to have such control over his trained muscles that they will respond quickly and accurately to orders. Such training should be started in infancy, in the form of guided play, as, for example, whittling, sewing, knitting, handling mechanical toys and tools, and playing musical instruments, and continued up to, and into, the period of entering a trade.

Schools Should Provide Mental Preparedness

The schools should render every student capable of filling some place worthily in the industries. The longer the student remains in school, the higher the position for which he should be prepared. The amount and nature of the training in the schools depends largely on the industrial work to be done, and will be possible of more accurate estimation constantly, as Scientific Management standardizes work and shows what the worker must be to be most efficient.

Vocational Guidance Must Provide Direction

As made most clear in Mr. Meyer Bloomfield's book, "Vocational Guidance," bureaus of competent directors stand ready to help the youth find that line of activity which he can follow best and with greatest satisfaction to himself. At present, such bureaus are seriously handicapped by the fact that little data of the industries are at hand, but this lack the bureaus are rapidly supplying by gathering such data as are available. Most valuable data will not be available until Scientific Management has been introduced into all lines.

Progress Demands Cooperation

Progress here, as everywhere, demands cooperation. The three sets of educators, — the teachers in the school, in the Vocational Guidance Bureaus, and in Scientific Management, must recognize their common work, and must cooperate to do it. There is absolutely no cause for conflict between the three; their fields are distinct, but supplementary. Vocational Guidance is the intermediary between the other two.

Summary

Results to the Work

Under the teaching of Traditional Management, the learner may or may not improve the quantity and quality of his work. This depends almost entirely on the particular teacher whom the learner happens to have. There is no standard improvement to the work.

Under the teaching of Transitory Management, the work gains in quantity as the methods become standardized, and quality is maintained or improved.

Under the teaching of Scientific Management, work, the quantity of work, increases enormously through the use of standards of all kinds; quantity is oftentimes tripled.

Under the teaching of Scientific Management, when the schools and Vocational Guidance movement cooperate, high output of required quality will be obtained at a far earlier stage of the worker's industrial life than is now possible, even under Scientific Management.

Results to the Worker

Under Traditional Management, the worker gains a knowledge of how his work can be done, but the method by which he is taught is seldom, of itself, helpful to him. Not being sure that he has learned the best way to do his work, he gains no method of attack. The result of the teaching is a habit of doing work which is good, or bad, as chance may direct.

Under Transitory Management, with the use of Systems as teachers, the worker gains a better method of attack, as he knows the reason why the prescribed method is prescribed. He begins to appreciate the possibilities and benefits of standardized teaching.

The method laid down under Scientific Management is devised to further the forming of an accurate accumulation of concepts, which results in a proper method of attack. The method of instruction under Scientific Management is devised to furnish two things:

1. A collection of knowledge relating in its entirety to the future work of the learner.
2. A definite procedure, that will enable the learner to apply the same process to acquiring knowledge of other subjects in the most economical and efficient way.

It teaches the learner to be observant of details, which is the surest method for further development of general truths and concepts.

The method of attack of the methods provided for in Scientific Management results, naturally, in a comparison of true data. This is the most efficient method of causing the learner to think for himself.

Processes differing but little, apparently, give vastly different results, and the trained habits of observation quickly analyse and determine wherein the one process is more efficient than the other.

This result is, of course, the one most desired for causing quick and intelligent learning.

The most valuable education is that which enables the learner to make correct judgments. The teaching under Scientific Management leads to the acquisition of such judgment, plus an all-around sense training, a training in habits of work, and a progressive development.

A partial topic list of the results may make more clear their importance.

1. Worker better trained for all work.
2. Habits of correct thinking instilled.
3. Preparedness provided for.
4. Productive and repetitive powers increased.
5. Sense powers increased.

6. Habits of proper reaction established.
7. "Guided original work" established.
8. System of waste elimination provided.
9. Method of attack taught.
10. Brain fully developed.
11. "Standard response" developed.
12. Opportunities and demands for "thinking" provided.
13. Self-reliance developed.
14. Love of truth fostered.
15. Moral sentiment developed.
16. Resultant happiness of worker.

Results to be Expected in the Future

When the schools, vocational guidance and teaching under Scientific Management cooperate, the worker will not only receive the benefits now obtained from Scientific Management, but many more. There will be nothing to unlearn, and each thing that is learned will be taught by those best fitted to teach it. The collection of vocational guidance data will begin with a child at birth, and a record of his inheritance will be kept. This will be added to as he is educated, and as various traits and tendencies appear. From this scientifically derived record will accrue such data as will assist in making clear exactly in what place the worker will be most efficient, and in what sphere he will be able to be most helpful to the world, as well as to himself. All early training will be planned to make the youth adept with his muscles, and alert, with a mind so trained that related knowledge is easily acquired.

When the vocation for which he is naturally best fitted becomes apparent, as it must from the study of the development of the youth and his desires, the school will know, and can give exactly, that training that is necessary for the vocation. It can also supplement his limitations intelligently, in case he decides to follow a vocation for which he is naturally handicapped.

This will bring to the industry learners prepared to be taught those things that characterize the industry, the "tricks of the trade," and the "secrets of the craft," now become standard, and free to all. Such teaching Scientific Management is prepared to give. The results of such teaching of Scientific Management will be a worker prepared in a short time to fill efficiently a position which will allow of promotion to the limit of his possibilities.

The result of such teaching will be truly educated workers, equipped to work, and to live, and to share the world's permanent satisfactions.

The effect of such education on industrial peace must not be underestimated. With education, including in education learning and culture, — prejudice will disappear. The fact that all men, those going into industries and those not, will be taught alike to be finger wise as well as book wise, up to the time of entering the industries, will lead to a better understanding of each other all through life.

The entire bearing of Scientific Management on industrial peace cannot be here fully discussed. We must note here the strong effect that teaching under Scientific Management will ultimately have on doing away with industrial warfare, — the great warfare of ignorance, where neither side understands the other, and where each side should realize that large immediate sacrifices should be made if necessary, that there may be obtained the great permanent benefit and savings that can be obtained only by means of the heartiest cooperation.

8

Incentives

Definition of Incentive

An "incentive" is defined by the Century Dictionary as "that which moves the mind or stirs the passions; that which incites or tends to incite to action; motive, spur." Synonyms — "impulse, stimulus, incitement, encouragement, goad."

Importance of the Incentive

The part that the incentive plays in the doing of all work is enormous. This is true in learning, and also in the performance of work which is the result of this learning: manual work and mental work as well. The business man finishing his work early that he may go to the baseball game; the boy at school rushing through his arithmetic that he may not be kept after school; the piece-worker, the amount of whose day's pay depends upon the quantity and quality he can produce; the student of a foreign language preparing for a trip abroad, — these all illustrate the importance of the incentive as an element in the amount which is to be accomplished.

Two Kinds of Incentives

The incentive may be of two kinds: it may be first of all, a return, definite or indefinite, which is to be received when a certain portion of the work is done, or it may be an incentive due to the working conditions themselves. The latter case is exemplified where two people are engaged in the same sort of work and start in to race one another to see who can accomplish the most, who can finish the fixed amount in the shortest space of time, or who can produce the best quality. The incentive may be in the form of some definite aim or goal which is understood by the worker himself, or it may be in some natural instinct which is roused by the work, either consciously to the worker, or consciously to the man who is assigning the work, or consciously to both, or consciously to neither one. In any of these cases it is a natural instinct that is being appealed to and that induces the man to do more work, whether he sees any material reward for that work or not.

Definitions of Two Types

We may call the incentive which utilizes the natural instinct, "direct incentive," and the incentive which utilizes these secondarily, through some set reward or punishment, "indirect incentive." This, at first sight, may seem a contradictory use of terms — it may seem that the reward would be the most direct of incentives; yet a moment's thought will cause one to realize that all the reward can possibly do is to arouse in the individual a natural instinct which will lead him to increase his work.

Indirect Incentives Include Two Classes

We will discuss the indirect incentives first as, contrary to the usual use of the word "indirect," they are most easy to estimate and to describe. They divide themselves into two classes, reward and punishment.

Definition of Reward

Reward is defined by the Century Dictionary as — "return, recompense, the fruit of one's labour or works; profit," with synonyms, "pay, compensation, remuneration, requital and retribution." Note particularly the word "retribution," for it is this aspect of reward, that is, the just outcome of one's act, that makes the reward justly include punishment. The word "reward" exactly expresses what management would wish to be understood by the incentive that it gives its men to increase their work.

Definition of Punishment

The word "punishment" is defined as — "pain, suffering, loss, confinement, or other penalty inflicted on a person for a crime or offense by the authority to which the offender is subject," with synonyms, "chastisement, correction, discipline."

The word punishment, as will be noted later, is most unfortunate when applied to what Scientific Management would mean by a penalty, though this word also is unfortunate; but, in the first place, there is no better word to cover the general meaning; and in the second place, the idea of pain and suffering, which Scientific Management aims to and does eliminate, is present in some of the older forms of management Therefore the word punishment must stand.

Rewards and Punishments Result in Action

There can be no doubt that a reward is an incentive. There may well be doubt as to whether a punishment is an incentive to action or not. This, however, is only at first glance, and the whole thing rests on the meaning of the word "action." To be active is certainly the opposite of being at rest. This being true, punishment is just as surely an incentive to action as is reward.

The man who is punished in every case will be led to some sort of action. Whether this really results in an increase of output or not simply determines whether the punishment is a scientifically prescribed punishment or not. If the punishment is of such a nature that the output ceases because of it, or that it incites the man punished against the general good, then it does not in any wise cease to be an active thing, but it is simply a wrong, and unscientifically assigned punishment, that acts in a detrimental way.

Soldiering Alone Cuts Down Activity

It is interesting to note that the greatest cause for cutting down output is related more closely to a reward than a punishment. Under such managements as provide no adequate reward for all, and no adequate assurance that all can receive extra rewards permanently without a cut in the rate, it may be advisable, for the worker's best interests, to limit output in order to keep the wages, or reward, up, and soldiering results. The evils of soldiering will be discussed more at length under the "Systems of Pay." It is plain, however, here that soldiering is the result of a cutting down of action, and it is self-evident that anything which cuts down action is harmful, not only to the individual himself, but to society at large.

Nature of Rewards and Punishments

Under all types of management, the principal rewards consist of promotion and pay, pay being a broad word used here to include regular wages, a bonus, shorter hours, other forms of remuneration or recompense; anything which can be given to the man who does the work to benefit him and increase his desire to continue doing the work. Punishments may be negative, that is, they may simply take the form of no reward; or they may be positive, that is, they may include fines, discharge, assignment to less remunerative or less desirable work, or any other thing which can be given to the man to show him that he has not done what is expected of him and, in theory at least, to lead him to do better.

Nature of Direct Incentives

Direct incentives will be such native reaction as ambition, pride and pugnacity; will be love of racing, love of play; love of personal recognition; will be the outcome of self-confidence and interest, and so on.

The Reward Under Traditional Management Unstandardized

As with all other discussions of any part or form of Traditional Management, the discussion of the incentive under Traditional Management is vague from the very nature of the subject. "Traditional" stands for vagueness and for variation, for the lack of standardization, for the lack of definiteness in knowledge, in process, in results. The rewards under Traditional Management, as under all types of management, are promotion and pay. It must be an almost unthinkably poor system of management, even under Traditional Management, which did not attempt to provide for some sort of promotion of the man who did the most and best work; but the lack of standardization of conditions, of instructions, of the work itself, and of reward, makes it almost impossible not only to give the reward, but even to determine who deserves the reward. Under Traditional Management, the reward need not be positive, that is, it might simply consist in the negation of some previously existing disadvantage. It need not be predetermined. It might be nothing definite. It might not be so set ahead that the man might look forward to it. In other words it might simply be the outcome of the good, and in no wise the incentive for the good. It need not necessarily be personal. It could be shared with a group, or gang, and lose all feeling of personality. It need not be a fixed reward or a fixed performance; in fact, if the management were Traditional it would be almost impossible that it would be a fixed reward. It might not be an assured reward, and in most cases it was not a prompt reward. These fixed adjectives describe the reward of Scientific Management — positive, predetermined, personal, fixed, assured and prompt. A few of these might apply, or none might apply to the reward under Traditional Management.

Reward a Prize Won by One Only

If this reward, whether promotion or pay, was given to someone under Traditional Management, this usually meant that others thereby lost it; it was in the nature of a prize which one only could attain, and which the others, therefore, would lose, and such a lost prize is, to the average man, for the time at least, a dampener on action. The rewarding of the winner, to the loss of all of the losers, has been met by the workmen getting together secretly, and selecting the winners for a week or more ahead, thus getting the same reward out of the employer without the extra effort.

Punishment Under Traditional Management Wrong in Theory

The punishment, under Traditional Management, was usually much more than negative punishment; that is to say, the man who was punished usually received much more than simply the negative return of getting no reward. The days of bodily punishment have long passed, yet the account of the beatings given to the galley slaves and to other workers in the past are too vividly described in authentic accounts to be lost from memory. Today, under Traditional Management, punishment consists of

1. fines, which are usually simply a cutting down of wages, the part deducted remaining with the company,

2. discharge, or
3. assignment to less pleasant or less desirable work.

This assignment is done on an unscientific basis, the man being simply put at something which he dislikes, with no regard as to whether his efficiency at that particular work will be high or not.

Results are Unfortunate

The punishment, under Traditional Management, is usually meted out by the foreman, simply as one of his many duties. He is apt to be so personally interested, and perhaps involved, in the case that his punishment will satisfy some wrong notions, impulse of anger, hate, or envy in him, and will arouse a feeling of shame or wounded pride, or unappreciation, in the man to whom punishment is awarded.

Direct Incentives not Scientifically Utilized

As for what we have called direct incentive, the love of racing was often used under Traditional Management through Athletic Contests, the faults in these being that the men were not properly studied, so that they could be properly assigned and grouped; care was not always exercised that hate should not be the result of the contest; the contest was not always conducted according to the rules of clean sport; the men slighted quality in hastening the work, and the results of the athletic contests were not so written down as to be thereafter utilized. Love of play may have been developed unconsciously, but was certainly not often studied. Love of personal recognition was probably often utilized, but in no scientific way. Neither was there anything in Traditional Management to develop self-confidence, or to arouse and maintain interest in any set fashion. Naturally, if the man were in a work which he particularly liked, which under Traditional Management was a matter of luck, he would be more or less interested in it, but there was no scientific way of arousing or holding his interest. Under Traditional Management, a man might take pride in his work, as did many of the old bricklayers and masons, who would set themselves apart after hours if necessary, lock themselves in, and cut bricks for a complicated arch or fancy pattern, but such pride was in no way fostered through the efforts of the management. Pugnacity was aroused, but it might have an evil effect as well as a good, so far as the management had any control. Ambition, in the same way, might be stimulated, and might not. There is absolutely nothing under Traditional Management to prevent a man being ambitious, gratifying his pride, and gratifying his pugnacity in a right way, and at the same time being interested in his work, but there was nothing under Traditional Management which provided for definite and exact methods for encouraging these good qualities, seeing that they developed in a proper channel, and scientifically utilizing the outcome again and again.

Pay for Performance Provided for by Transitory Management

Under Transitory Management, as soon as practicable, one bonus is paid for doing work according to the method prescribed. As standardization takes place, the second bonus for completing the task in the time set can be paid. As each element of Scientific Management is introduced, incentives become more apparent, more powerful, and more assured.

Direct Incentives more Skillfully Used

With the separating of output, and recording of output separately, love of personal recognition grew, self-confidence grew, interest in one's work grew. The Athletic Contest is so conducted that love of speed, love of play, and love of competition are encouraged, the worker constantly feeling that he can indulge in these, as he is assured of "fair play."

Incentives Under Scientific Management Constructive

It is most important, psychologically and ethically, that it be understood that Scientific Management is not in any sense a destructive power. That only is eliminated that is harmful, or wasteful, or futile; everything that is good is conserved, and is utilized as much as it has ever been before, often much more than it has ever been utilized. The constructive force, under Scientific Management, is one of its great life principles. This is brought out very plainly in considering incentives under Scientific Management. With the scientifically determined wage, and the more direct and more sure plan of promotion, comes no discard of the well-grounded incentives of older types of management. The value of a fine personality in all who are to be imitated is not forgotten; the importance of using all natural stimuli to healthful activity is appreciated. Scientific Management uses all these, in so far as they can be used to the best outcome for workers and work, and supplements them by such scientifically derived additions as could never have been derived under the older types.

Characteristics of the Reward

Rewards, under Scientific Management are —

(a) positive; that is to say, the reward must be a definite, positive gain to the man, and not simply a taking away of some thing which may have been a drawback.

(b) predetermined; that is to say, before the man begins to work it must be determined exactly what reward he is to get for doing the work.

(c) personal; that is, individual, a reward for that particular man for that particular work.

(d) fixed, unchanged. He must get exactly what it has been determined beforehand that he shall get.

(e) assured; that is to say, there must be provision made for this reward before the man begins to work, so that he may be positive that he will get the reward if he does the work. The record of the organization must be that rewards have always been paid in the past, therefore probably will be in the future.

(f) the reward must be prompt; that is to say, as soon as the work has been done, the man must get the reward. This promptness applies to the announcement of the reward; that is to say, the man must know at once that he has gotten the reward, and also to the receipt of the reward by the man.

Positive Reward Arouses Interest and Holds Attention

The benefit of the positive reward is that it arouses and holds attention. A fine example of a reward that is not positive is that type of "welfare work" which consists of simply providing the worker with such surroundings as will enable him to work decently and without actual discomfort. The worker, naturally, feels that such surroundings are his right, and in no sense a reward and incentive to added activity. The reward must actually offer to the worker something which he has a right to expect only if he earns it; something which will be a positive addition to his life.

Predetermined Reward Concentrates Attention

The predetermined reward allows both manager and man to concentrate their minds upon the work. There is no shifting of the attention, while the worker wonders what the reward that he is to receive will be. It is also a strong factor for industrial peace, and for all the extra activities which will come when industrial conditions are peaceful.

Personal Reward Conserves Individuality

The personal reward is a strong incentive toward initiative, towards the desire to make the most of one's individuality. It is an aid toward the feeling of personal recognition. From this personal reward come all the benefits which have been considered under individuality.

Fixed Reward Eliminates Waste Time

The fact that the reward is fixed is a great eliminator of waste to the man and to the manager both. Not only does the man concentrate better under the fixed reward, but the reward, being fixed, need not be determined anew, over and over again; that is to say, every time that kind of work is done, simultaneous with the arising of the work comes the reward that is to be paid for it. All the time that would be given to determining the reward, satisfying the men and arguing the case, is saved and utilized.

Assured Reward Aids Concentration

The assured reward leads to concentration, — even perhaps more so than the fact that the reward is determined. In case the man was not sure that he would get the reward in the end, he would naturally spend a great deal of time wondering whether he would or not. Moreover, no immediate good fortune counts for much as an incentive if there is a prospect of bad luck following in the immediate future.

Need for Promptness Varies

The need for promptness of the reward varies. If the reward is to be given to a man of an elementary type of mind, the reward must be immediately announced and must be actually given very promptly, as it is impossible for anyone of such a type of intellect to look forward very far. A man of a high type of intellectual development is able to wait a longer time for his reward, and the element of promptness, while acting somewhat as an incentive, is not so necessary.

Under Scientific Management, with the ordinary type of worker on manual work, it has been found most satisfactory to pay the reward every day, or at the end of the week, and to announce the score of output as often as every hour. This not only satisfies the longing of the normal mind to know exactly where it stands, but also lends a fresh impetus to repeat the high record. There is also, through the prompt reward, the elimination of time wasted in wondering what the result will be, and in allaying suspense. Suspense is not a stimulus to great activity, as anyone who has waited for the result of a doubtful examination can testify, it being almost impossible to concentrate the mind on any other work until one knows whether the work which has been done has been completed satisfactorily or not.

Promptness Always an Added Incentive

There are many kinds of life work and modes of living so terrible as to make one shudder at the thoughts of the certain sickness, death, or disaster that are almost absolutely sure to follow such a vocation. Men continue to work for those wages that lead positively to certain death, because of the immediateness of the sufficient wages, or reward. This takes their attention from their ultimate end. Much more money would be required if payment were postponed, say, five years after the act, to obtain the services of the air-man, or the worker subject to the poisoning of some branches of the lead and mercury industries.

If the prompt reward is incentive enough to make men forget danger and threatened death, how much more efficient is it in increasing output where there is no such danger.

Immediate Reward not Always Preferable

There are cases where the prompt reward is not to be preferred, because the delayed reward will be greater, or will be available to more people Such is the case with the reward that comes from unrestricted output.

For example, — the immediacy of the temporarily increased reward caused by restricting output has often led the combinations of working men to such restriction, with an ultimate loss of reward to worker, to employer, and to the consumer.

Rewards Possible of Attainment by All

Every man working under Scientific Management has a chance to win a reward. This means not only that the man has a "square deal," for the man may have a square deal under Traditional Management in that he may have a fair chance to try for all existing rewards. There is more than this under Scientific Management. By the very nature of the plan itself, the rewards are possible of achievement by all; any one man, by winning, in no way diminishes the chances of the others.

Rewards of Management Resemble Rewards of Workers

So far the emphasis, in the discussion of reward, has been on the reward as given to the worker, and his feeling toward it. The reward to the management is just as sure. It lies in the increased output and therefore the possibility of lower costs and of greater financial gain. It is as positive; it is as predetermined, because before the reward to the men is fixed the management realizes what proportion that reward will bear to the entire undertaking, and exactly what profits can be obtained. It is a fundamental of Scientific Management that the management shall be able to prophesy the outputs ahead. It will certainly be as personal, if the management side is as thoroughly systematized as is the managed; it will be as fixed and as assured, and it certainly is as prompt, as the cost records can be arranged to come to the management every day, if that is desired.

Results of Such Rewards

There are three other advantages to management which

might well be added here. First, that a reward such as this attracts the best men to the work; second, that the reward, and the stability of it, indicates the stability of the entire institution, and thus raises its standing in the eyes of the community as well as in its own eyes; and third, that it leads the entire organization, both managed and managing, to look favourably at all standardization. The standardized reward is sure to be attractive to all members. As soon as it is realized that the reason that it is attractive is because it is *standardized*, the entire subject of standardization rises in the estimation of every one, and the introduction of standards can be carried on more rapidly, and with greater success.

Rewards Divided into Promotion and Pay

Rewards may be divided into two kinds; first, promotion and, second, pay. Under Scientific Management promotion is assured for every man and, as has been said, this promotion does not thereby hold back others from having the same sort of promotion. There is an ample place, under Scientific Management, for every man to advance. Not only is the promotion sure, thus giving the man absolute assurance that he will advance as his work is satisfactory, but it is also gradual. The promotion must be by degrees, otherwise the workers may get discouraged, from finding their promotion has come faster than has their ability to achieve, and the lack of attention, due to being discouraged, may be contagious. It is, therefore, of vital importance that the worker be properly selected, in order that, in his advancement and promotion, he shall be able to achieve his task after having been put at the new work. He must be advanced and promoted in a definite line of gradual development, in accordance with a fully conceived plan. This should be worked out and set down in writing as a definite plan, similar to the plan on the instruction card of one of his tasks.

Promotion may be to Places Within or Without the Business

In many lines of business, the business itself offers ample opportunity for promoting all men who can "make good" as rapidly as they can prepare themselves for positions over others, and for advancement; but under Scientific Management provision is made even in case the business does not offer such opportunities. This is done by the management finding places outside their own organization for the men who are so trained that they can be advanced.

Such Promotion Attracts Workers

While at first glance it might seem a most unfortunate thing for the management to have to let its men go, and while, as Dr. Taylor says, it is unfortunate for a business to get the reputation of being nothing but a training school, on the other hand, it has a very salutary effect upon the men to know that their employers are so disinterestedly interested in them that they will provide for their future, even at the risk of the individual business at which they have started having to lose their services. This will not only, as Dr. Taylor makes clear, stimulate many men in the establishment whose men go on to take the places of those who are promoted, but will also be a great inducement to other men to come into a place that they feel is unselfish and generous.

Subdivisions of "Pay." — Under "Pay" we have included eight headings:

1. Wages
2. Bonus
3. Shorter hours
4. Prizes other than money
5. Extra knowledge
6. Method of attack
7. Good opinion of others
8. Professional standing.

Relation Between Wages and Bonus

Wages and bonus are closely related. By wages we mean a fixed sum, or minimum hourly rate, that the man gets in any case for his time, and by bonus we mean additional money that he receives for achievement of method, quantity or quality. Both might very properly be included under wages, or under money received for the work, or opportunities for receiving money for work, as the case might be. In the discussion of the different ways of paying wages under Scientific Management, there will be no attempt to discuss the economic value of the various means; the different methods will simply be stated, and the psychological significance will be, as far as possible, given.

Before discussing the various kinds of wages advised by the experts in Scientific Management, it is well to pause a moment to name the various sorts of methods of compensation recognized by authorities. David F. Schloss in his "Method of Industrial Remuneration" divides all possible ways of gaining remuneration into three —

1. the different kinds of wages
    - time wage
    - piece wage
    - task wage
    - progressive wage
    - collective piece wage
    - collective task wage
    - collective progressive wage
    - contract work
    - cooperative work with
2. profit sharing, and
3. industrial cooperation. These are defined and discussed at length in his book in a lucid and simple manner.

It is only necessary to quote him here as to the relationship between these different forms, where he says, page 11, — "The two leading forms of industrial remuneration under the Wages System are time wages, and piece wages. Intermediate between these principal forms, stands that known as task wage, while supplemental to these two named methods, we find those various systems which will here be designated by the name of Progressive Wages." Day Work Never Scientific

The simplest of all systems, says Dr. Taylor in "A Piece Rate System," paragraph 10, in discussing the various forms of compensation "is the Day Work plan, in which the employees are divided into certain classes, and a standard rate of wages is paid to each class of men," He adds — "The men are paid according to the position which they fill, and not according to their individual character, energy, skill and reliability," The psychological objection to day work is that it does not arouse interest or effort or hold attention, nor does it inspire to memorizing or to learning.

It will be apparent that there is no inducement whatever for the man to do more than just enough to retain his job, for he in no wise shares in the reward for an extra effort, which goes entirely to his employer. "Reward," in this case, is usually simply a living wage, — enough to inspire the man, if he needs the money enough to work to hold his position, but not enough to incite him to any extra effort.

It is true that, in actual practice, through the foreman or some man in authority, the workers on day work may be "speeded up" to a point where they will do a great deal of work; the foreman being inspired, of course, by a reward for the extra output, but, as Dr. Taylor says, paragraph 17 — "A Piece Rate System," this sort of speeding up is absolutely lacking in self-sustaining power. The moment that this rewarded foreman is removed, the work will again fall down. Therefore, day wage has almost no place in ultimate, scientifically managed work.

Piece Work Provides Pay in Proportion to Work Done

Piece Work is the opposite of time work, in that under it the man is paid not for the time he spends at the work, but for the amount of work which he accomplishes. Under this system, as long as the man is paid a proper piece rate, and a rate high enough to keep him interested, he will have great inducements to work. He will have a chance to develop individuality, a chance for competition, a chance for personal recognition. His love of reasonable racing will be cultivated. His love of play may be cultivated.

All of these incentives arise because the man feels that his sense of justice is being considered; that if the task is properly laid out, and the price per piece is properly determined, he is given a "square deal" in being allowed to accomplish as great an amount of work as he can, with the assurance that his reward will be promptly coming to him.

Danger of Rate Being Cut

Piece work becomes objectionable only when the rate is cut. The moment the rate is cut the first time, the man begins to wonder whether it is going to be cut again, and his attention is distracted from the work by his debating this question constantly. At best, his attention wanders from one subject to the other, and back again. It cannot be concentrated on his work. After the rate has been cut once or twice, — and it is sure to be cut unless it has been set from scientifically derived elementary time units, — the man loses his entire confidence in the stability of the rate, and, naturally, when he loses this confidence, his work is done more slowly, due to lack of further enthusiasm. On the contrary, as long as it is to his advantage to do the work and he is sure that his reward will be prompt, and that he will always get the price that has been determined as right by him and by the employers for his work, he can do this work easily in the time set. As soon as he feels that he will not get it, he will naturally begin to do less, as it will be not only to his personal advantage to do as little as possible, but also very much to the advantage of his fellows, for whom the rate will also be cut.

Task Wage Contains no Incentive to Additional Work

What Schloss calls the Task Wage would, as he well says, be the intermediate between time or day wage and piece wage; that is, it would be the assigning of a definite amount of work to be done in definite time, and to be paid for by a definite sum. If the task were set scientifically, and the time scientifically determined, as it must naturally be for a scientific task, and the wage adequate for that work, there would seem to be nothing about this form of remuneration which could be a cause of dissatisfaction to the worker. Naturally, however, there would be absolutely no chance for him to desire to go any faster than the time set, or to accomplish any more work in the time set than that which he was obliged to, in that he could not possibly get anything for the extra work done.

Worth of Previous Methods in the Handling

It will be noted in the discussion of the three types of compensation so far discussed, that there is nothing in them that renders them unscientific. Any one of the three may be used, and doubtless all are used, on works which are attempting to operate under Scientific Management. Whether they really are scientific methods of compensation or not, is determined by the way that they are handled. Certainly, however, all that any of these three can expect to do is to convince the man that he is being treated justly; that is to say, if he knows what sort of a contract he is entering into, the contract is perfectly fair, provided that the management keeps its part of the contract, pays the agreed-upon wage.

In proceeding, instead of following the order of Schloss we will follow the order, at least for a time, of Dr. Taylor In "A Piece Rate System"; this for two reasons:

First, for the reason that the "Piece Rate System" is later than Schloss' book, Schloss being 1891, and the "Piece Rate" being 1895; in the second place that we are following the Scientific Management side in distinction to the general economic side, laid down by Schloss. There is, however, nothing in our plan of discussion here to prevent one's following fairly closely in the Schloss also.

The Gain-sharing Plan

We take up, then, the Gain-sharing Plan which was invented by Mr. Henry R. Towne and used by him with success in the Yale & Towne works. This is described in a paper read before the American Society of Mechanical Engineers, in professional paper No. 341, in 1888 and also in the Premium Plan, Mr. Halsey's modification of it, described by him in a paper entitled the "Premium Plan of Paying for Labour," American Society of Mechanical Engineers, 1891, Paper 449. In this, in describing the Profit-sharing Plan, Mr. Halsey says — "Under it, in addition to regular wages, the employees were offered a certain percentage of the final profits of the business. It thus divides the savings due to increased production between employer and employe."

Objections to this Plan

We note here the objection to this plan: First, — "The workmen are given a share in what they do not earn; second, the workmen share regardless of individual deserts; third, the promised rewards are remote; fourth, the plan makes no provision for bad years; fifth, the workmen have no means of knowing if the agreement is carried out." Without discussing any farther whether these are worded exactly as all who have tried the plan might have found them, we may take these on Mr. Halsey's authority and discuss the psychology of them. If the workmen are given a share in what they do not earn, they have absolutely no feeling that they are being treated justly. This extra reward which is given to them, if in the nature of a present, might much better be a present out and out. If it has no scientific relation to what they have gotten, if the workmen share regardless of individual deserts, this, as Dr. Taylor says, paragraph 27 in the "Piece Rate System," is the most serious defect of all, in that it does not allow for recognition of the personal merits of each workman. If the rewards are remote, the interest is diminished. If the plan makes no provision for bad years, it cannot be self-perpetuating. If the workmen have no means of knowing if the agreement will be carried out or not, they will be constantly wondering whether it is being carried out or not, and their attention will wander.

The Premium Plan

The Premium Plan is thus described by Mr. Halsey — "The time required to do a given piece of work is determined from previous experience, and the workman, in addition to his usual daily wages, is offered a premium for every hour by which he reduces that time on future work, the amount of the premium being less than his rate of wages. Making the hourly premium less than the hourly wages is the foundation stone upon which rest all the merits of the system."

Dr. Taylor's Description of this Plan

Dr. Taylor comments upon this plan as follows:

"The Towne-Halsey plan consists in recording the quickest time in which a job has been done, and fixing this as a standard. If the workman succeeds in doing the job in a shorter time, he is still paid his same wages per hour for the time he works on the job, and, in addition, is given a premium for having worked faster, consisting of from one-quarter to one-half the difference

between the wages earned and the wages originally paid when the job was done in standard time," Dr. Taylor's discussion of this plan will be found in "Shop Management," paragraphs 79 to 91.

Psychologically, the defect of this system undoubtedly is that it does not rest upon accurate scientific time study, therefore neither management nor men can predict accurately what is going to happen. Not being able to predict, they are unable to devote their entire attention to the work in hand, and the result cannot be as satisfactory as under an assigned task, based upon time study. The discussion of this is so thorough in Dr. Taylor's work, and in Mr. Halsey's work, that it is unnecessary to introduce more here.

Profit-sharing

Before turning to the methods of compensation which are based upon the task, it might be well to introduce here mention of "Cooperation," or "Profit-sharing," which, in its extreme form, usually means the sharing of the profits from the business as a whole, among the men who do the work. This is further discussed by Schloss, and also by Dr. Taylor in paragraphs 32 to 35, in "A Piece Rate System"; also in "Shop Management," quoting from the "Piece Rate System," paragraphs 73 to 77.

Objections to Profit-sharing

The objections, Dr. Taylor says, to cooperation are, first in the fact that no form of cooperation has been devised in which each individual is allowed free scope for his personal ambition; second, in the remoteness of the reward; third, in the unequitable division of the profits. If each individual is not allowed free scope, one sees at once that the entire advantage of individuality, and of personal recognition, is omitted. If the reward is remote, we recognize that its power diminishes very rapidly; and if there cannot be equitable division of the profits, not only will the men ultimately not be satisfied, but they will, after a short time, not even be satisfied while they are working, because their minds will constantly be distracted by the fact that the division will probably not be equitable, and also by the fact that they will be trying to plan ways in which they can get their proper share. Thus, not only in the ultimate outcome, but also during the entire process, the work will slow up necessarily, because the men can have no assurance either that the work itself, or the output, have been scientifically determined.

Scientific Management Embodies Valuable Elements of Profit-sharing

Scientific Management embodies the valuable elements of profit-sharing, namely, the idea of cooperation, and the idea that the workers should share in the profit.

That the latter of these two is properly emphasized by Scientific Management is not always understood by the workers. When a worker is enabled to make three or four times as much output in a day as he has been accustomed to, he may think that he is not getting his full share of the "spoils" of increased efficiency, unless he gets a proportionately increased rate of pay. It should, therefore, be early made clear to him that the saving has been caused by the actions of the management, quite as much as by the increased efforts for productivity of the men. Furthermore, a part of the savings must go to pay for the extra cost of maintaining the standard conditions that make such output possible. The necessary planners and teachers usually are sufficient as object-lessons to convince the workers of the necessity of not giving all the extra savings to the workers.

It is realized that approximately one third of the extra profits from the savings must go to the employer, about one third to the employees, and the remainder for maintaining the system and carrying out further investigations.

This once understood, the satisfaction that results from a cooperative, profit-sharing type of management will be enjoyed.

The five methods of compensation which are to follow are all based upon the task, as laid down by Dr. Taylor; that is to say, upon time study, and an exact knowledge by the man, and the employers, of how much work can be done.

Differential Rate Piece Work the Ultimate Form of Compensation

Dr. Taylor's method of compensation, which is acknowledged by all thoroughly grounded in Scientific Management to be the ultimate form of compensation where it can be used, is called Differential Rate Piece Work. It is described in "A Piece Rate System," paragraphs 50 to 52, as follows: —

"This consists, briefly, in paying a higher price per piece, or per unit, or per job, if the work is done in the shortest possible time and without imperfection, than is paid if the work takes a longer time or is imperfectly done. To illustrate — suppose 20 units, or pieces, to be the largest amount of work of a certain kind that can be done in a day. Under the differential rate system, if a workman finishes 20 pieces per day, and all of these pieces are perfect, he receives, say, 15 cents per piece, making his pay for the day 15 times 20 = $3.00. If, however, he works too slowly and turns out only, say 19 pieces, then instead of receiving 15 cents per piece he gets only 12 cents per piece, making his pay for the day 12×19= $2.28, instead of $3.00 per day. If he succeeds in finishing 20 pieces — some of which are imperfect — then he should receive a still lower rate of pay, say 10¢ or 5¢ per piece, according to circumstances, making his pay for the day $2.00 or only $1.00, instead of $3.00."

Advantages of this System

This system is founded upon knowledge that for a large reward men will do a large amount of work. The small compensation for a small amount of work — and under this system the minimum compensation is a little below the regular day's work — may lead men to exert themselves to accomplish more work. This system appeals to the justice of the men, in that it is more nearly an exact ratio of pay to endeavour.

Task Work with a Bonus

The Task work with Bonus system of compensation, which is the invention of Mr. H.L. Gantt, is explained in "A Bonus System of Rewarding Labour," paper 923, read before the American Society of Mechanical Engineers, December, 1901, by Mr. Gantt. This system is there described as follows: —

"If the man follows his instructions and accomplishes all the work laid out for him as constituting his proper task for the day, he is paid a definite bonus in addition to the day rate which he always gets. If, however, at the end of the day he has failed to accomplish all of the work laid out, he does not get his bonus, but simply his day rate."

Advantages of Task Work with a Bonus

The psychological advantage of the task with a Bonus is the fact that the worker has the assurance of a living wage while learning, no matter whether he succeeds in winning his bonus or not. In the last analysis, it is "day rate" for the unskilled, and "piece rate" for the skilled, and it naturally leads to a feeling of security in the worker. Mr. Gantt has so admirably explained the advantages, psychological as well as industrial, of his system, that it is unnecessary to go farther, except to emphasize the fine feeling of brotherhood which underlies the idea, and its expression.

The Differential Bonus System

The Differential Bonus System of Compensation is the invention of Mr. Frederick A. Parkhurst, and is described by him in his book "Applied Methods of Scientific Management."

"The time the job should be done in is first determined by analysis and time study. The bonus is then added above the day work line. No bonus is paid until a definitely determined time is realized. As the time is reduced, the bonus is increased."

Three Rate with Increased Rate System

The Three Rate System of Compensation is the invention of Mr. Frank B. Gilbreth and consists of day work, i.e., a day rate, or a flat minimum rate, which all who are willing to work receive until they can try themselves out; of a middle rate, which is given to the man when he accomplishes the work with exactness of compliance to prescribed motions, according to the requirements of his instruction card; and of a high rate, which is paid to the man when he not only accomplishes the task in accordance with the instruction card, but also within the set time and of the prescribed quality of finished work.

Advantage of this System

The advantage of this is, first of all, that the man does not have to look forward so far for some of his reward, as it comes to him just as soon as he has shown himself able to do the prescribed methods required accurately. The first extra reward is naturally a stimulus toward winning the second extra reward. The middle rate is a stimulus to endeavour to perform that method which will enable him easiest to achieve the accomplishment of the task that pays the highest wage. The day rate assures the man of a living wage. The middle rate pays him a bonus for trying to learn. The high rate gives him a piece rate when he is skilled.

Lastly, as the man can increase his output, with continued experience, above that of the task, he receives a differential rate piece on the excess quantity, this simply making an increasing stimulus to exceed his previous best record.

All Task Systems Investigate Loss of Bonus

Under all these bonus forms of wages, if the bonus is not gained the fact is at once investigated, in order that the blame may rest where it belongs. The blame may rest upon the workers, or it may be due to the material, which may be defective, or different from standard; it may be upon the supervision, or some fault of the management in not supplying the material in the proper quality, or sequence, or a bad condition of tools or machinery; or upon the instruction card. The fact that the missing of the bonus is investigated is an added assurance to the workman that he is getting the "square deal," and enlists his sympathy with these forms of bonus system, and his desire to work under them. The fact that the management will investigate also allows him to concentrate upon output, with no worry as to the necessity of his investigating places where he has fallen short.

Necessity for Workers Bearing this Loss

In any case, whether the blame for losing the bonus is the worker's fault directly or not, he loses his bonus. This, for two reasons; in the first place, if he did not lose his bonus he would have no incentive to try to discover flaws before delays occurred; he would, otherwise, have an incentive to allow the material to pass through his hands, defective or imperfect as the case might be. This is very closely associated with the second reason, and that is; that the bonus comes from the savings caused by the plan of management, and that it is necessary that the workers as well as the management shall see that everything possible tends to increase the saving. It is only as the worker feels that his bonus is a part of the saving, that he recognizes the justice of his receiving it, that it is in no wise a gift to him, simply his proper share, accorded not by any system of philanthropy, or so-called welfare work, but simply because his own personal work has made it possible for the management to hand back his share to him.

Users of any Task System Appreciate other Task Systems

It is of great importance to the workers that the users of any of these five methods of compensation of Scientific Management are all ready and glad to acknowledge the worth of all these systems. In many works more than one, in some all, of these systems of payment may be in use. Far from this resulting in confusion, it simply leads to the understanding that whatever is best in the particular situation should be used. It also leads to a feeling of stability everywhere, as a man who has worked under any of these systems founded on time study can easily pass to another. There is also a great gain here in the doing away of industrial warfare.

Shorter Hours and Holidays Effective Rewards

Probably the greatest incentive, next to promotion and more pay, are shorter hours and holidays. In some cases, the shorter hours, or holidays, have proven even more attractive to the worker than the increase of pay. In Shop Management, paragraph 165, Dr. Taylor describes a case where children working were obliged to turn their entire pay envelopes over to their parents. To them, there was no particular incentive in getting more money, but, when the task was assigned, if they were allowed to go as soon as their task was completed, the output was accomplished in a great deal shorter time. Another case where shorter hours were successfully tried, was in an office where the girls were allowed the entire Saturday every two weeks, if the work was accomplished within a set amount of time. This extra time for shopping and matinees proved more attractive than any reasonable amount of extra pay that could be offered.

Desire for Approbation an Incentive

Under "Individuality" were discussed various devices for developing the individuality of the man, such as his picture over a good output or record. These all act as rewards or incentives.

How successful they would be, depends largely upon the temperament of the man and the sort of work that is to be done. In all classes of society, among all sorts of people, there is the type that loves approbation. This type will be appealed to more by a device which allows others to see what has been done than by almost anything else. As to what this device must be, depends on the intelligence of the man.

Necessity for Cooperation a Strong Incentive

Under Scientific Management, many workers are forced by their coworkers to try to earn their bonuses, as "falling down on" tasks, and therefore schedules, may force them to lose their bonuses also.

The fact that, in many kinds of work, a man falling below his task will prevent his fellows from working, is often a strong incentive to that man to make better speed. For example, on a certain construction job in Canada, the teamsters were shown that, by their work, they were cutting down working opportunities for cart loaders, who could only be hired as the teamsters hauled sufficient loads to keep them busy.

Value of Knowledge Gained an Incentive to a Few Only

Extra knowledge, and the better method of attack learned under Scientific Management, are rewards that will be appreciated by those of superior intelligence only.

They will, in a way, be appreciated by all, because it will be realized that, through what is learned, more pay or promotion is received, but the fact that this extra knowledge, and better method of attack, will enable one to do better in all lines, not simply in the line at which one is working, and will render one's life more full and rich, will be appreciated only by those of a wide experience.

Acquired Professional Standing a Powerful Incentive

Just as the success of the worker under Scientific Management assures such admiration by his fellow-workers as will serve as an incentive toward further success, so the professional standing attained by success in Scientific Management acts as an incentive to those in more responsible positions.

As soon as it is recognized that Scientific Management furnishes the only real measure of efficiency, its close relationship to professional standing will be recognized, and the reward which it can offer in this line will be more fully appreciated.

Punishments Negative and Positive

Punishments may be first negative, that is, simply a loss of promised rewards. Such punishments, especially in cases of men who have once had the reward, usually will act as the necessary stimulus to further activity. Punishments may also be positive, such things as fines, assignment to less pleasant work, or as a last resort, discharge.

Fines Never Accrue to the Management

Fines have been a most successful mode of punishment under Scientific Management. Under many of the old forms of management, the fines were turned back to the management itself, thus raising a spirit of animosity in the men, who felt that everything that they suffered was a gain to those over them.

Under Scientific Management all fines are used in some way for the benefit of the men themselves. All fines should be used for some benefit fund, or turned into the insurance fund. The fines, as has been said, are determined solely by the disciplinarian, who is disinterested in the disposition of the funds thus collected.

As the fines do not in any way benefit the management, and in fact rather hurt the management in that the men who pay them, no matter where they are applied, must feel more or less discouraged, it is, naturally, for the benefit of the management that there shall be as few fines as possible. Both management and men realize this, which leads to industrial peace, and also leads the managers, the functional foremen, and in fact every one, to eliminate the necessity and cause for fines to as great an extent as is possible.

Assignment to Less Pleasant Work Effective Punishment

Assignment to less pleasant work is a very effective form of discipline. It has many advantages which do not show on the surface, The man may not really get a cut in pay, though his work be changed, and thus the damage he receives is in no wise to his purse, but simply to his feeling of pride. In the meantime, he is gaining a wider experience of the business, so that even the worst disadvantage has its bright side.

Discharge to be Avoided Wherever Possible

Discharge is, of course, available under Scientific Management, as under all other forms, but it is really less used under Scientific Management than under any other sort, because if a man is possibly available, and in any way trained, it is better to do almost anything to teach him, to assign him to different work, to try and find his possibilities, than to let him go, and have all that teaching wasted as far as the organization which has taught it is concerned.

Discharge a Grave Injury to a Worker

Moreover, Scientific Management realizes that discharge may be a grave injury to a worker. As Mr. James M. Dodge, who has been most successful in Scientific Management and is noted for his good work for his fellow-men, eloquently pleads, in a paper on "The Spirit in Which Scientific Management Should Be Approached," given before the Conference on Scientific Management at Dartmouth College, October, 1911:

"It is a serious thing for a worker who has located his home within reasonable proximity to his place of employment and with proper regard for the schooling of his children, to have to seek other employment and readjust his home affairs, with a loss of time and wages. Proper management takes account not only of this fact, but also of the fact that there is a distinct loss to the employer when an old and experienced employe is replaced by a new man, who must be educated in the methods of the establishment. An old employe has, in his experience, a potential value that should not be lightly disregarded, and there should be in case of dismissal the soundest of reasons, in which personal prejudice or temporary mental condition of the foreman should play no part. "Constant changing of employees is not wholesome for any establishment, and the sudden discovery by a foreman that a man who has been employed for a year or more is 'no good' is often a reflection on the foreman, and more often still, is wholly untrue. All working men, unless they develop intemperate or dishonest habits, have desirable value in them, and the conserving and increasing of their value is a duty which should be assumed by their superiors."

Punishment can Never be Entirely Abolished

It might be asked why punishments are needed at all under this system; that is, why positive punishments are needed. Why not merely a lack of reward for the slight offenses, and a discharge if it gets too bad? It must be remembered, however, that the punishments are needed to insure a proper appreciation of the reward.

If there is no negative side, the beauty of the reward will never be realized; the man who has once suffered by having his pay cut for something which he has done wrong, will be more than ready to keep up to the standard. In the second place, unless individuals are punished, the rights of other individuals will, necessarily, be encroached upon. When it is considered that under Scientific Management the man who gives the punishment is the disinterested disciplinarian, that the punishment is made exactly appropriate to the offense, and that no advantage from it comes to any one except the men themselves, it can be understood that the psychological basis is such as to make a punishment rather an incentive than a detriment.

Direct Incentives Numerous and Powerful

As for the direct incentives, these are so many that it is possible to enumerate only a few. For example —

This may be simply a result of love of speed, love of play, or love of activity, or it may be, in the case of a man running a machine, not so much for the love of the activity as for a love of seeing things progress rapidly. There is a love of contest which has been thoroughly discussed under "Athletic Contests," which results in racing, and in all the pleasures of competition.

Racing Directed Under Scientific Management

The psychology of the race under Scientific Management is most interesting.

The race is not a device of Scientific Management to speed up the worker, any speed that would be demanded by Scientific Management beyond the task-speed would be an unscientific thing. On the other hand, it is not the scope of Scientific Management to bar out any contests which would not be for the ultimate harm of the workers.

Such interference would hamper individuality; would make the workers feel that they were restricted and held down. While the workers are, under Scientific Management, supposed to be under the supervision of some one who can see that the work is only such as they can do and continuously thrive, any such interference as, for example, stopping a harmless race, would at once make them feel that their individual initiative was absolutely destroyed.

It is not the desire of Scientific Management to do anything of that sort, but rather to use every possible means to make the worker feel that his initiative is being conserved.

All "Native Reactions" Act as Incentives

Pride, self-confidence, pugnacity, — all the "native reactions" utilized by teaching serve as direct incentives.

Results of Incentives to the Work

All incentives in every form of management, tend, from their very nature, to increase output. When Scientific Management is introduced, there is selection of such incentives as will produce greatest amount of specified output, and the results can be predicted.

Results of Incentives to the Worker

Under Traditional Management the incentives are usually such that the worker is likely to overwork himself if he allows himself to be driven by the incentive. This results in bodily exhaustion. So, also, the anxiety that accompanies an unstandardized incentive leads to mental exhaustion. With the introduction of Transitory Management, danger from both these types of exhaustion is removed. The incentive is so modified that it is instantly subject to judgment as to its ultimate value.

Scientific Management makes the incentives stronger than they are under any other type, partly by removing sources of worry, waste and hesitation, partly by determining the ratio of incentive to output. The worker under such incentives gains in bodily and mental poise and security.

9

Welfare and Development

Definition of Welfare

"Welfare" means "a state or condition of doing well; prosperous or satisfactory course or relation; exemption from evil;" in other words, well-being.

This is the primary meaning of the word. But, today, it is used so often as an adjective, to describe work which is being attempted for the good of industrial workers, that any use of the word welfare has that fringe of meaning to it.

"Welfare" Here Includes Two Meanings

In the discussion of welfare in this chapter, both meanings of the word will be included.

"Welfare" under each form of management will be discussed, first, as meaning the outcome to the men of the type of management itself; and second, as discussing the sort of welfare work which is used under that form of management.

Discussion of First Answers, Three Questions

A discussion of welfare as the result of work divides itself naturally into three parts, or three questions:

What is the effect upon the physical life?

What is the effect upon the mental life?

What is the effect upon the moral life?

Under Traditional Management no Physical Improvement

The indefiniteness of Traditional Management manifests itself again in this discussion, it being almost impossible to make any general statement which could not be controverted by particular examples; but it is safe to say that in general, under Traditional Management, there is not a definite physical improvement in the average worker. In the first place, there is no provision for regularity in the work. The planning not being done ahead, the man has absolutely no way of knowing exactly what he will be called upon to do. There being no measure of fatigue, he has no means of knowing whether he can go to work the second part of the day, say, with anything like the efficiency with which he could go to work in the first part of the day. There being no standard, the amount of work which he can turn out must vary according as the tools, machinery and equipment are in proper condition, and the material supplies his needs.

No Good Habits Necessarily Formed

In the second place, under Traditional Management there are no excellent habits necessarily formed. The man is left to do fairly as he pleases, if only the general outcome be considered sufficient by those over him. There may be a physical development on his part, if the work be of a kind which can develop him, or which he likes to such an extent that he is willing to do enough of it to develop him physically; this liking may come through the play element, or through the love of work, or through the love of contest, or through some other desire for activity, but it is not provided for scientifically, and the outcome cannot be exactly predicted. Therefore, under Traditional Management there is no way of knowing that good health and increased strength will result from the work, and we know that in many cases poor health and depleted strength have been the outcome of the work. We may say then fairly, as far as physical improvement is concerned that, though it might be the outcome of Traditional Management, it was rather in spite of Traditional Management, in the sense at least that the management had nothing to do with it, and had absolutely no way of providing for it. The moment that it was provided for in any systematic way, the Traditional Management vanished.

No Directed Mental Development

Second, mental development. Here, again, there being no fixed habits, no specially trained habit of attention, no standard, there was no way of knowing that the man's mind was improving. Naturally, all minds improve merely with experience. Experience must be gathered in, and must be embodied into judgment. There is absolutely no way of estimating what the average need in this line would be, it varies so much with the temperament of the man. Again, it would usually be a thing that the man himself was responsible for, and not the management, certainly not the management in any impersonal sense. Some one man over an individual worker might be largely responsible for improving him intellectually. If this were so, it would be because of the temperament of the overman, or because of his friendly desire to impart a mental stimulus; seldom, if ever, because the management provided for its being imparted. Thus, there was absolutely no way of predicting that wider or deeper interest, or that increased mental capacity, would take place.

Moral Development Doubtful

As for moral development, in the average Traditional Management it was not only not provided for, but rather doubtful. A man had very little chance to develop real, personal responsibilities, in that there was always some one over him who was watching him, who disciplined him and corrected him, who handed in the reports for him, with the result that he was in a very slight sense a free agent. Only men higher up, the foremen and the superintendents could obtain real development from personal responsibilities. Neither was there much development of responsibility for others, in the sense of being responsible for personal development of others. Having no accurate standards to judge by, there was little or no possibility of appreciation of the relative standing of the men, either by the individual of himself, or by others of his ability. The man could be admired for his strength, or his skill, but not for his real efficiency, as measured in any satisfactory way. The management taught self-control in the most rudimentary way, or not at all. There was no distinct goal for the average man, neither was there any distinct way to arrive at such a goal; it was simply a case, with the man lower down, of making good for any one day and getting that day's pay. In the more enlightened forms of Traditional Management, a chance for promotion was always fairly sure, but the moment that the line of promotion became assured, we may say that Traditional Management had really ceased, and some form of Transitory Management was in operation.

"Square Deal" Lacking

Perhaps the worst lack under Traditional Management is the lack of the "square deal." In the first place, even the most efficient worker under this form of management was not sure of his place. This not only meant worry on his part, which distracted his attention from what he did, but meant a wrong attitude all along the line.

He had absolutely no way of knowing that, even though he did his best, the man over him, in anger, or because of some entirely ulterior thing, might not discharge him, put him in a lower position. So also the custom of spying, the only sort of inspection recognized under Traditional Management of the most elementary form, led to a feeling on the men's part that they were being constantly watched on the sly, and to an inability to concentrate.

This brought about an inability to feel really honest, for being constantly under suspicion is enough to poison even one's own opinion of one's integrity. Again, being at the beck and call of a prejudiced foreman who was all-powerful, and having no assured protection from the whims of such a man, the worker was obliged, practically for self-protection, to try to conciliate the foremen by methods of assuming merits that are obvious, on the surface. He ingratiates himself in the favour of the foreman in that way best adapted to the peculiarities of the character of the foreman, sometimes joining societies, or the church of the foreman, sometimes helping him elect some political candidate or relative; at other times, by the more direct method of buying drinks, or taking up a subscription for presenting the foreman with a gold watch, "in appreciation of his fairness to all;" sometimes by consistently losing at cards or other games of chance. When it is considered that this same foreman was probably, at the time, enjoying a brutal feeling of power, it is no wonder that no sense of confidence of the "square deal" could develop.

There are countless ways that the brutal enjoyment of power could be exercised by the man in a foreman's position. As has already been said, some men prefer promotion to a position of power more than anything else. Nearly all desire promotion to power for the extra money that it brings, and occasionally, a man will be found who loves the power, although unconsciously, for the pleasure he obtains in lording over other human beings.

This quality is present more or less in all human beings. It is particularly strong in the savage, who likes to torture captured human beings and animals, and perhaps the greatest test for high qualifications of character and gentleness is that of having power over other human beings without unnecessarily accenting the difference in the situation. Under Military Management, there is practically no limit to this power, the management being satisfied if the foreman gets the work out of the men, and the men having practically no one to appeal to, and being obliged to receive their punishment always from the hands of a prejudiced party.

Little Possibility of Development of Will

Being under such influence as this, there is little or no possibility of the development of an intelligent will. The "will to do" becomes stunted, unless the pay is large enough to lead the man to be willing to undergo abuses in order to get the money. There is nothing, moreover, in the aspect of the management itself to lead the man to have a feeling of confidence either in himself, or in the management, and to have that moral poise which will make him wish to advance.

Real Capacity not Increased

With the likelihood of suspicion, hate and jealousy arising, and with constant preparations for conflict, of which the average union and employers' association is the embodiment, naturally, real capacity is not increased, but is rather decreased, under this form of management, and we may ascribe this to three faults:

First, to lack of recognition of individuality, — men are handled mostly as gangs, and personality is sunk.

Second, to lack of standardization, and to lack of time study, that fundamental of all standardization, which leads to absolute inability to make a measured, and therefore scientific judgment, and

Third, to the lack of teaching; to the lack of all constructiveness.

These three lacks, then, constitute a strong reason why Traditional Management does not add to the welfare of the men.

Little Systematized Welfare Work Under Traditional Management

As for welfare work, — that is, work which the employers themselves plan to benefit the men, if under such work be included timely impulses of the management for the men, and the carrying of these out in a more or less systematic way, it will be true to say that such welfare work has existed in all times, and under all forms of management. The kind-hearted man will show his kind heart wherever he is, but it is likewise true to say that little systematic beneficial work is done under what we have defined as Traditional Management.

Definite Statements as to Welfare Under Transitory Management Difficult to Make

It is almost impossible to give any statement as to the general welfare of workers under Transitory Management, because, from the very nature of the case, Transitory Management is constantly changing. In the discussion of the various chapters, and in showing how individuality, functionalization, measurement, and so on, were introduced, and the psychological effect upon the men of their being introduced, welfare was more or less unsystematically considered. In turning to the discussion under Scientific Management and showing how welfare is the result of Scientific Management and is incorporated in it, much as to its growth will be included.

Welfare Work Under Transitory Management is Usually Commendable

As to the welfare work under Transitory Management, much could be said, and much has been said and written. Typical Welfare Work under Transitory Management deserves nothing but praise. It is the result of the dedication of many beautiful lives to a beautiful cause. It consists of such work as building rest rooms for the employees, in providing for amusements, in providing for better working conditions, in helping to better living conditions, in providing for some sort of a welfare worker who can talk with the employees and benefit them in every way, including being their representative in speaking with the management.

An Underlying Flaw is Apparent

There can be no doubt that an enormous quantity of good has been done by this welfare work, both positively, to the employees themselves, and indirectly, to the management, through fostering a kinder feeling. There is, however, a flaw to be found in the underlying principles of this welfare work as introduced in Transitory Management, and that is that it takes on more or less the aspect of a charity, and is so regarded both by the employees and by the employer. The employer, naturally, prides himself more or less upon doing something which is good, and the employe naturally resents more or less having something given to him as a sort of charity which he feels his by right.

Its Effect is Detrimental

The psychological significance of this is very great. The employer, feeling that he has bestowed a gift, is, naturally, rather chagrined to find it is received either as a right, or with a feeling of resentment. Therefore, he is often led to decrease what he might otherwise do, for it is only an unusual and a very high type of mind that can be satisfied simply with the doing of the good act, without the return of gratitude. On the other hand, the employe, if he be a man of pride, may resent charity even in such a general form as this, and may, with an element of rightness, prefer that the money to be expended be put into his pay envelope, instead. If it is simply a case of better working conditions, something that improves him as an efficient worker for the management, he will feel that this welfare work is in no sense something which he receives as a gift, but rather something which is his right, and which benefits the employer exactly as much, if not more than it benefits him.

Welfare Work Not Self-perpetuating

Another fault which can be found with the actual administration of the welfare work, is the fact that it often disregards one of the fundamental principles of Scientific Management, in that the welfare workers themselves do not train enough people to follow in their footsteps, and thus make welfare self-perpetuating.

In one case which the writer has in mind, a noble woman is devoting her life to the welfare of a body of employees in an industry which greatly requires such work. The work which she is doing is undoubtedly benefiting these people in every aspect, not only of their business but of their home lives, but it is also true that should she be obliged to give up the work, or be suddenly called away, the work would practically fall to pieces. It is built up upon her personality, and, wonderful as it is, its basis must be recognized as unscientific and temporary.

Scientific Provision for Welfare Under Scientific Management

Under Scientific Management general welfare is provided for by: —

The effect that the work has on physical improvement. This we shall discuss under three headings —

1. the regularity of the work.
2. habits.
3. physical development.

As for the regularity of the work — we have;

(a) The apportionment of the work and the rest. Under Scientific Management, work time and rest time are scientifically apportioned. This means that the man is able to come to each task with the same amount of strength, and that from his work he gains habits of regularity.

(b) The laying out of the work. The standards upon which the instruction cards are based, and the method of preparing them, assure regularity.

(c) The manner of performing the work. Every time that identical work is done, it is done in an identical manner.

The resulting regularity has an excellent effect upon the physical welfare of the worker.

Habits, under Scientific Management;

(a) are prescribed by standards. The various physical habits of the man, the motions that are used, having all been timed and then standardized, the worker acquires physical habits that are fixed.

(b) are taught; therefore they are not remote but come actually and promptly into the consciousness and into the action of the worker.

(c) are retained, because they are standard habits and because the rewards which are given for using them make it an object to the worker to retain them.

(d) are reënforced by individuality and functionalization; that is to say, the worker is considered as an individual, and his possibilities are studied, before he is put into the work; therefore, his own individuality and his own particular function naturally reënforce those habits which he is taught to form. These habits, being scientifically derived, add to physical improvement.

Physical development;

(a) is fostered through the play element, has been scientifically studied, and is utilized as far as possible; the same is true of the love of work, which is reënforced by the fact that the man has been placed where he will have the most love for his work.

(b) is insured by the love of contest, which is provided for not only by contest with others, but by the constant contest of the worker with his own previous records. When he does exceed these records he utilizes powers which it is for his good physically, as well as otherwise, to utilize.

Results of Physical Improvement

This regularity, good habits, and physical development, result in good health, increased strength and a better appearance. To these three results all scientific managers testify. An excellent example of this is found in Mr. Gantt's "Work, Wages and Profits," where the increased health, the better color and the better general appearance of the workers under Scientific Management is commented on as well as the fact that they are inspired by their habits to dress themselves better and in every way to become of a higher type. Mental Development

Welfare under Scientific Management is provided for by Mental Development. This we may discuss under habits, and under general mental development.

1. As for habits we must consider;
   (a) Habits of attention. Under Scientific Management, as we have shown, attention must become a habit. Only when it does become a habit, can the work required be properly performed, and the reward received. As only those who show themselves capable of really receiving the reward are considered to be properly placed, ultimately all who remain at work under Scientific Management must attain this habit of attention.
   (b) Habit of method of attack. This not only enables the worker to do the things that he is assigned satisfactorily, but also has the broadening effect of teaching him how to do other things, i.e., showing him the "how" of doing things, and giving him standards which are the outcome of mental habits, and by which he learns to measure.
2. General mental development is provided for by the experience which the worker gets not only in the general way in which all who work must give experience, but in the set way provided for by Scientific Management. This is so presented to the worker that it becomes actually usable at once. This not only allows him to judge others, but provides for self-knowledge, which is one of the most valuable of all of the outcomes of Scientific Management. He becomes mentally capable

of estimating his own powers and predicting what he himself is capable of doing. The outcome of this mental development is

(a) wider interest.

(b) deeper interest.

(c) increased mental capabilities.

The better method of attack would necessarily provide for wider interest. The fact that any subject taken up is in its ultimate final unit form, would certainly lead to deeper interest; and the exercise of these two faculties leads to increased mental capabilities.

Moral Development

Moral development under Scientific Management results from the provisions made for cultivating —

1. Personal responsibility is developed by;

   (a) Individual recognition. When the worker was considered merely as one of a gang, it was very easy for him to shift responsibilities upon others. When he knows that he is regarded by the management, and by his mates, as an individual, that what he does will show up in an individual record, and will receive individual reward or punishment, necessarily personal responsibility is developed.

   Moreover, this individual recognition is brought to his mind by his being expected to fill out his own instruction card. In this way, his personal responsibility is specifically brought home to him.

   (b) The appreciation which comes under Scientific Management. This appreciation takes the form of reward and promotion, and of the regard of his fellow-workers; therefore, being a growing thing, as it is under Scientific Management, it insures that his personal responsibility, shall also be a growing thing, and become greater the longer he works under Scientific Management.

2. Responsibility for others is provided for by the interrelation of all functions. It is not necessary that all

workers under Scientific Management should understand all about it. However, many do understand, and the more that they do understand, the more they realize that everybody working under Scientific Management is more or less dependent upon everybody else. Every worker must feel this, more or less, when he realizes that there are eight functional bosses over him, who are closely related to him, on whom he is dependent, and who are more or less dependent upon him. The very fact that the planning is separated from the performing, means that more men are directly interested in any one piece of work; in fact, that every individual piece of work that is done is in some way a bond between a great number of men, some of whom are planning and some of whom are performing it. This responsibility for others is made even more close in the dependent bonuses which are a part of Scientific Management, a man's pay being dependent upon the work of those who are working under him. Certainly, nothing could bring the fact more closely to the attention of each and every worker under this system, than associating it with the pay envelope.

3. Appreciation of standing is fostered by;
   (a) individual records. Through these the individual himself knows what he has done, his fellows know, and the management knows.
   (b) comparative records, which show even those who might not make the comparison, exactly how each worker stands, with relation to his mates, or with relation to his past records.

   This appreciation of standing is well exemplified in the happy phrasing of Mr. Gantt — "There is in every workroom a fashion, or habit of work, and the new worker follows that fashion, for it isn't respectable not to. The man or woman who ignores fashion does not get much pleasure from associating with those that follow it, and the new member consequently tries to fall in with the sentiment of the community. Our chart shows that the stronger the sentiment in favour of industry is, the harder the new member tries and the sooner he succeeds."

4. Self-control is developed by;
   (a) the habits of inhibition fostered by Scientific Management, — that is to say, when the right habits are formed, necessarily many wrong habits are eliminated. It becomes a part of Scientific Management to inhibit all inattention and wrong habits, and to concentrate upon the things desired. This is further aided by
   (b) the distinct goal and the distinct task which Scientific Management gives, which allow the man to hold himself well in control, to keep his poise and to advance steadily.
5. "Squareness." This squareness is exemplified first of all by the attitude of the management. It provides, in every way, that the men are given a "square deal," in that the tasks assigned are of the proper size, and that the reward that is given is of the proper dimensions, and is assured. This has already been shown to be exemplified in many characteristics of Scientific Management, and more especially in the inspection and in the disciplining.

Moral Development Results in Contentment, Brotherhood and the "Will To Do".

The three results of this moral development are;

1. Contentment is the outgrowth of the personal responsibility, the appreciation of standing, and the general "squareness" of the entire plan of Scientific Management.
2. The idea of brotherhood is fostered particularly through the responsibility for others, through the feeling that grows up that each man is dependent upon all others, and that it is necessary for every man to train up another man to take his place before he can be advanced. Thus it comes about that the old caste life, which so often grew up under Traditional Management, becomes abolished, and there ensues a feeling that it is possible

for any man to grow up into any other man's place. The tug-of-war attitude of the management and men is transformed into the attitude of a band of soldiers scaling a wall. Not only is the worker pulled up, but he is also forced up from the bottom.

3. The "will to do" is so fostered by Scientific Management that not only is the worker given every incentive, but he, personally, becomes inspired with this great desire for activity, which is after all the best and finest thing that any system of work can give to him.

Interrelation of Physical, Mental and Moral Development

As to the interrelation of physical, mental and moral development, it must never be forgotten that the mind and the body must be studied together, and that this is particularly true in considering the mind in management.

For the best results of the mind, the body must be cared for, and provided for, fully as much as must the mind, or the best results from the mind will not, and cannot, be obtained.

Successful management must consider the results of all mental states upon the health, happiness and prosperity of the worker, and the quality, quantity and cost of the output. That is to say, unless the mind is kept in the right state, with the elimination of worry, the body cannot do its best work, and, in the same way, unless the body is kept up to the proper standard, the mind cannot develop.

Therefore, a really good system of management must consider not only these things separately, but in their interrelation, — and this Scientific Management does.

Result of Physical, Mental and Moral Development is Increased Capacity

The ultimate result of all this physical improvement, mental development and moral development is increased capacity, increased capacity not only for work, but for health, and for life in general.

Welfare Work an Integral Part of Scientific Management

Strictly speaking, under Scientific Management, there should be no necessity for a special department of Welfare Work. It should be so incorporated in Scientific Management that it is not to be distinguished. Here the men are looked out for in such a way under the operation of Scientific Management itself that there is no necessity for a special welfare worker. This is not to say that the value of personality will disappear under Scientific Management, and that it may not be necessary in some cases to provide for nurses, for physical directors, and for advisers. It will, however, be understood that the entire footing of these people is changed under Scientific Management. It is realized under Scientific Management that these people, and their work, benefit the employers as much as the employees. They must go on the regular payroll as a part of the efficiency equipment. The workers must understand that there is absolutely no feeling of charity, or of gift, in having them; that they add to the perfectness of the entire establishment.

Summary

Results of Welfare to the Work

Because of Welfare Work, of whatever type, more and better work is accomplished, with only such expenditure of effort as is beneficial to the worker. Not only does the amount of work done increase, but it also tends to become constant, after it has reached its standard expected volume.

Result of Welfare Work to the Worker

This description of welfare of the men under Scientific Management, in every sense of the word welfare, has been very poor and incomplete if from it the reader has not deduced the fact that Scientific Management enables the worker not only to lead a fuller life in his work, but also outside his work; that it furnishes him hours enough free from the work to develop such things as the work cannot develop; that it furnishes him with health and interest enough to go into his leisure hours with a power to develop himself there; that it furnishes him with a broader outlook, and, best of all, with a capacity of judging for himself what he needs most to get. In other words, if Scientific Management is what it claims to be, it leads to the development of a fuller life in every sense of the word, enabling the man to become a better individual in himself, and a better member of his community. If it does not do this it is not truly Scientific Management. Miss Edith Wyatt has said, very beautifully, at the close of her book, "Making Both Ends Meet" : "No finer dream was ever dreamed than that the industry by which the nation lives, should be so managed as to secure for the men and women engaged in it their real prosperity, their best use of their highest powers. How far Scientific Management will go toward realizing the magnificent dream in the future, will be determined by the greatness of spirit and the executive genius with which its principles are sustained by all the people interested in its inauguration, the employers, the workers and the engineers."

We wish to modify the word "dream" to the word "plan." The plan of Scientific Management is right, and, as Miss Wyatt says, is but waiting for us to fulfil the details that are laid out before us.

10

Vocational Education and Employability

Vocational education or *vocational education and training* (VET) prepares trainees for jobs that are based on manual or practical activities, traditionally non-academic, and totally related to a specific trade, occupation, or *vocation*. It is sometimes referred to as *technical education* as the trainee directly develops expertise in a particular group of techniques or technology.

Vocational education may be classified as teaching procedural knowledge. This can be contrasted with declarative knowledge, as used in education in a usually broader scientific field, which might concentrate on theory and abstract conceptual knowledge, characteristic of tertiary education. Vocational education can be at the secondary or post-secondary level and can interact with the apprenticeship system. Increasingly, vocational education can be recognised in terms of recognition of prior learning and partial academic credit towards tertiary education (e.g., at a university) as credit; however, it is rarely considered in its own form to fall under the traditional definition of higher education.

Up until the end of the twentieth century, vocational education focused on specific trades such as, for example, those of automobile mechanic or welder, and it was therefore associated with the activities of lower social classes. As a consequence, it carries some social stigma. Vocational education is related to the age-old apprenticeship system of learning. However, as the labour market becomes more specialized and economies demand higher levels of skill, governments and businesses are increasingly investing in the future of vocational education through publicly funded training organizations and subsidized apprenticeship or traineeship initiatives for businesses. At the post-secondary level vocational education is typically provided by an institute of technology, or by a local community college.

Vocational education has diversified over the 20th century and now exists in industries such as retail, tourism, information technology, funeral services and cosmetics, as well as in the traditional crafts and cottage industries.

Employability

Employability refers to a person's capability of gaining initial employment, maintaining employment, and obtaining new employment if required. In simple terms, employability is about being capable of getting and keeping fulfilling work. More comprehensively, employability is the capability to move self-sufficiently within the labour market to realise potential through sustainable employment. For individuals, employability depends on the knowledge, skills and abilities (KSAs) they possess, the way they use those assets and present them to employers, and the context (e.g. personal circumstances and labour market environment) within which they seek work.

Employability is a two-sided equation and many individuals need various forms of support to overcome the physical and mental barriers to learning and personal development (i.e. updating their assets). Employability is not just about vocational and academic skills. Individuals need relevant and usable labour market information to help them make informed decisions about the labour market options available to them. They may also need support to realise when such information would be useful, and to interpret that information and turn it into intelligence.

Finally, people also need the opportunities to do things differently, to access relevant training and, most crucially, employment. Both the supply and demand of labour need to be taken into account when defining employability, which is often dependent on factors outside of an individual's control.

Employability was one of the four 'pillars' of the European Employment Strategy until its reformulation in 2000, along with entrepreneurship, adaptability and equal opportunities. It has thus also been a key theme of the EQUAL Community Initiative. For individuals, employability depends on:

- their assets in terms of the knowledge, skills and attitudes they possess
- the way they use and deploy those assets
- the way they present them to employers
- crucially, the context (e.g. personal circumstances and labour market environment) within which they seek work.

The balance of importance between and within each element will vary for groups of individuals, depending on their relationship to the labour market.

Government policy is aimed:

- more at the development and accreditation of knowledge and vocational skills than at the 'softer' skills and attitudes
- more on the demonstration of assets than their deployment — particularly for adults (e.g. lack of provision of a careers education and guidance service for adults)
- more at individuals looking to enter the labour market (e.g. from education or unemployment) than within
- more on the individual and the supply side, than on employers and the demand side (i.e. the labour market contextual factors).

Four Components of Employability

This suggests that we can separate out four main elements in respect of individuals' employability: the first three are analogous to the concepts of production, marketing and sales, and the fourth the marketplace in which they operate.

Assets

An individual's 'employability assets' comprise their knowledge (i.e. what they know), skills (what they do with what they know) and attitudes (how they do it). There are a number of detailed categorisations in the literature which, for instance, distinguish between:

- 'baseline assets' such as basic skills and essential personal attributes (such as reliability and integrity).
- 'intermediate assets' such as occupational specific skills (at all levels), generic or key skills (such as communication and problem solving) and key personal attributes (such as motivation and initiative), and
- 'high level assets' involving skills which help contribute to organizational performance (such as team working, self management, commercial awareness etc.)

Further key points from the literature include the importance of the transferability of these skills from one occupational or business context to another for employability and the increased attention employers are paying to the softer attitudinal skills in selecting employees. Merely being in possession of employer-relevant knowledge, skills and attitudes is not enough for an individual to either 'move self-sufficiently' in the modern labour market or 'realise their potential'. People also need the capability to exploit their assets, to market them and sell them.

Deployment

These are a linked set of abilities which include:

- Career management skills and life skills — commonly identified as self-awareness (i.e. diagnosing occupational interests and abilities), opportunity awareness (knowing what work opportunities exist and their entry requirements i.e. labour market knowledge), decision-making skills (to develop a strategy of getting from where you are to where you want to be) and transition skills. The latter generally includes:
- Job search skills — i.e. finding suitable jobs. Access to formal and informal networks is an important component of job search and employability.
- Strategic approach — being adaptable to labour market developments and realistic about labour market opportunities, be occupationally and locationally mobile.

There is obviously an important inter-relationship between assets and deployment. The extent to which an individual is aware of what they possess in terms of knowledge, skills and attitudes and its relevance to the employment opportunities available may affect their willingness to undertake training and other activities designed to upgrade their skills etc.

Presentation

Another key aspect of employability is being able to get a particular job, once identified — sometimes included under career management skills, but is given prominence as a separate element here due to its crucial importance to securing employment. It centres around the ability to demonstrate 'employability' assets and present them to the market in an accessible way. This includes:

- the presentation of CVs etc., (including Records of Achievement)
- the qualifications individuals possess (both academic and vocational), perhaps accredited through prior learning
- references and testimonies
- interview technique, and, of particular importance,
- work experience/track record.

In the Context of Personal Circumstances and the Labour Market

Finally and crucially, the ability to realise or actualise 'employability' assets depends on the individual's personal and external circumstances and the inter-relationship between the two. This includes:

- personal circumstances — e.g. caring responsibilities, disabilities, and household status can all affect their ability to seek different opportunities and will vary during an individual's life cycle; while
- external factors such as macro-economic demand and the pattern and level of job openings in their labour market, be it local or national; labour market regulation and benefit rules; and employer recruitment and selection behaviour.

Priorities for Action

For the state, as well as raising the skill profile of the existing workforce, especially at lower levels to boost flexibility and competitiveness, there are a number of potential priority groups including:

- labour market entrants
- labour market re-entrants
- disadvantaged groups
- insecure or under-utilised employees.

Where different policies may need to be targeted according to different circumstances.

For employers the priorities might be to help key groups of staff to develop both those assets which have explicit, immediate value to the organization as well as those transferable ones which have a wider, longer term currency, thereby engendering a sense of security, encouraging commitment, risk-taking and flexibility among employees.

For the individual the need is to boost those aspects of their employability which will most enhance their opportunities in the light of their circumstances.

Issues for Public Policy

The above definition of employability provides a basis for analysing the policies affecting the employability of certain groups (e.g. 16 and 17-year-old school leavers), or conversely how major policy initiatives (e.g. the New Deal) impact on employability. A brief review of government initiatives in this area suggests that policy is aimed:

- more at the development and accreditation of knowledge and vocational skills than at the 'softer' skills and attitudes
- more on the demonstration of assets than their deployment — particularly for adults (e.g. lack of provision of a careers education and guidance service for adults)
- more at individuals looking to enter the labour market (e.g. from education or unemployment) than within

- more on the individual and the supply side, than on employers and the demand side (i.e. the labour market contextual factors).

This policy orientation may reflect a variety of factors such as difficulties in defining, assessing and verifying 'soft skills', and difficulties identifying and accessing specific groups of employees at which to target limited resources.

Thus some key questions for future policy interventions include:

- who are the priority groups
- where the most serious gaps are for such groups be they related to e.g. which assets, dimensions of deployment or presentational skills
- how these gaps might best be remedied and
- which of the arms of public policy are best placed to add such value and how through interventions.

Finally, whatever the interventions, they need to be evaluated so that lessons can be fed back into further improvements and to the decision to continue with, change or stop such interventions. Potential measures include those relating to input measures, e.g. possession of vocational qualifications, or the receipt of careers management training; perception measures, e.g. the views of employers and the workforce of their employability; and outcome measures, e.g. the speed at which people are able to get jobs or 'measurements of failure', e.g. the numbers or proportion of people with difficulty finding or keeping work, or the number of job changes, however defined. Obviously there is room for some combination of all three. Whatever route is chosen, it is important to take account of the overall state of the labour market and how it is changing, to take account of any dead-weight effect and assess true additionality.

Duality of Employability

An alternative account of employability takes a more relative approach. Brown and Hesketh define employability as 'the relative chances of getting and maintaining different kinds of employment' (2004).

While most people view employability in absolute terms, focussing on the need for individuals to obtain credentials, knowledge and social status, the concept of employability can also be seen as subjective and dependent on contextual factors. 'Employability not only depends on whether one is able to fulfil the requirements of specific jobs, but also on how one stands relative to others within a hierarchy of job seekers'. Taking the supply and demand of labour into account challenges the idea that credentials, knowledge and social status alone will guarantee a good position in the labour market.

With the move to a more knowledge based economy, it is widely thought that there is an increasing demand for high-calibre managerial talent. However, a focus on obtaining skills in order to gain good employment has led to an over-supply of graduates and a larger number of contenders chasing the same top jobs. Brown and Hesketh argue that there is a clear mismatch between individuals' expectations of employability and the realities posed by the labour market.

Under these conditions, students will use a number of tactics in the labour market to maintain competitive advantage. Brown and Hesketh identify two ideal types of individuals entering the labour market. Those who will do anything to get a top job are classed as 'players'. Players are not afraid to take on a different identity if they feel that is what the employer is looking for. The second type, 'purists', are those who believe that job market outcomes should reflect meritocratic achievement. For purists it is important to maintain an authentic sense of self as this will ensure a good fit between individual capabilities and occupational demands. Purists may be as competitive as Players but feel that Players are cheating in order to get ahead.

This view of employability incorporates the dual aspects of supply and demand of labour to show that advancing one's position in the labour market by gaining credentials is partially dependent on structural factors outside the individual's control. The recent financial crisis demonstrates that global economic factors can and do have a significant impact on the likelihood of an individual securing a job regardless of their skills, credentials and social status.

Increasing Human Efficiency by Live Factors in Management

The modern business man is the true heir of the old magicians. Every thing he touches seems to increase ten or a hundredfold in value and usefulness. All the old methods, old tools, old instruments have yielded to his transforming spell or else been discarded for new and more effective substitutes. In a thousand industries the profits of today are wrung from the wastes or unconsidered trifles of yesterday.

The only factor which has withstood this wizard touch is man himself. Development of the instruments of production and distribution has been so great it can hardly be measured: the things themselves have been so changed that few features of their primitive models have been retained.

Our railroad trains, steamships, and printing presses preserve a likeness more apparent than actual. Our telephones, electric lights, gas engines, and steam turbines, our lofty office buildings and huge factories crowded with wonderful automatic machinery are creations of the generation of business men and scientists still in control of them. By comparison the increase in human efficiency during this same period (except where the worker is the slave of the machine, compelled to keep pace with it or lose his place) has been insignificant.

Reasons for this disproportion are not lacking. The study of the physical antedates the study of the mental always. In the history of the individual as well as of nations, knowledge of the psychical has dragged far behind mastery of tangible objects. We come in contact with our physical environment and adjust ourselves to it long before we begin to study the acts by which we have been able to control objects around us.

It was inevitable, therefore, that attention should have been concentrated upon the material and mechanical side of production and distribution. Results there were so tangible, so easily figured. For example, if the speed of a drill or the strokes of a punch press were multiplied, the increase would be easily recognized. The whole country, too, was absorbed in invention, in the development of tools to accomplish what had always required hand labour. The effort was not so much to increase the efficiency of the individual worker— though many wise and far-sighted employers essayed studies and experiments with varying success—as to displace the human factor altogether.

As the functions and limitations of machinery have become clearer in recent years, business men have generally recognized the importance of the human factor in making and marketing products. Selecting and handling men is of much more significance today than ever before in the history of the world —the more so as organizations have increased in size and scope and the individual employee is farther removed from the head and assigned greater responsibilities.

It is not a difficult task to build and equip a factory, to choose and stock a store. The problems of power and its transmission come nearer solution every day. Physics and chemistry have revealed the secrets of raw materials.

For any given service, the manufacturer can determine the cheapest and most suitable metal, wood, or fabric which will satisfy his requirements, and the most economical method of treating it. Of the elements involved in production or distribution, the human factor is today the most serious problem confronting the business man. The individual remains to be studied, trained, and developed—to be brought up to the standard of maximum results already reached by materials and processes.

Few employers can gather a force of efficient workers and keep them at their best. Not only is it difficult to select the right men but it is even harder to secure top efficiency after they are hired. Touching this, there will be no dispute. Experts in shop management go even farther. F. W. Taylor, who has made the closest and most scientific study, perhaps, of actual and potential efficiency among workers, declares that:—

"A first-class man can, in most cases, do from two to four times as much as is done on the average."

"This enormous difference," Mr. Taylor goes on to say, "exists in all the trades and branches of labour investigated, from pickand-shovel men all the way up the scale to machinists and other skilled workmen. The multiplied output was not the product of a spurt or a period of overexertion; it was simply what a good man could keep up for a long term of years without injury to his health, become happier, and thrive under."

Ask the head of any important business what is the first qualification of a foreman or manager, and he will tell you "ability to handle men."

Men who know how to get maximum results out of machines are common; the power to get the maximum of work out of subordinates or out of yourself is a much rarer possession.

Yet this power is not necessarily a sixth sense or a fixed attribute of personality. It is based on knowledge of the workings of the other man's mind, either intuitive or acquired. It is the purpose of this and succeeding chapters to consider some of the aspects of human nature that can be turned to advantage in the cultivation of individual efficiency and the elimination of lost motion and wasted effort.

In a thousand instances, in factory and market place, unrecognized use has been made of the principles of psychology by business men to influence other men and to attain their ends. For the science of psychology is in respect to certain data merely common sense, the wisdom of experience, analysed, formulated, and codified. It has taken its place, alongside physics and chemistry, as the ally and employee of trade and industry.

The time has come when a man's knowledge of his business, if the larger success is to be won, must embrace an understanding of the laws which govern the thinking and acting of the men who make and sell his products as well as those others who buy and consume them.

The achievements of the human mind and the human body seem to many to be out of the range of possible improvement through application of any science which deals with these human activities. Muscular strength and mental efficiency seem to be fixed quantities not subject to increase or improvement.

The contention here supported, however, is that human efficiency is a variable quantity which increases and decreases according to law. By the application of known physical laws the telephone and the telegraph have supplanted the messenger boy. By the laws of psychology applied to business equally astounding improvements are being and will be secured.

Employers sometimes find that their men are not working well, that they loaf and kill time on every possible occasion.

The men are not trying and are indifferent to results. Under such circumstances a new foreman, the dismissal of the poorer workmen, modification of the wage scale or method of payment, or some other device may correct the evil and induce the men to exert themselves.

Again, the men are working industriously and may feel that an increase in output would be injurious to health or even impossible. They think they are doing their best; while the employer himself may feel that he is achieving but little, although he assumes that he is doing as much as it is wise to attempt. For instance, Mr. Taylor, in his studies, found that both employers and men had only a vague conception of what constituted a full day's work for a first-class man. The good workmen knew they could do more than the average; but refused to believe when, after close observation and careful timing of the elements of each operation, they were shown that they could accomplish twice or three times as much as their customary tasks.

Actual instances prove that great increase of work and results can be secured by outside stimulus and by conscious effort.

If there is one place where the limit of exertion can be counted upon, it is in an intercollegiate athletic contest. While taking part in football games, I frequently observed that my team would be able to push the opposing team halfway across the field. Then the tables would be turned and my team would give ground. At one moment one team would seem to possess much superior physical strength to the other; the next moment the equilibrium would be changed apparently without cause. Often, however, the weaker team would rally in response to the captain's coaching. On the field a player frequently finds himself unable to exert himself. His greatest effort is necessary to force himself to work. In such a mental condition a vigorous and enthusiastic appeal from the coach may supply the needed stimulus and stir him to sudden display of all his strength.

I recently conducted a series of experiments on college athletes to determine whether coaching could actually increase a man's strength when he was already trying his "best," and whether he could continue to work after he was "completely exhausted." I put each man at work on machines which allowed him to exert himself to his utmost and measured his accomplishment. While he was thus employed, the coach began urging him to increase his exertion. Ordinarily the increase was marked—sometimes as much as fifty per cent.

Again, when the man had exhausted himself without coaching, the extra demand would be made on him; usually he was able to continue, even though without the coaching he had been unable to do any more. There was, of course, a point of exhaustion at which the coaching ceased to be effective.

The tests proved conclusively that when a man is doing what he believes to be his best, he is still able to do better; when he is completely exhausted, he is, under proper stimulus, able to continue.

Before a horse is started in a race it is vigorously exercised, "warmed up." To the uninitiated this process seems so strenuous as to defeat its purpose by wearing out the strength of the horse. Every horseman knows, however, that the animal cannot attain top speed till after it has undergone this severe discipline.

In training for a contest an athlete usually takes long runs. Soon after the start he feels weary and exhausted, but, by disregarding this feeling and continuing to run, a sudden change comes over him commonly known as "getting his second wind."

Thus the runner feels wave upon wave of exhaustion followed by waves of invigoration. Had he stopped when he first began to tire, he never would have known of his wonderful reserve fund of strength which can be drawn upon only by passing through the feeling of exhaustion. He seems to be able to tap deeper and deeper reservoirs of strength.

Many men have never discovered their reserve stores of strength because they have formed the fixed habit of quitting at the first access of weariness.

Thus they never become conscious of the wonderful resources which might be used if they were willing to disregard the trifling wave of weariness.

Our best energies are not on the surface and are not available without great exertion. We have to warm up and get our second wind before we are capable of our best physical or mental accomplishments. All our muscular and psychical processes are dependent upon the activity of the nervous system. This activity seems to be at its best only after repeated and vigorous stimulation and after it has reached down to profound and widely distributed centers.

Most of us never know of our possible achievements because we have never warmed up and got our second wind in our business or professional affairs.

When an individual succeeds in tapping his reserve energies, others marvel at the tremendous tasks he accomplishes. They judge in terms of superficial energy, and for such the results would, of course, be impossible, even though many of the admiring spectators could actually equal or excel the deed.

Consider for a moment the work achieved by Mr. Edward Payson Weston who recently walked the entire distance from New York to San Francisco without halt or rest in one hundred and four days. Throughout the entire journey Mr. Weston covered about fifty miles daily, once attaining the remarkable distance of eighty-seven miles in twenty-four hours. Though Mr. Weston is seventy years of age, at the close of the walk he seemed to be relatively free from exhaustion and undaunted in spirit.

The work accomplished by such men as Gladstone and Roosevelt is incomprehensible to most of us who have never undertaken more than puny tasks. These men retain their strength and in no way seem to be undermining their health by the accomplishment of their Herculean labours. Body and mind seem to respond to the demands made upon them. Their periods of sleep and their vacations seem to be no more than the hours and days of rest required by those of us who accomplish infinitely less.

No need, however, to go beyond the field of business or industry to find men whose super-energy has carried them to epochial discoveries or feats of organization. The invention of the incandescent lamp by Edison is said to have been accomplished, for instance, only after forty-eight hours' continuous concentration on the final problem of finding the right carbon filament and determining the proper degree of vacuum in the inclosing bulb. Months of experiment and research had gone before; eighteen hours a day in the labouratory had been no uncommon thing for the inventor and his assistants, but in the last strenuous grapple with success his own physical and mental powers were alone equal to the strain. Not once during the two days and nights did he rest or sleep or take his attention from the successive tests which led up to the assembling of the lamp which lights the world's work and play.

The steel blade that is used seems to last as long as the one which is allowed to lie idle. The wearing out in the one case does not seem to be more destructive than the rusting out in the other.

We have a choice between wearing out and rusting out. Most of us unwittingly have chosen the rusting process.

This, indeed, may be said to be Edison's regular method of work, as it is the method of many other men who have accomplished great things in science and industry. Both mind and body have been trained and accustomed to exertions which seem quite impossible to ordinary individuals.

Many persons find that increased intellectual activity results in less fatigue and greater achievements. As a student I did my best work and enjoyed it most the year I carried the greatest number of courses and assumed the most outside duties. In my capacity as adviser to college students I find many who are able to accomplish thirty per cent more work than is expected of college students but fail to do equally well the regular amount. There are others who can carry the regular amount but not more without injury to their health.

College grades afford a means of recording intellectual efficiency directed toward particular problems. With no apparent change in bodily conditions the same student frequently increases his efficiency a hundred per cent. The increase seldom has an injurious effect on health, but is merely evidence of the fact that he has suddenly wakened up and is applying energies which before were undiscovered. A slow walk for a single mile leaves many persons "dragged out" and exhausted, but a brisk walk of the same or a greater distance results in invigoration and recuperation. Likewise the droning over an intellectual task results in exhaustion, while vigorous treatment whets the appetite for additional problems. This swift, decisive attack on problems was the method of Edward H. Harriman, who crowded into ten years the railroad achievements of an extraordinary lifetime. Decisions involving expenditure of many millions of dollars were arrived at so quickly as to seem off-hand, even reckless. In reality, they were the products of brief periods of intense application in which he reviewed all the conditions and elements involved, and forged his conclusion, as it were, at white heat. Back of each decision was exact and thorough knowledge of the physical and traffic conditions of each of his railroads. In the case of the Union Pacific, at least, he gained this mastery by patient, intensive study of each grade and curve and freight-producing town on its 1800 miles of track.

The inhabitant of the torrid zone upon moving to a northern climate is severely affected by the chill of the atmosphere. The discomfort may last for days or months, but he becomes acclimated and is able to withstand the cold without serious discomfort. Likewise the inhabitant of a cool climate feels exhausted by the heat of the torrid zone. In some cases he is unable to accustom himself to the change, but in many instances the acclimatization follows rapidly and leaves the individual well fortified against the dangers of excessive heat.

Persons who have accustomed themselves to stimulants of any sort are completely depleted if they are unable to get the special form to which they have been accustomed. This holds true for tobacco, morphine, coffee, and many other forms of stimulants actually indulged in by many persons. If they are able to resist the temptation and deny themselves the stimulant, the period of exhaustion soon disappears and the subject may even lose all craving for that which formerly seemed essential to his very existence. The quantity which we eat is partly a matter of habit. There is doubtless a minimum of nourishment which is absolutely necessary for health and strength. On the other hand there is doubtless a maximum limit which cannot be passed without serious injury. Our bodies seem to demand the amount of food to which we have accustomed them. If we should increase the amount ten or twenty per cent, we might, for a while, feel some discomfort from it, but soon our system would begin to demand the greater quantity and we could not again return to the lighter diet without a period of discomfort.

Likewise the amount of food which most of us consume could be reduced materially with no permanent injury or reduction of energy or danger to health. Following the reduction would be a period of discomfort and probable reduction of weight. This period would last for but a relatively short time, after which we would again strike a physiological equilibrium such that an increase of food would not be craved nor be of any benefit. Any great increase in the amount of physical or mental work results in a feeling of weariness which is usually sufficient to cause us to return to our habitual amount of expenditure of energy. Our system is, however, wonderful in its capacity to adjust itself to changed demands which come upon it, whether these demands be in the nature of changes in temperature, in stimulants, in nourishment, or in the expenditure of physical or mental energy.

There is, of course, a limit to possible human achievements. There are resources which may not be exhausted without serious injury to health. Those who accomplish most, however, compare favourably with others in length of days and retention of health.

While overwork has its place among the things which reduce energy and shorten life, it is my opinion that overwork is not so dangerous or so common as is ordinarily supposed.

In not a few industries, the dominant house or firm has for its head a man past seventy who still keeps a firm and vigorous grip on the business: men like Richard T. Crane of Chicago, E. C. Simmons of St. Louis, and James J. Hill, whose careers are records of intense industry and absorbed devotion to the work in hand.

Many persons confuse overwork with what is really underwork accompanied with worry or unhygienic practices.

A recent writer on sociology calls attention to the fact that nervous prostrations and general breakdowns are most common among those members of society who achieve the least and who may be regarded as parasites. Exercise both of brain and of muscle is necessary for growth and for health.

Those nations which expend the most energy are probably the ones among whom longevity is greatest and the mortality rate the lowest. In the city of Chicago there are many conditions adverse to health of body and mind, yet the city is famous for its relatively low mortality as a parallel fact. It is also affirmed that the average Chicago man works longer hours and actually accomplishes more than the average man elsewhere. This excess in the expenditure of energy—in so far as it is wisely spent—may be one of the reasons for the excellent health record of the city.

In every walk of life we see that the race is not to the swift nor the battle to the strong. We all know men clearly of secondary ability who nevertheless occupy high positions in business and state. We are acquainted also with men of excellent native endowment who still have never risen above the ranks of mediocrity.

Human efficiency is not measured in terms of muscular energy nor of intellectual grasp. It is dependent upon many factors other than native strength of mind and body.

The attitude which one takes toward life in general and toward his calling in particular is of more importance than native ability. The man with concentration, or the power of continued enthusiastic application, will surpass a brilliant competitor if this latter is careless and indifferent towards his work. Many who have accomplished great things in business, in the professions, and in science have been men of moderate ability. For testimony of this fact take this striking quotation from Charles Darwin.

"I have no great quickness of apprehension or wit, which is so remarkable in some clever men," he writes. "I am a poor critic.... My power to follow a long and purely abstract train of thought is very limited; and therefore I never could have succeeded with metaphysics or mathematics. My memory is extensive, yet hazy; it suffices to make me cautious by vaguely telling me that I have observed or read something opposed to the conclusion which I am drawing, or on the other hand in favour of it. So poor in one sense is my memory, that I have never been able to remember for more than a few days a single date or a line of poetry. I have a fair share of invention, and of common sense or judgment, such as every fairly successful lawyer or doctor must have, but not, I believe, in any higher degree." This is presumably an honest statement of fact, and in addition it should be remembered that Darwin was always physically weak, that for forty years he was practically an invalid and able to work for only about three hours a day. In these few hours he was able to accomplish more, however, than other men of apparently superior ability who were able to work long hours daily for many years. Darwin made the most of his ability and increased his efficiency to its maximum.

For a parallel in business, Cyrus H. McCormick might be named. The inventor of the reaper and builder of the first American business which covered the world was not a man of extraordinary intellect, wit, or judgment. He had, however, the will and power to focus his attention on a single question until the answer was evolved. Again and again, his biographers tell us, he pursued problems which eluded him far into the night and he was frequently found asleep at his desk the morning following. When roused, instead of seeking rest, he addressed his task again and usually overcame his obstacle before leaving it.

All these considerations point to one conclusion. It is quite certain, then, that most of us are whiling away our days and occupying positions far below our possibilities. A corollary to this statement is Mr. Taylor's conclusion that "few of our best-organized industries have attained the maximum output of first-class men."

Not to give too wide application to his discovery that the average day's work is only half or less than half what a first-class man can do, it is more than probable that the average man could, with no injury to his health, increase his efficiency fifty per cent. We are making use of only part of our existing mental and physical powers and are not taxing them beyond their strength. Increased accomplishments, and heightened efficiency would cultivate and develop them, would waken the latent powers and tap hidden stores of energy within us, would widen the fields in which we labour and would open up to us new and wider horizons of honourable and profitable activity.

Imitation as A Means of Increasing Human Efficiency

Twenty years ago the head of an industry now in the million-a-month class sat listening to his "star" salesman. The latter, in the first enthusiasm of discovery and creation, was telling how he had developed the company's haphazard selling talk and had taken order after order with a standard approach, demonstration, and summary of closing arguments. To prove the effectiveness of "the one best way," he challenged his employer to act as a customer, staged the little drama he had arranged, secured admissions of savings his machine would make, ultimately cornered the other, and sold him. "That's great," the owner declared the instant he had surrendered to the salesman's logic. "If we can get all our agents to learn and use this new method of yours, we'll double our business in three years."

Then followed discussion of the means by which the knowledge could be spread. "I've got it," the manager announced at last. "I'll telegraph five or six men to come in"— he named the agents within a night's ride of the factory—"and you can show them how you sold fifteen machines last week.

"We could take down your talk in shorthand and send it to them, but that wouldn't do the business. I want them to watch you sell, to study how you make your points, how you introduce yourself, how you get your man's attention, how you bring out his objections and meet them, how you lead up to the signing minute, and show him where to sign. _*What you say_ is about half the trick: _*how you say it_ is the convincing part— the thing the slowest man in the force by watching you can learn more quickly than the smartest could work out at home."

The result of that conference was one of the earliest organized training schools for salesmen in the country. It was an unconscious, but none the less certain, utilization of the instinct of _*imitation_ for increasing the efficiency in employees. Since then, business has borrowed many well-recognized principles from psychology and pedagogy and adapted them to the same end.

Many important houses have grafted the school upon their organizations and teach not only raw and untrained employees, but provide instruction calculated to make workmen and clerks masters of their jobs and also to fit them for advancement to higher and more productive planes. Teaching is by example rather than by precept, just as it was in the old apprentice system.

The newer method uses even more than the older a perfect example of the process and the product for the learner's imitation and makes them the basis of the instruction.

No man was made to live alone. For an individual, existence entirely independent of other members of the race is the conception of a dreamer; apart from others one would fail to become human. Modern psychology has abandoned the individualistic and adopted the social point of view. We no longer think of imitation as a characteristic only of animals, children, and weak-minded folk.

We have come to see that imitation is the greatest factor in the education of the young and a continuous process with all of us. The part of wisdom, then, is to utilize this power from which we cannot escape, by setting up a perfect copy for imitation.

The child brought up by a Chinaman imitates the sounds he hears, hence speaks Chinese; brought up in an American home, English is his speech—ungrammatical or correct according to the usage of his companions. If one boy in a group walks on stilts or plays marbles, the others follow his example. If a social leader rides in an automobile, wears a Panama hat, or plays golf, all the members of this circle are restless till they have the same experience. The same phenomenon is seen in the professions and in business. If one bank decides to erect a building for its own use, other banks in the city begin to consult architects. If one manufacturer or distributor in a given field adopts a new policy in manufacturing or in extending his trade zone, his rivals immediately consider plans of a similar sort. Partly, of course, this act is defensive. In the main, however, imitation and emulation are at the bottom of the move.

For the sake of clearness, in studying acts of imitation we separate them into two classes—voluntary imitation (also called conscious imitation) and instinctive_ imitation.

A peculiar signature may strike my fancy so that consciously and deliberately I may try to imitate it. This is a clear case of voluntary imitation. Threading crowded city streets, I see a man crossing at a particular point and voluntarily follow in his path. In writing letters or advertisements or magazine articles, I analyse the work of other men and consciously imitate what seems best. Or I observe a fellow-labourer working faster than I, and forthwith try to catch and hold his pace.

The contagion of yawning, on the other hand, is instinctive imitation. Also when in a crowd during the homeward evening rush, we instinctively quicken our pace though there may be no reason for hurry.

For precisely similar reasons, a "loafer" or a careless or inefficient workman will lower the efficiency or slow up the production of the men about him, no matter how earnest or industrious their natural habits. Night work by clerks, also, is taken by some office managers to indicate a slump in industry during the day. To correct this the individuals who are drags on the organization are discovered, and either are revitalized or discharged. I have seen more than one machine shop where production could have been materially raised by the simple expedient of weeding out the workmen who were satisfied with a mere living wage earned by piecework, thereby setting a dilatory example to the rest; and replacing them with fresh men ambitious to earn all they could, who would have been imitated by the others.

In these instances it is assumed that the imitation is not voluntary, but that we unconsciously imitate whatever actions happen to catch our attention. For the negative action, the "slowing down" process, we have the greater affinity simply because labour or exertion is naturally distasteful. One such influence or example, therefore, may sway us more than a dozen positive impulses towards industry.

Imitation thus broadly considered is seen to be of the utmost importance in every walk of life. The greatest and most original genius is in the main a creature of imitation. By imitation he reaches the level of knowledge and skill attained by others; and upon this foundation builds his structure of original and creative thought, experiment, and achievement. Furthermore he does not imitate at random; but concentrates his activity on those things and persons in the line of his pursuits. Among my associates are both industrious and shiftless individuals. I instinctively imitate the actions of all those with whom I come in contact; but if I am sufficiently ambitious, I will consciously imitate the acts of the industrious. This patterning after energetic models will render me more active and efficient than would have been possible for me without such examples.

Imitation, accordingly, is an imperative factor both in self-development and in the control of groups of individuals. Knowing that I instinctively imitate all sorts of acts, I must take care that only the right sort shall catch my attention_.

And since imitation is a most effective aid in development, I must provide myself with the best models. To reduce my tendency to idleness or procrastination I must avoid the companionship of the shiftless. To acquire ease and accuracy in the use of French, I must consort with masters of that tongue.

In handling others, the same rule holds;

To profit from the instinctive imitation of my men, I must control their environment in shop or office and make sure that examples of energy and efficiency are numerous enough to catch their attention and establish, as it were, an atmosphere of industry in the place_.

There are instances in which it would be to the mutual interest of employer and employee to increase the speed of work, but conditions may limit or forbid the use of pacemakers. In construction work and in some of the industries where there are minute subdivision of operations and continuity of processes this method of increasing efficiency is very commonly applied. In many factories, however, such an effort to "speed up" production might stir resentment, even among the pieceworkers, and have an effect exactly opposite to that desired. The alternative, of course, is for the employer to secure unconscious pacemakers by providing incentives for the naturally ambitious men in the way of a premium or bonus system or other reward for unusual efficiency.

To take advantage of their conscious or voluntary imitation, workpeople must be provided with examples which appeal to them as admirable and inspire the wish to emulate them. A common application of this principle is seen in the choice of department heads, foremen, and other bosses. Invariably these win promotion by industry, skill, and efficiency greater than that displayed by their fellows, or by all-round mastery of their trades which enable them to show their less efficient mates how any and all operations should be conducted.

This focusing of attention upon individuals worthy of imitation has been carried much farther by various companies. Through their "house organs"—weekly or monthly papers published primarily for circulation within the organization—they make record of every incident reflecting unusual skill, initiative, or personal power in an individual member of the organization.

A big order closed, a difficult contract secured, a complex or delicate operation performed in less than the usual time, a new personal record in production, the invention of an unproved method or machine—whatever the achievement, it is described and glorified, its author praised and held up for emulation. This, indeed, is one of the methods by which the larger sales organizations have obtained remarkable results.

Graphically told, the story of an important sale with the salesman's picture alongside makes double use of the instinct of imitation. It suggests forcibly that every man in the field can duplicate the achievement and tells how he can do it.

Frequently, examples of initiative and efficiency are borrowed from outside organizations. "Carrying a message to Garcia" has long been a business synonym for immediate and effective execution of orders. One big company, employing thousands of mechanics and developing all its executives and skilled experts from boys and men within the organization, has printed in its house organ studies of all the great American and English inventors from Stephenson and Fulton to Edison and Westinghouse. These histories emphasize the facts that these men were self taught and bench-trained, and that their achievements can be imitated by every intelligent mechanic in the organization. In teaching and learning by imitation certain modifying facts are to be kept constantly in mind. We tend to imitate everything which catches our attention, but certain things appeal more powerfully than others.

The acts of those whom I admire are particularly contagious, but I remain indifferent to the acts of those who are uninteresting. Acts showing a skill to which I aspire are immediately imitated, while acts representing stages of development from which I have escaped are less likely to be imitated. We imitate the acts of hearty, jovial individuals more than the acts of others. This point cannot be pressed too far since a surly and selfish individual often seems to corrupt a whole group. Also it is not always the acts which I admire that are imitated. If I am frequently with a lame person, I am in danger of acquiring a limp; one who stutters is clearly injurious to my freedom of speech; round shouldered friends may at first cause me to straighten up, but soon I am in danger of a droop.

That imitation is merely something to be avoided by teachers, employers, and foremen is an idea soon banished when the importance and complexity of the process is comprehended. In teaching we find precept inferior to example wherever the latter is possible. Particularly in teaching all sorts of acts of skill the imitation of perfect models is the first resort. In business, however, insufficient consideration has been given to the possibilities of imitation in increasing human efficiency.

In increasing the efficiency of your employees do you utilize imitation by

(1) placing efficient workmen where they may be imitated by the less efficient?

(2) having the men visit highly efficient establishments?

(3) bringing to the attention of your men the lives of successful men and the work of successful houses?

(4) bringing frequently to the attention of the men model methods of work?

(5) Have you observed any pronounced instance of increase or decrease in the work of a department due to imitation?

The men interviewed took a decided interest in the subject, and their answers contained much of general value. Some admitted that they had never made any conscious effort to utilize imitation as implied in the first four questions. Many others had made particular use of one or more of the methods. A few of the firms interviewed had employed all four methods with entire satisfaction.

The following is a fair representative of the answers. It is the response of a very successful general manager of a railroad:—

"I beg to give you below the answer to the questions which you have asked:—

"1. The superintendent and foremen in our shops are the most efficient we can find. They are imitated, and thus influence the less efficient.

"2. We have the heads of our departments visit other shops to see how they are progressing in the same line. If they notice anything that is better than what we have as to the output of work, we imitate it by following their methods.

"3. We have not made a practice of bringing to the attention of our employees the lives of successful men or the work of successful houses.

"4. We keep standard models of the different kinds of work in plain view of the men. If there is any doubt in their minds, they can study these models.

"5. We have observed a pronounced increase in the work of our shops, due to imitation, since in lining up our organization we put the most competent men we have at the head.

Their influence over the men in their charge increases the work, as there is no question that a good leader is imitated by the men, and the company is benefited by this imitation."

Judged by the results of the investigation the most common use of imitation is in the training or "breaking in" of new employees. The accepted plan is to pick out the most expert and intelligent workman available and put the new man in his charge.

By observing the veteran and imitating his actions, working gradually from the simpler operations to the more complex, the beginner is able to master technic and methods in the shortest possible time. The psychological moment for such instruction, of course, is the first day or the first week. New men learn much more readily than those who have become habituated to certain methods or tasks; not having had time or opportunity to experiment and learn wrong methods, they have nothing to unlearn in acquiring the right. They fall into line at once and adopt the stride and the manner of work approved by the house.

This is the specific process by which the most advanced industrial organizations develop machine hands and initiate skilled mechanics into house methods and requirements. It has been largely used by public service corporations—street-car motormen and conductors, for instance, learning their duties almost entirely by observation of experienced men either in formal schools or on cars in actual operation. Many large commercial houses give new employees regular courses in company methods before intrusting work to them; the instructor is some highly efficient specialist, who shows the beginner how to get output and quality with the least expenditure of time and energy. The same method has been adapted by leading manufacturers of machines, who call their mechanics or assemblers together at intervals and have the most expert among them show how they conduct operations in which they have attained special skill.

In the training of salesmen imitation has received its widest application in teaching new men the elements of salesmanship; in showing them how to make the individual sale; in giving old men the best and newest methods—all by imitation.

Not only is the recruit to the selling ranks in formal schools given repeated examples of the most effective ways to approach customers, to demonstrate the house goods and secure the order; but the more progressive companies, after this preliminary instruction, assign him to a training ground where he accompanies one of the company's best salesmen and merely observes how actual sales are made. Then the new man is sent out alone; usually he fails to secure as large an order as the house wants. Again the star salesman takes him in hand, analyzes the student's approach and demonstration, points out their weaknesses and, going back with the new man, makes the right kind of approach and secures a satisfactory order. For the beginner this is the most vivid lesson in salesmanship; he cannot but model his next selling effort on the lines proved so effective. The use of imitation, however, is carried further. In the monthly or semiannual district conventions of salesmen which most big organizations call, the newest and most effective selling methods are staged for the instruction both of new men and veterans. The district leader in sales, for example, or the man who has closed an order by a new or unusual argument is pitted against a salesman equally able, and the whole force sees how the successful man secured his results.

Educational trips to other factories were employed by several firms to stimulate mental alertness and the instinct of imitation in their men. These trips usually supplemented some sort of suggestion system for encouraging employees to submit to the management ideas for improving methods, machines, or products.

Cash payments were made for each suggestion adopted, quarterly prizes of ten to fifty dollars were awarded for the most valuable suggestions; and finally a dozen or a score of the men submitting the best ideas were sent on a week's tour of observation to other industrial centers and notable plants. In some instances the expense incurred was considerable, but the companies considered the money well spent. Not only were the men making helpful suggestions the very ones who would observe most wisely and profit most extensively from such educational trips, but they would bring back to their everyday tasks a new perspective, see them from a new angle, and frequently offer new suggestions which would more than save or earn the vacation cost.

Business managers, it was made plain, are coming more and more to depend upon imitation as one of the great forces in securing a maximum of efficiency without risking the rupture or rebellion which might follow if the same efficiency were sought by force or by any method of conscious compulsion. Tactfully suggested, the examples for imitation will lead men where no amount of argument or reasonable compensation will drive them. I am therefore led to suggest the following uses of imitation for increasing the efficiency of the working force.

In breaking in new recruits they should be set to imitate expert workmen in all the details possible. Gang foremen and superintendents should always be capable of "showing how" for the sake of the men under them.

The better workmen should, where possible, be located so that they will be observed by the other employees.

Inefficient help should be avoided since the example of the less efficient should become the model for the larger group.

Educational trips or tours of inspection should be regularly encouraged for both workmen and superintendents.

The deeds of successful houses should be brought to the attention of employees. Where conditions admit, pacemakers should be retained in various groups to key up the other men.

Favorable conditions should be provided for conscious and instinctive imitation for all the members of the plant.

Persons who are sociable and much liked are imitated more than others, and if efficient, are particularly valuable; but if inefficient, are especially detrimental to others. At the formal and informal meetings of the men of a house or a department, demonstrations of how to do certain definite things are very interesting and helpful to all concerned. Demonstrations should be more common.

11

Competition in Organization

Competition as a Means of Increasing Human Efficiency

Thirty years ago American steel makers were astonishing the world with new production records. What English ironmasters, intrenched in their supremacy for centuries, had regarded as a standard week's output for Bessemer converters, their young rivals in mills about the Great Lakes were doubling, trebling, and even further increasing. Hardly a month passed without a new high mark and a shift in possession of the leadership.

To this remarkable increase in efficiency William R. Jones—"Captain Bill" Jones as he was familiarly known—contributed more than any other operating man. He was a genius among executives as well as an inventor of resource and initiative—a natural leader and handler of men. When he was asked by the British Iron and Steel Institute in 1881, to explain the reasons for the amazing development in the United States, he attributed it to organization spirit of the workmen and the rivalry among the various mills.

"So long as the record made by a mill stands first," he wrote, "its workmen are content to labour at a moderate rate. But let it be known that some other establishment has beaten that record and there is no content until the rival's record is eclipsed."

It was on this idea of competition for efficiency—of production as a game and achievement as a goal—that the wonderful growth of the steel industry was based_. On the intensive development of this idea by Andrew Carnegie, within his expanding organization, hinged the tremendous progress and profits of the Carnegie Company. "The little boss" matched furnace against furnace, mill against mill, superintendent against superintendent. He scanned his weekly and monthly reports not merely for records of output, but for comparative consumption of ore, fuel, and other supplies, for time and labour costs in proportion to product.

If a superintendent, foreman, or gang failed to respond to this urging, failed to get into the race for the famous broom which crowned the stack of the champion Carnegie mill or furnace, the parallel showing of the other mills became a club to drive the laggards into line. So intense was the competition, so sharp the verbal goads applied that Jones, after resigning in indignation, parodied in sarcastic notes in this manner the Carnegie fashion of bringing executives to task: "Puppy dog number three, you have been beaten by puppy dog number two on fuel. Puppy dog number two, you are higher on labour than puppy dog number one."

How effective was this system of pitting man against man, plant against plant, was shown by the dominant position of the Carnegie Company in the trade when the Steel Corporation was launched and by the staggering value put upon its business. Indirect testimony of the same fact was given another time by Jones when he refused thousands of dollars in yearly royalties for the use of his inventions by outside companies, this though the men who sought them were personal friends and his contract with the Carnegie Company allowed such licenses. His excuse was eloquent of the power residing in the C rnegie contest for efficiency and results: leadership for his charge, the Edgar Thompson works, in output and costs, meant more to him than money and a chance to help his friends.

The Carnegie system was one of the most comprehensive applications in business of man's instinct of competition to the work of increasing individual and organization efficiency.

In the handling of executives it was carried to such extremes as few great managers would approve today. Undeniably, however, the contest idea was an important influence in the building up of a vast business in relatively brief time, while the influence on the pace of the whole industry gave the United States its present supremacy in steel and iron. It survives in the parallel comparisons of records with which the Steel Corporation measures the efficiency of its units of production and keeps its mill superintendents to the mark. It is utilized, in some degree and in varying departments, by hundreds of successful houses.

Let us analyse the facts, the habits of thought, the emotions behind competition and determine where and how it may be applied to the task of increasing our own and our employees' efficiency.

The experienced horseman knows that a horse is unable to attain his greatest speed apart from a pacemaker. The horse needs the stimulus of an equal to get under way quickly, to strike his fastest gait and to keep it up. In this particular an athlete in sprinting is like the horse. He is unable by sheer force of will to run a hundred yards in ten seconds. To achieve it he needs a competitor who will push him to his utmost effort.

The struggle for existence, one of the main factors in the evolution of man, has raged most fiercely among equals; without it, development scarcely would have been possible. So fundamental has been this struggle that the necessity for it has become firmly established within us. We require it to stimulate us to attain our highest ends.

As is made evident by a consideration of imitation we are eminently social creatures. We imitate the acts of those about us. Imitation is, however, only the first stage of our social relationship. We first imitate and then compete. I purchase an automobile in imitation of the acts of my friends, but I compete with them by securing a more powerful or swifter car. By erecting a new building because some other banker has done so, the second individual does more than imitate. He competes with the first by planning to erect a more magnificent structure and on a more commanding site. Or a great retail store, announcing a "February sale" of "white goods" or furniture, invariably tries to surpass the bargains offered by rival establishments. We do indeed imitate and compete with all our associates, but those whom we recognize as our peers are the ones who stimulate us more to the instinctive acts of imitation and competition.

Our actual equals stimulate us less than those whom we recognize as the peers of our ideal selves—of ourselves as we strive and intend to become. The man on the ladder just above me stirs me irresistibly.

The effect of one individual upon others, then, is not confined to imitation. There is a constant tendency to vary from and to excel the model. My devotion to golf is mainly due to he example of some of my friends. My ambition is to outplay these same friends. Imitation and competition, apparently antagonistic, are in reality the two expressions for our social relationships. We first imitate and then attempt to differentiate ourselves from our companions.

The manufacturer or merchant imitates his competitor, but tries also to surpass him. Indeed it is a truism that competition is the life of trade. In the shop and in the office, on the road and behind the counter, in all buying and selling, competition is essential to the greatest success. Competition, the desire to excel, is universal and instinctive. It gives a zest to our work that would otherwise be lacking. In every sphere of human activity competition seems essential for securing the best results.

We assume ordinarily that competition exists only between individuals. As a matter of fact, a slight degree of competition may be aroused between a man's present efforts and his previous records.

While not so tense or so compelling as is competition between individuals, it has the advantage of avoiding the creation of jealousies. In all the more exciting and stimulating games, rivalry between individuals is a prominent feature. In golf the game is frequently played without this factor, the only competition being with previous records or with the mythical Bogy.

Such competition adds considerable zest to the game, and the same principle is applicable to business. The most compelling rivalry is between peers; without this, however, it is possible to pit the possibilities of the present month against the achievements of the previous four weeks or the past year or even against a hypothetical individual "bogy." This bogy may be fixed by the executive, and the man induced to compete with it. Thus the dangers of competition may be minimized and the advantages of the human instinctive desire for competition be gained.

In the average well-organized business the carrying out of such a plan would not be difficult. Studying the previous records of his men, a manager or foreman could determine what each individual bogy should be. The employee should know just what the _*record is_ that he is competing with, and that his success or failure would be recorded to his credit or otherwise. Above all, the bogy must be fair and within the power of the man to accomplish.

Competition need not be confined to individuals. Frequently one city finds a stimulus in competing with another. Nations compete with one another. In any organization one section may compete with another.

In an army there may be competition between regiments. Within the regiment there may be the keenest rivalry between the different companies. We are such social creatures that we easily identify ourselves with our block, our street, our town, our social set, our party, our firm, or our department in the firm. Like teams in any game or sport, these groups may be rendered self-conscious and thus made units for competition. It is possible to create such units for competition in business organizations. In some instances individual employees of one firm are pitted against those of a competing firm, the contest proving stimulating to the men in both. In other instances the competition is restricted to the house, and similar departments or sections are the units.

The closer the parallel between the units and their activities, as in the Carnegie blast furnaces and steel mills, the more interesting and effective the competition becomes. This principle has received widest recognition and achieved greatest success in the sales department. Here individuals are on a footing of approximate equality or may be given equality by a system of handicaps based on conditions in their territories. Success has also attended the pitting of selling districts against each other. These larger competing units work against bogies of the same character as do the individual ones. The whole house may be keyed up to surpass previous records or to attain some fixed standard. To ascertain to what extent the principle of competition was consciously employed by business firms and what methods were used to apply it in increasing the efficiency of the men, a number of successful business firms were asked the following questions:—

How do you utilize competition in increasing efficiency among your employees?_

(1) Do you regard it as unwise to stimulate competition in any form?

(2) Do you encourage men to excel their own records of previous years?

(3) Do you encourage competition between men in the same department?

(4) Do you encourage competition between your own departments?

(5) Do you encourage competition with departments of competing establishments?

(6) In competition do you make it fair by "handicapping" your men?

What reward does the winner receive, e.g_.:—

(1) Monetary reward?

(2) Promotion?

(3) Public commendation?

In answers by equally successful managers great diversity of opinion prevailed. Some men were afraid of all forms of competition_.

They believed that cooperation was essential to success and that any form of competition among the men tended to lessen such cooperation. Most of the men interviewed believed that competition when wisely handled is very effective in stimulating the men. Of course, most firms try in some way to encourage their men to excel their record of previous years. The inquiry developed, however, that a few are unwilling to employ competition even in this mild form as a means to increased efficiency. Most of the firms made conscious use of this principle and were convinced of its potency.

Competition between men in the same department was approved by a majority of the firms, and its adaptability to the selling department was especially emphasized. But some of the best houses will permit no such competition. The diversity in opinion was very pronounced in answering this question.

As to encouraging competition between departments in the same firm, no general answer is satisfactory. Organizations differ widely. In many houses such competition is not practicable; in others it certainly is not to be encouraged. In many organizations which would admit of such competition the experiment had not been tried. In others it has become a regular practice and is looked upon with favour.

In competition between members of the same department or between departments the danger of jealousy and enmity seems to be so real that the greatest caution has to be observed in managing the contests. When such caution is exercised, the results are ordinarily reported upon favourably.

As to encouraging competition with departments of rival establishments, the diversity of business makes general statements unilluminating. Even where such a course is possible, some managers reject the practice as unwise. They believe that it is not best to recognize other houses or to consider them in this particular. A few firms report that they are able to stimulate their men successfully in this way, even though the conditions for such a contest are difficult to handle. Of those who utilize competition a few houses employ no handicaps to put their men on the same level and make success equally possible to all.

The principle of handicaps is so manifestly fair that organizers of contests can hardly afford to neglect this essential to the widest interest and participation in the competition_. If the little man in a country territory doesn't feel that he has a fighting chance to equal or surpass the man in the big agency, he makes no attempt to qualify. And the purpose of every contest, of course, is to get every man into the game.

Touching monetary rewards for the winners, there is practical unanimity of opinion. The winner should receive a prize in cash or its equivalent. Usually the effort is to distribute the prizes so that all who excel their average records receive compensation and recognition for the additional work. In many instances unusual increases in sales or output are rewarded by a higher rate of compensation.

That success in contests should influence promotion was generally agreed. The knowledge and energy shown are indications of capacity to occupy a better position_. The contest merely reveals such capacity; the promotion might well follow as part of the prize for the winner or winners.

Public commendation of winners in competitions is held by many firms to be bad policy. There is fear that such commendation might render the participant conceited and unfit for further usefulness. A majority of firms, however, give the widest possible publicity to such commendation. This, indeed, is the reward most generally used and apparently most keenly desired by employees. Reproduction of photographs of the winners in the house organ with an account of their achievements is the commonest acknowledgment of their success, though posting the names of the winners in various parts of the establishment is the method employed by smaller houses.

Many important houses use competition as part of their regular equipment for handling and energizing men_.

Particularly is this true of manufacturers and distributors of specialties, patented machines, trade-marked goods and lines, and wholesalers whose travellers are selling in territories where conditions are generally the same. Several firms of this sort make conscious and elabourate use of the instinct of competition in their ordinary scheme of management.

A concrete and typical illustration of its application to selling is afforded by the experience and the undoubted success of one of the largest specialty houses which distributes its products direct to the consumer.

The sales force numbers about 500 men, and executives of wide experience declare that the organization is, of its size, the most efficient in the United States. Analysis of this company's methods is most illuminating and suggestive because every phase of the instinct of competition has been exploited to the advantage of both the house and its employees.

The medium of competition is a series of contests—monthly, quarterly, even yearly which bring into play all the motives urging individuals to maximum effort and industry desire to beat bogy, ambition to win in individual contest with immediate neighbours and against the whole organization, team spirit in the matching of one group of agencies against another group, and finally organization spirit in the battle of the whole force to equal or surpass the mark which has been set for it.

The first and basic contest here is that of the individual salesman against his bogy or "sales quota_."

This quota, the monthly amount of business which each agency should produce, has been worked out with great care and has a scientific foundation. Since the great bulk of sales are made to retail merchants, the possibilities of each territory are determined by reckoning the total population of all towns containing three retailers rated by commercial agencies. For normal months there is a standard quota, a little above the monthly average of all agencies the previous year, reckoned against their total urban populations. In "rush" months, this quota is advanced from fifteen to forty per cent, as the judgment of the sales manager dictates. If general and trade conditions lead him to believe, for instance, that the month of May should produce $1,000,000 in orders, while the sum of the usual quotas is $800,000, he calls for an overplus of twenty per cent. The territory containing one per cent of the total urban population of the country, as reckoned, would then be expected to make sales equal to $10,000. This would be the agency quota for the month, and the first and most important task of the agent would be to secure it.

Because all quotas, both normal and special, are figured on the productive population of the territories and standings may be calculated by percentages, it follows that all agents are on terms of equality_.

This is essential in a contest for individual leadership as well as in team or organization matches. For at least eight months of the year, there is such a competition for the best selling record in the entire force. Variety is given to these contests and the interest of the men sustained by changing the terms of the competition. One month the chief prize will be given to the salesman who secures his quota at the earliest date; next month the award will be for the individual who first obtains a fixed sum in orders, usually $2500; leadership the third month will go to the man who gets the highest per cent of his quota during the entire period; again, the honor will fall to the agent whose net sales total the greatest for the month.

Further changes are rung and the inspirational effect of the contest immensely increased by enlarging the conditions so that every third or fourth agent is able to qualify for the month's honours and a prize_.

Here, for instance, besides the prize for the first agent selling $2500, there will be prizes— like hats, umbrellas, and so on—for every man who closes $2500 in orders before the twentieth of the month, with the attendant publicity of having his portrait and his record printed in the house organ which goes to every agent in the field and every department and executive at the factory. Before leaving the individual contests, mention should be made of the "star" club of agents who sell $30,000 or more during the year; the presidency going to the agent who first secures that total, the other official positions falling to his nearest rivals in the order in which they finish.

The team and organization contests are usually carried on simultaneously with the individual competitions. These range from matches between the forces of the big city offices, like New York, Chicago, and St. Louis, upward to district contests in which each team represents from thirty to fifty salesmen and finally to international "wars" where the American organization is pitted against all the agents abroad. Challenges from one district to another usually precipitate the district competitions; once a year there is a three months' general contest in which all the districts take part for the championship of the whole selling force.

To announce contests is a simple matter; to organize and execute them so that they are of benefit is much more difficult_.

Unless the interest of the men is focused on the contests, they are not worth while. To make them successful the firm under consideration utilized the following devices:— During the contest the house organ appeared often and was devoted almost exclusively to the contest. In it the record of each salesman was printed, his quota, his sales to date, and other pertinent information. The sheet was edited by a "sporting editor," and great tact and skill were displayed in giving the contest the atmosphere of an actual race or game. In addition the sales manager, the district managers, and the house executives wrote letters and telegrams of encouragement, and even made trips to the agencies that got under way too slowly.

The unique feature of the contest was the manner in which the "sporting editor" gave actuality to the contests by pictorial representations. One competition took the form of a shooting match. The house organ contained an enormous target with two rings and a bull's eye. When a salesman qualified with orders for $625, he was credited with a shot inside the outer ring and his name was printed there. With $1250 in sales, he moved into the inner ring, and when his orders amounted to $2500, he was credited with a bull's eye and his name blazoned in the centre space.

Another contest was represented as a balloon race between the different districts. Each district was given a balloon, and as sales increased, the airship mounted higher. On the balloon the name of the district leader in sales was printed, while cartoons enlivened the race by showing the expedients, in terms of orders, by which the district managers and their crews sought to drive their airships higher. Each issue of the house organ showed the current standing of the districts by the heights of their balloons. This conception of the selling contest was very successful. "Going up—going up—how far are you up now?" was used as a call, and it seemed to strike the men and inspire them. It became the greeting of the salesmen when they met, and irresistibly produced a feeling of competition and a desire to have the district balloon go higher.

Other ingenious fancies by which the contests were given the appeal and interest of popular sports was their conception as a baseball game, a football game, an automobile race, a Marathon run, and so on.

In providing prizes, the firm was rather generous, though the expense was never great. While the contest was in progress, all those who were really "in the running" had the satisfaction of honourable mention, with their photographs reproduced in the house bulletin. This honor and publicity was the chief reward received by the great majority of contestants, and was adequate. Minor prizes were offered on conditions, allowing a large number to qualify, and tempting virtually everybody to make an effort to win one. The value of the prizes did not need to be great, for each man was impressed with the idea that his comrades were watching him, that they observed every advance or retrogression. Success in the contest meant "making good" in the eyes of the other salesmen as well as in the eyes of his superiors. This desire for social approval and the spirited comment of the editor had a marked influence on the efficiency of many of the younger salesmen_.

These special contests were conducted chiefly during the "rush" seasons, when activity and efficiency of salesmen meant greater returns to the house. Because of their varied forms the contests did not become monotonous, and thus fail in their effect. During the three or four "big" selling months when special quotas were announced, an individual pocket schedule was mailed to each man, showing how much business he must close each day to keep pace with "Mr. Quota," the constant competitor.

The most industrious and ambitious men are stimulated by competition; with the less industrious such a stimulation is often wonder working in its effects_.

For many positions in the business world a hypothetical bogy should be created after the style of the quota referred to above.

To increase the feeling of comradeship and promote cooperation between the men the entire organization or single sections of it occasionally should be made the unit of competition. This is perhaps the most helpful form of competition, but it is hard to execute.

Valuable prizes should always be given to the winners. This "need" may not necessarily be monetary.

Promotion should not depend upon success in contests, but such success may be well reckoned in awarding promotions.

Public commendation for success in competition costs the company little and is greatly appreciated by the winner. There seems to be no reason why the head of the house should not assist in the presentation.

The most essential factor in creating interest in a contest is the skill of the "sporting editor" in injecting the real spirit of the game into each contest, thus securing wide publicity, and enlisting the cooperation of large numbers of participants.

Prizes should be widely distributed, so that the greatest number may be encouraged. A fair system of handicapping should be adopted in every case where equal opportunity to win is not possessed by all. Previous records often make successful bogies, and should be more extensively employed.

It is possible to carry on contests between individuals in the same department without jealousies, but skill is required to conduct them. There is the danger that individuals will seek to win by hindering others as well as by exerting themselves. Where it is not possible to carry on a contest and retain a feeling of comradeship between the men, no competition should be encouraged.

12

Loyalty in Organization

As a Means of Increasing Human Efficiency

Delayed by a train of accidents, a big contractor faced forfeiture of his bond on a city tunnel costing millions of dollars. He had exhausted his ingenuity and his resources to comply with the terms of his contract, but had failed. Because public opinion had been condemning concessions on other jobs on flimsy grounds, the authorities refused to extend the time allowed for completing the work. By canceling the contract, collecting the penalty, and reletting the task, the city would profit without exceeding its legal rights.

In his dilemma, he called his foremen together and explained the situation to them. "Tell the men," he said. Many of these had been members of his organization for years, moving with him from one undertaking to the next, looking to him for employment, for help in dull seasons or in times of misfortune, repaying him with interest in their tasks and a certain rough attachment.

He had been unusually considerate, adopting every possible safeguard for their protection, recognizing their union, employing three shifts of men, paying more than the required scale when conditions were hard or dangerous.

A score of unions were represented in the organization: miners, masons, carpenters, plasterers, engineers, electricians, and many grades of helpers. Learning his plight, they rallied promptly to his aid. They appealed to their trades and to the central body of unions to intervene in his behalf with the city officials. How One Considerate Employer was protected by his Men. As taxpayers, voters, and members of an organization potentially effective in politics, they approached the mayor and the department heads concerned. They pointed out— what was true—that the city's negligence in prospecting and charting the course of the tunnel was partly responsible for the contractor's failure. They pleaded that the city should make allowances rather than interrupt their employment, and that the delay in the work would counterbalance any advantage contingent on forfeiture. They promised also that if three additional months were given the contractor, they would _*do all in their power to push construction_.

The mayor yielded; the extension was granted. And the men made their promise good literally, waiving jealously guarded rights and sparing no effort to forward the undertaking. The miners, masons, carpenters, and specialists in other lines in which additional skilled men could not be secured laboured frequently in twelve-hour shifts and accepted only the regular hourly rate for the overtime. With such zeal animating them, only one conclusion was possible. The tunnel was entirely completed before the ninety days of grace had expired.

Here was loyalty as stanch and effective as that which wins battlefields and creates nations. It increased the efficiency of the individual workers; it greatly augmented the effectiveness of the organization as a whole. It was developed, without appeal to sentiment, under conditions which make for division rather than cooperation between employer and employee. The men were unionists; wages, hours, and so on, were contract matters with the boss. Yet in an emergency, the tie between the tunnel builder and his men was strong enough to stand the strain of the fatiguing and long-continued effort necessary to complete the job and save the former from ruin. Like incidents, on perhaps a smaller and less dramatic scale, are not uncommon; but the historian of business has not yet risen to make them known.

Loyalty, to Nation or Organization, Shows Itself in an Emergency

As with patriotism, business loyalty needs some such crisis as this to evoke its expression. In peace the patriotism of citizens is rarely evident and is frequently called in question. In America we sometimes assume that it is a virtue belonging only to past generations. But every time the honor or integrity of the country is threatened, a multitude of eager citizens volunteer in its defence. Likewise, many a business man who has come to think hi , workmen interested only in the wages he pays them, discovers in his hour of need an unsuspected asset in their devotion to the welfare of the business, and their willingness to make sacrifices to bring it past the cape of storms.

Study of any field, of any single house, or of any of the periods of depression which have afflicted and corrected our industrial progress, will convince one of the unfailing and genuine loyalty of men to able and considerate employers. So generally true is this, indeed, that "house patriotism," "organization spirit," or "loyalty to the management" is accepted by all great executives as one of the essential elements in the day-by-day conduct of their enterprises.

Striking exhibitions of this loyalty may wait for an emergency. Unless it exists, however, unless it is apparent in the daily routine, there is immediate and relentless search for the antagonistic condition or method, which is robbing the force of present efficiency and future power. Cooperation of employees is the first purpose of organization. Without loyalty and team work the higher levels in output, quality, and service are impossible.

Loyalty on Part of Employer Begets Loyalty in his Workers

The importance of loyalty in business could not readily be overestimated, even though its sole function were to secure united action on the part of the officers and men. Where no two men or groups of men were working to counter purposes, but all are united in a common purpose, the gain would be enormous, even though the amount of energy put forth by the individuals was not increased in the least. When to this fact of value in organized effort we add the accompanying psychological facts of increased efficiency by means of loyalty, we then begin to comprehend what it means to have or to lack loyalty.

The amount of work accomplished by an individual is subject to various conditions. The whole intellect, feeling, and will must work in unity to secure the best results. Where there is no heart in the work (absence of feeling) relatively little can be accomplished, even though the intellect be convinced and the will strained to the utmost. The employee who lacks loyalty to his employer can at least render but half-hearted service even though he strive to his utmost and though he be convinced that his financial salvation is dependent upon efficient service. *The employer who secures the loyalty of his men not* only secures better service, but he enables his men to accomplish more with less effort *and less exhaustion*. The creator of loyalty is a public benefactor.

Such loyalty is always reciprocal. The feeling which workmen entertain for their employer is usually a reflection of his attitude towards them. Fair wages, reasonable hours, working quarters and conditions of average comfort and healthfulness, and a measure of protection against accident are now no more than primary requirements in a factory or store. Without them labour of the better, more energetic types cannot be secured in the first place or held for any length of time. And the employer who expects, in return for these, any more than the average of uninspired service is sure to be disappointed. If he treats his men like machines, looks at them merely as cogs in the mechanism of his affairs, they will function like machines or find other places. If he wishes to stir the larger, latent powers of their brains and bodies, thereby increasing their efficiency as thinkers and workers, he must recognize them as men and individuals and give in <p 83> some measure what he asks. He must identify them with the business, and make them feel that they have a stake in its success and that the organization has an interest in the welfare of its men. The boss to whom his employees turn in any serious perplexity or private difficulty for advice and aid is pretty apt to receive more than the contract minimum of effort every day and is sure of devoted service in any time of need.

The Effect of Personal Relations in creating Loyalty in a Force

It is on this personal relationship, this platform of mutual interests and helpfulness, that the success and fighting strength of many oneman houses are built. As in the contractor's dilemma already cited, it bears fruit in the fighting zeal, the keener interest, and the extra speed and effort which workers bring to bear on their individual and collective tasks. All the knowledge and skill they possess are thrown into the scale; their quickened intelligences reach out for new methods and short cuts; when the crisis has passed, there may be a temporary reaction, but there is likely to be a permanent advance both in individual efficiency and organization spirit.

On the employer's side, this feeling is expressed in the surrender of profits to provide work in dull seasons; in the retention of aged mechanics, labourers, or clerks on the payroll after their usefulness has passed; in pensions; in a score of neighbourly and friendly offices to those who are sick, injured, or in trouble. A reputation for "taking care of his men" has frequently been a bulwark of defence to the small manufacturer or trader assailed by a greedy larger rival.

Personality is, beyond doubt, the primitive wellspring of loyalty. Most men are capable of devotion to a worthy leader; few are ever zealots for the sake of a cause, a principle, a party, or a firm. All these are too abstract to win the affection of the average man. It is only when they become embodied in an individual, a concrete personality which stirs our human interest, that they become moving powers. The soldiers of the Revolution fought for Washington rather than for freedom; Christians are loyal to Christ rather than to his teachings; the voter cheers his candidate and not his party; the employee is loyal to the head of the house or his immediate foreman and not to the generality known as the House. Loyalty to the individuals constituting the firm may ultimately develop into house loyalty. To attempt to create the latter sentiment, however, except by first creating it for the men higher up is to go contrary to human nature—always an unwise expenditure of energy.

Human Sympathy as a Factor in Developing Loyalty in Men

In developing loyalty, human sympathy is the greatest factor. If an executive of a company is confident that his directors approve his policies, appreciate his obstacles, and are ready to back him up in any crisis, his energy and enthusiasm for the common object never flag. If department heads and foremen are assured that the manager is watching their efforts with attention and regard, approving, supporting, and sparing them wherever possible, they will anticipate orders, assume extra burdens, and fling themselves and their forces into any breach which may threaten their chief's program.

If a workman, clerk, or salesman knows that his immediate chief is interested in him personally, that he understands what service is being rendered and is anxious to forward his welfare as well as that of the house, there is no effort, inconvenience, or discomfort which he will not undertake to complete a task which the boss has undertaken. Throughout the entire organization, the sympathy and cooperation of the men above with the men below is essential for securing the highest degree of loyalty. No assumed or manufactured sympathy, however, will take the place of the genuine article.

Personal Relationship with Workers as Basis for Creating Loyalty

The effectiveness of human sympathy in creating loyalty is most apparent in one-man businesses where the head of the house is in personal contact with all or many of his employees. This personal touch, however, is not necessarily limited to the small organization. Many men have employed thousands and secured it. Others have succeeded in impressing their personalities, and demonstrating their sympathy upon large forces, though their actual relations were with a few. The impression made upon these and the loyalty created in them were sufficient to permeate and influence the entire body. Potter Palmer, the elder Armour, Marshall Field, and Andrew Carnegie were among the hundreds of captains who made acquaintance with the men in the ranks the cornerstone on which they raised their trade or industrial citadels.

When the size of the organization precludes personal contact, or when conditions remove the executive to a distance, the task of maintaining touch is frequently and successfully intrusted to a lieutenant in sympathy with the chief's ideals and purposes. He may be the head of a department variously styled, —

adjustments, promotion and discharge, employment, labour,—but his express function is to restore to an organization the simple but powerful human relation without which higher efficiency cannot be maintained. In factories and stores employing many women this understudy to the manager is usually a woman, who is given plenary authority in the handling of her charges, in reviewing disputes with foremen, and in finding the right position for the misplaced worker. Whether man or woman, this representative of the manager hears all grievances, reviews all discharges, reductions, and the like, and makes sure that the employee receives a little more than absolute justice.

Many successful merchants and manufacturers, however, disdain agents and intermediaries in this relation and are always accessible to every man in their organizations; holding that, since the cooperation of employees is the most important single element in business, the time given to securing it is time well spent.

Even though human sympathy may well be regarded as the most important consideration in increasing loyalty, it is not sufficient in and of itself. The most patriotic citizens are those who have, served the state. They are made loyal by the very act of service. They have assumed the responsibility of promoting the welfare of the state, and their patriotism is thereby stimulated and given concrete outlet. A paternalistic government in which the citizens had every right but no responsibility would develop beggars rather than patriots.

Similarly in a business house ideally organized to create loyalty, each employee not only feels that his rights are protected, but also feels a degree of responsibility for the success and for the good name of the house. He feels that his task or process is an essential part of the firm's activity; and hence is important and worthy of his best efforts. To cement this bond and make closer the identification of the employee with the house many firms encourage their employees to purchase stock in the company. Others have worked out profit-sharing plans by which their men share in the dividends of the good years and are given a powerful incentive to promote teamwork and the practice of the economies from which the overplus of profit is produced.

Loyalty may be Developed by Education in House History and Policies

The stability of a nation depends on the patriotism of its citizens. Among methods for developing this patriotism, _*education_ ranks as the most effective. In the public schools history is taught for the purpose of awakening the love and loyalty of the rising generations. The founders, builders, and saviours of the country, the great men of peace and war who have contributed to its advancement, are held up for admiration. From the recital of what country and patriotism meant to Washington, Jefferson, Lincoln, Grant, and a host of lesser heroes, the pupils come to realize what country should, and does, mean to them. They become patriotic citizens.

Grounding the New Employee in Company Traditions and Ideals

In like manner the history of any house can be used to inspire loyalty and enthusiasm among its employees. Business has not been slow to borrow the methods and ideals of education, but the writer has been unable to discover any company which makes adequate use of this principle. That this loyalty may be directed to the house as a whole, and not merely to immediate superiors, every employee should be acquainted with the purposes and policies of the company and should understand that the sympathy which he discovers in his foreman is a common characteristic of the whole organization, clear up to the president. The best way to teach this is by example— by incidents drawn from the past, or by a review of the development of the company's policy.

To identify one's self with a winning cause, party, or leader, also, is infinitely easier than to be loyal to a loser. For this reason the study of the history of the firm may well include its trade triumphs, past and present; the remarkable or interesting uses to which its products have been put; the honor or prestige which its executives or members of the organization have attained; and the hundred other items of human interest which can be marshaled to give it house personality. All this would arouse admiration and appreciation in employees, would stir enthusiasm and a desire to contribute to future achievements, and would foster an unwillingness to leave the organization. Some companies have begun in this direction. New employees, by way of introduction, listen to lectures, either with or without the accompaniment of pictures, which review what the house has accomplished, define its standing in the trade, analyse its products and their qualities or functions, sketch the plan and purpose of its organization, and touch upon the other points of chief human interest. Other companies put this information in booklets. Still others employ their house organs to recall and do honor to the interesting traditions of the company as well as to exploit the successful deeds and men of the moment. An organized and continuous campaign of education along this line should prove an inexpensive means of increasing loyalty and efficiency among the men. To the mind of the writer, it seems clear that the future will see pronounced advances in this particular.

Personality can be overdone, however. Workers instinctively give allegiance to strong, balanced men, but resent and combat egotism unchecked by regard for others' rights. Exploitation of the employer's or foreman's personality will do more harm than good unless attended by consideration for the personality of the employee. The service of more than one important company has been made intolerable for men of spirit and creative ability by the arrogant and dominating spirit of the management. The men who continue to sacrifice their individuality to the whim or the arbitrary rule of their superiors, in time lose their ambition and initiative; and the organization declines to a level of routine, mechanical efficiency only one remove from dryrot.

How Efficiency and Loyalty of Workers may be Capitalized

Conservation and development of individuality in workers may be made an important factor in creating loyalty as well as in directly increasing efficiency. Great retail stores put many department heads into business for themselves, giving them space, light, buying facilities, clerks, and purchasing and advertising credit as a basis of their merchandising; then requiring a certain percentage of profit on the amount allowed them. The more successful of Marshall Field's lieutenants were taken into partnership and, as in the case of Andrew Carnegie and his "cabinet of young geniuses," were given substantial shares of the wealth they helped to create. Some industries and stores carry this practice to the point of making specialized departments entirely independent of the general buying, production, and selling organizations whenever these fall short of the service offered outside; while the principle of stock distribution or other forms of profit sharing has been adopted by so many companies that it has come to be a recognized method of promoting loyalty.

Regard for the employee's personality must be carried down in an unbroken chain through all the ranks. It may be broken at any step in the descent by an executive or foreman who has not himself learned the lesson that loyalty to the house includes loyalty to the men under him.

It is not uncommon, in some American houses, to find three generations of workers — grandfather, father, and apprentice son— rendering faithful and friendly service; or to discover a score of bosses and men who have spent thirty or forty years—their entire productive lives—in the one organization. Where such a bond exists between employer and employees, it becomes an active, unfailing force in the development of loyalty, not only among the veterans, but also among the newest recruits for whom it realizes an illustration of what true cooperation means.

Many Examples of the Loyalty of Executives for their Men in Danger

This double loyalty—to the chief and to the organization—is not a plant of slow growth. Few mine accidents or industrial disasters occur without bringing to merited, but fleeting, fame some heroic superintendent or lesser boss who has risked his own life to save his men or preserve the company's property. The same sense of responsibility extends to every grade. Give a man the least touch of authority and he seems to take on added moral stature. The engineer who clings to his throttle with collision imminent has his counterparts in the "handy man" who braves injury to slip a belt and save another workman or a costly machine, and in the elevator conductor who drives his car up and down through flames and smoke to rescue his fellows. Such efficiency and organization spirit is the result of individual growth as well as the impression of the employer's personality upon his machine.

A Disloyal Sales Manager and his Influence on his Force

On the other hand, lack of loyalty on the part of employers towards their men is almost as common as failing devotion on the part of workers. Too many assume that the mere providing of work and the payment of wages give them the right to absolute fidelity, even when they take advantage of their men. The sales manager concerned in the following incident refused to believe that his attitude towards his men had anything to do with the lack of enthusiasm and low efficiency in his force.

An experienced salesman who had lost his position because of the San Francisco fire applied to the sales manager for a position. He was informed that there were fifteen applicants for the Ohio territory, but that the place would be given to him because of his better record. The manager laid out an initial territory in one corner and ordered the salesman to work it first.

Working this territory, the salesman secured substantial orders, but refrained from "over-selling" any customer, gave considerable time to missionary work and to cultivating the acquaintance of buyers. His campaign was planned less for immediate results than for the future and for the effect on the larger field of the state. Having no instructions as to pushing his wider campaign, in about sixty days he asked for instructions. In answer he was ordered home and discharged on the ground that business was dull and that he had been a loss to the house. During the sixty days he had been working on a losing commission basis with the expectation of taking his profits later. Investigation disclosed that he was but one of five salesmen to whom the Ohio territory had been assigned simultaneously. Of the five, one other also had made good and had been retained because he could be secured for less money.

This multiple try-out policy is entirely fair when the applicants know the conditions. But to lead each applicant to believe that he has been engaged subject only to his ability to make good is manifestly unjust. The facts are bound to come out sooner or later and create distrust among all employees of the house. Loyalty is strictly reciprocal. If an employee feels that he has no assurance of fair treatment, his attitude towards the firm is sure to be negative. Even the man who secures the position will recognize the firm's lack of candor and will never give his employers the full measure of cooperation which produces maximum efficiency.

The "square deal," indeed, is the indispensable basis of loyalty and efficiency in an organization. The spirit as well as the letter of the bargain must be observed, else the workmen will contrive to even up matters by loafing, by slighting the work, or by a minimum production. This means a loss of possible daily earnings. On the other hand, employees never fail to recognize and in time respect the executive who holds the balance of loyalty and justice level between them and the business.

Fair wages, reasonable hours, working quarters and conditions of average comfort and healthfulness, ordinary precautions against accidents, and continuous employment are all now regarded as primary requirements and are not sufficient to create loyalty in the men. More than this must be done.

The chief executive should create such a spirit that his officers shall turn to him for help when in perplexity or difficulty. The superintendent and officers or bosses should sustain this same sympathetic relationship toward their men that the executive has toward his officers. A reputation for taking care of his men is a thing to be sought in a chief executive as well as in all underofficers.

Personal relationships should be cultivated. In some large organizations the chief executive may secure this personal touch with individuals through an agent or through a department known as the department of "promotion and discharge," "employment," or "labour." In others, occasional meetings on a level of equality may be brought about through house picnics, entertainments, vacation camps, and so on, where employer and employee meet each other outside their usual business environment.

It is not worth while to attempt to develop loyalty to the house until there has been developed a loyalty to the personalities representing the house. Loyalty in business is in the main a reciprocal relationship. The way to begin it is for the chief to be loyal to his subordinates and to see to it that all officers are loyal to their inferiors. When loyalty from above has been secured, loyalty from the ranks may readily be developed. The personality of the worker must be respected by the employer. "Giving a man a chance" to develop himself, allowing him to express his individuality, is the surest way of enlisting the interest and loyalty of a creative man.

To identify the interests of employees with the interests of the house, various plans of profit sharing, sale of stock to employees, pensions, insurance against sickness and accident, and so on, have been successfully applied by many companies.

So far as possible, responsibility for the success of the house should be assumed by all employees. In some way the workmen should feel that they are in partnership with the executives. We easily develop loyalty for the cause for which we have taken responsibility or rendered a service.

Creating Loyalty to Firm Itself by Educational Campaign

A perpetual campaign of publicity should be maintained for the benefit of every man in the employ of the house. In this there should be a truthful but emphatic presentation of acts of loyalty on the part of either employers or workmen. Everything connected with the firm which has human interest should be included in this history. This educational campaign should change the loyalty to the _*men_ in the firm into loyalty to the _*firm_ itself. It should be an attempt to give the firm a personality, and of such a noble character that it would win the loyalty of the men. This could be accomplished at little expense and with great profit.

Bibliography

Aamodt, Michael G.: *Applied Industrial / Organizational Psychology*. Pacific Grove, CA: Brooks/Cole, 1999.

Ahmad, S. Fayyaz : *Organisational Behaviour*, Atlantic, Delhi, 2008.

Anderson, N.: *Handbook of industrial, work and organizational psychology*, Thousand Oaks, CA: Sage Publications Ltd., 2002.

Asch, M : *Abnormal and Developmental Psychology*, Ivy Pub, Delhi, 2003.

Bernstein, I.: *Psychometric theory*, New York: McGraw-Hill, 1994.

Chandra, S.S. : *Advanced Industrial Psychology*, Atlantic, Delhi, 2004.

Dibbern, Jens : *Evidence of Cultural, Industry and Functional Differences,* Physica Verlag Heidelberg, 2004.

Dicken, P. : *Wheels of Change, the Automobile Industry*, London, 2007.

Dubey, K.C. : *Experimental and Developmental Psychology*, Omega Pub, Delhi, 2009.

Dunnette, M. D.: *Handbook of industrial and organizational psychology*. Chicago: Rand McNally, 1976.

Grace, G. : *Leadership: Beyond Educational Development*, London, Falmer, 1995.

Hayduk, L.A.: *Structural equations modeling with LISREL*. Baltimore, MD: Johns Hopkins University Press, 1987.

Kumar, Arvind : *Industrial Pollution and Management*, APH, Delhi, 2004.

Lawson, Robert B., and Zheng Shen: *Organizational Psychology: Foundations and Applications*. New York: Oxford University Press, 1998.

Mckenna, S.: *Business Psychology and Organisational Behaviour*, Taylor and Francis, Delhi, 2010.

Mehrotra, Anju : *Leadership Styles of Principals — Authoritarian and Task Oriented*, Mittal Pub, Delhi, 2005.

Muchinsky, Paul M.: *Psychology Applied to Work*. Belmont, CA: Wadsworth, 1999.

Murthy, J. Krishna : *Administration and Organisation of Physical Education and Sports*, Commonwealth, Delhi, 2005.

Parker, Barbara : *Introduction to Globalization and Business: Relationships and Responsibilities*, Response, Delhi, 2005.

Pathak, Bachcha : *Industrial Policy of India : Changing Facets*, Deep and Deep, Delhi, 2007.

Rastogi, P.N. : *Management of Technology and Innovation : Competing Through Technological Excellence*, Response, Delhi, 2009.

Rathod, P B : *Dynamics of Political Psychology*, ABD Pub, Delhi, 2008.

Sagar, G. Vidya : *Pharmaceutical Organizational Management*, Pharma Book Syndicate, Delhi, 2005.

Schultz, Duane P.: *Psychology and Work Today*. Upper Saddle River, NJ: Prentice Hall, 1998.

Stone, Philip: *Organizational Psychology*. Brookfield, VT: Ashgate Publishing Co., 1997.

Suri, R.K. : *Dynamics of Industrial Relations*, Pentagon Press, Delhi, 2007.

Tiwari, Saurabh Kumar : *Psychological Perspectives of Organizational Commitment*, Concept Pub, Delhi, 2009.

Vaknin, Sam : *A Textbook of Organizational Psychology*, Dominant Pub, Delhi, 2010.

Index

S

T

U

V

W

□□□